ORIGINAL NARRATIVES
OF EARLY AMERICAN HISTORY

REPRODUCED UNDER THE AUSPICES OF THE
AMERICAN HISTORICAL ASSOCIATION

GENERAL EDITOR, J. FRANKLIN JAMESON, PH.D., LL.D., LITT.D.

DIRECTOR OF THE DEPARTMENT OF HISTORICAL RESEARCH IN THE
CARNEGIE INSTITUTION OF WASHINGTON

NARRATIVES
OF THE INDIAN WARS

1675—1699

EDITED BY

CHARLES H. LINCOLN, PH.D.

New York

BARNES & NOBLE, INC.

CONTENTS

NARRATIVES OF THE INDIAN WARS

EDITED BY CHARLES H. LINCOLN

CONTENTS

A RELACION OF THE INDYAN WARRE, BY JOHN EASTON, 1675

INTRODUCTION

FEW students of American colonial history have failed to observe the difference in method employed by France and by England in their respective efforts to control the new continent. The government at Paris sent out its colonists, took much interest in their welfare, and weakened them by its excessive care. The English immigrants came to America of their own accord, developed along paths of their own choosing, and prospered under British neglect.

As the mother country treated her representatives in America so the colonists treated the Indians. From his arrival on the St. Lawrence the Frenchman regarded the Indian as a possible friend, and joined with him in his wars as well as in his hunting expeditions. No efforts were spared to cement an alliance between the two races, an alliance which gave the profits of the fur-trade to France and enabled the French in America to resist for a hundred and fifty years a much greater number of English rivals. Very different was the behavior of the New Englander toward the Indian. Nothing could induce him to regard the red man as an equal, although in no English colony save Pennsylvania was the Indian better treated. Massachusetts tried to educate the Indian, endeavored to convert him to Christianity, traded with him, and fought with him, but neither people felt at home in the presence of the other.

In another and not less vital way the policies of the French and English toward the Indians differed. The French were directed by a single head, and under that direction maintained a consistent attitude toward their neighbors. The English, lacking the direction of an efficient central government, fol-

3

lowed as many methods in their dealings with the Indians as there were colonies in America. Intercolonial jealousies prevented that union against the Indians which won the Five Nations to the Dutch in New York and the Huron Confederation to the French along the line of the Great Lakes.

In few sections of America were these jealousies more rampant than in New England, where New Hampshire was in fear of absorption by Massachusetts and where Rhode Island had an additional fear of Plymouth and Connecticut. One attempt at united policy against the Indians was made even in New England. Following their bitter war against the Pequots, Massachusetts, Plymouth, Connecticut, and New Haven formed the New England Confederation of 1643, a union of the four governments for defensive purposes. Whether because of this alliance, or because of the memories of the Pequot war, the borders of New England were undisturbed by the Indians for thirty years. Then came an outbreak which threatened to overthrow all government by the English in that portion of America. It would seem as if the Indians had observed the jealousy existing between Rhode Island and her neighbors and had formed a loose confederacy among themselves in order to make one strong united fight against the invader of their lands and dignities.

King Philip's war covered about two years of New England's history. It was the most prolonged Indian war in which the New England colonies ever engaged, and when estimated in life and property few wars have occasioned greater loss to their participants. The cost to the Indians can only be guessed at, but one-tenth of the adult males of Massachusetts were killed or captured by the Indians, and two-thirds of her towns and villages suffered directly from Indian raids during this war. The loss in Rhode Island was no less, and while Connecticut was somewhat more fortunate in her location her fighting strength was seriously depleted.

It is most fitting that the first narrative of this Indian war series should be that of a Rhode Islander. That colony had been denied admittance into the New England Confederation of 1643, and feared that an Indian war would give Plymouth or Connecticut an opportunity to encroach upon her boundaries. Rhode Island was the home of the Narragansetts, the most important of Philip's allies and whose chief, Canonchet, was at least the equal of Philip in conducting the war, if not the foremost to arouse the various tribes for a united assault upon New England. In Rhode Island occurred the Swamp Fight, perhaps the most important battle of the war, and in the same colony was located Mount Hope, or Montop, the capital of Philip and the scene of his final defeat.

In no contemporary account of the war do we find more evidence of a desire to be impartial. Some have found the reason for John Easton's impartiality in his aversion to all fighting and in Rhode Island's equal fear of Massachusetts and of Indian conquest. Increase Mather indeed accused Easton of favoring the Indians, remarking that this narrative was "written by a Quaker in Road Island, who pretends to know the Truth of Things"; but that it was "fraught with worse Things than meer Mistakes." A more moderate view is that the boundary disputes may have urged Easton to emphasize the possibility of maintaining peace with the Indians by arbitration were it not for the indiscretion of their white neighbors. Easton regarded the Indians more kindly than did Mather or the authors of our other narratives, but we shall not be far astray if we consider him as expressing the Rhode Island rather than the Indian point of view. His condemnation of the colonists in certain acts is shown, as in his account of the conference between Indian and white, but this is not accompanied by indiscriminate praise of Indian motives and methods. The Rhode Island writer intends to be fair and is reasonably successful in this intent.

Easton's birth and surroundings aided him in this effort. He was the son of Nicholas Easton, a Friend, who came to New England in 1634 and settled at Ipswich. From this Massachusetts town he moved successively to Newbury and Hampton, where he is said to have built the first English house. In 1638 Nicholas Easton was driven from Massachusetts by religious intolerance; he settled a year later at Newport, again building the first English house. There he held important positions until 1675, dying in Newport soon after his last term as governor of the colony. His son John, the author of our narrative, was born in 1617 and accompanied his father in his various removes. He was attorney-general of Rhode Island for much of the time between 1652 and 1674, and fifteen years after the death of his father John Easton also became governor of the colony.

Easton was about sixty years old at the time of the events recounted in the following narrative. It was written by a person of mature years and of conservative temperament, a person well fitted to give a judicial account of the origin of the war and a careful estimate of its participants. The original narrative remains in manuscript form in the New York State Library. We are indebted to Mr. Peter Nelson, of the archives of that state, for collation of our text with the original. A printed edition limited to one hundred copies was published in Albany in 1858 under the careful editing of Franklin B. Hough. The importance of the narrative and inaccessibility of this edition warrant its republication at this time. The care with which it was written may lead the reader to wish that the record covered a greater period of the war, but the fact that Easton's father was governor of Rhode Island from 1672 to 1674 and that the son was deputy governor (1674–1676) when the war opened may have given the son a peculiar fitness as a historian of the war's beginning which he would not have retained for its later history.

A RELACION OF THE INDYAN WARRE, BY Mr. EASTON, OF ROADE ISLD., 1675

a true relation of wt I kno and of reports, and my understanding Conserning the begining and progres of the war now betwen the English and the indians.

In the winter in the year 1674 an indian was found dead, and by a Corener iquest of Plimoth Coleny judged murdered. he was found dead in a hole thro ies broken in a pond with his gun and sum foulle by him. sum English suposed him throne in sum indians that I judged intelegabell and impartiall in that Case did think he fell in and was so drouned and that the ies did hurt his throat as the English saied it was cut, but acnoledged that sumtimes naty[1] indians wold kill others but, not as ever thay herd to obscuer as if the dead indian was not murdered. the dead indian was caled Sausimun[2] and a Christian that could read and write. report was he was a bad man that king Philop got him to write his will and he made the writing for a gret part of the land to be his but read as if it had bine as Philop wold, but it Came to be knone and then he run away from him. now one indian informed that 3 indians had murdered him, and shewed a Coat that he said thay gave him to Conseall them, the indians report that the informer had played away his Coate, and these men sent him

[1] Naughty, *i. e.*, wicked.

[2] This name is written Sosoman, Sassamon, Sausaman, and Sausimun, all abbreviations of his own spelling Wussausmon. He was a preacher to the Indians and possibly to Philip himself. Sausaman was born in Punkapog (now Canton, Massachusetts), was given the Christian name of John, was brought up by the English, and used frequently by them as an interpreter in negotiations with the Indians. He was used also as a scribe by Alexander and by Philip, the former granting him lands near Assawomset pond in Middleborough, Plymouth County, Massachusetts. It was here, as stated in the text, that his dead body was found January 29, 1674/5.

7

that coate, and after demanded pay and he not to pay so
acused them, and knoing it wold pleas the English so to think
him a beter Christian, and the reporte Came, that the 3
indians had confesed and acused Philop so to imploy them,
and that the English wold hang Philop, so the indians wear
afraid, and reported that the English had flatred them (or by
threts) to bely Philop that thay might kill him to have his
Land and that if Philop had dun it it was ther Law so to
execute home[1] ther kings judged deserved it that he had no
Case to hide it.

so Philop kept his men in arems. Plimoth Governer, required him to disband his men, and informed him his jelosy
was falce. Philop ansered[2] he wold do no harem, and thanked
the Governer for his information. the 3 indians wer hunge,
to the last denied the fact, but one broke the halter as it is
reported then desiere to be saved and so was a litell while
then confesed thay 3 had dun the fact and then he was hanged[3]
and it was reported Sausimun before his death had informed
of the indian plot and that if the indians knew it thay wold
kill him, and that the hethen might destroy the English for
ther wickedness as god had permited the heathen to destroy
the iserallits[4] of olde, so the English wear afraid and Philop
was afraid and both incresed in arems but for 40 years time
reports and jelosys of war had bine veri frequent that we did
not think that now a war was breking forth, but about a wecke
before it did we had Case to think it wold,[5] then to indever to
prevent it, we sent a man to Philop that if he wold Cum to the

[1] Whom.

[2] Other accounts say that Philip paid no attention to the court and made
no effort to clear himself of complicity or suspicion. The governor of Plymouth
colony was Josiah Winslow.

[3] For a different account of the manner in which the Indians had come to
kill Sausimun see *The Present State of New England*, p. 24, *post*. It is not certain
that the three men were hanged. One is reported to have been reprieved for
a time and shot later. The jury trying the accused consisted of four Indians
and twelve whites. One bit of evidence is stated by Increase Mather: "When
Tobias came near the dead body, it fell a bleeding on fresh, as if it had been
newly slain."

[4] Israelites.

[5] Four years earlier peace had been made at Taunton on April 12, 1671, but
since that time the Indians had been reported as dissatisfied with the conditions
imposed upon them and as preparing for a renewal of the war.

fery[1] we wold Cum over to speke with him. about 4 mile
we had to Cum thether. our mesenger Come to them, thay
not awar of it behaved themselefs as furious but sudingly
apesed when thay understood who he was and what he came
for. he Called his counsell and agreed to Cum to us came
himself unarmed and about 40 of his men armed. then 5[2]
of us went over. 3 wear magestrats. we sate veri frindly
together.[3] we told him our bisnes was to indever that thay
might not reseve or do rong. thay said that was well thay
had dun no rong, the English ronged them, we saied we knew
the English saied the indians ronged them and the indians
saied the english ronged them but our desier was the quarell
might rightly be desided in the best way, and not as dogs
desided ther quarells. the indians owned that fighting was
the worst way then thay propounded how right might take
plase, we saied by arbetration. thay saied all English agred
against them, and so by arbetration thay had had much rong,
mani miles square of land so taken from them for English wold
have English Arbetrators, and once thay wer perswaided to
give in ther arems, that therby Jelosy might be removed and
the English having ther arems wold not deliver them as thay
had promised, untill thay consented to pay a 100po, and now
thay had not so much land or muny, that thay wear as good
be kiled as leave all ther liveflyhode.[4] we saied thay might
Choose a indian king, and the English might Choose the
Governer of new yorke[5] that nether had Case to say ether
weare parties in the diferans. thay saied thay had not herd
of that way and saied we onestly spoke so we wear perswaided

---

    [1] Trip's Ferry.   [2] The reading is probably 5, possibly 50.

    [3] No other contemporary historian has given an account of this conference.
Possibly no other colony could have secured a conference with Philip at this
time, but Rhode Island had been more friendly with the Indians than had Massachusetts or Plymouth.

    [4] A reference to the treaty at Taunton, which the Indians had interpreted as
meaning a temporary surrender of arms brought to the meeting-place but which
the English had construed as a permanent giving up of all arms in possession of
the various tribes represented. On Philip's proposition a meeting of the New
England Commissioners was held September 29, 1671, which resulted in the aban-
donment by the English of their construction of the treaty, conditional upon
the payment by the Indians of £100 as stated in the text. This condition the
Indians here declare to be impracticable.

    [5] Sir Edmund Andros.

if that way had bine tendered thay wold have acsepted. we
did indever not to here ther Cumplaints, saied it was not
Convenient for us now to Consider of, but to indever to prevent war, saied to them when in war against English blud was
spilt that ingadged all Englishmen for we wear to be all under
one king. we knew what ther Cumplaints wold be, and in
our Colony had removed sum of them in sending for indian
rulers in what[1] the Crime Conserned indians lives which thay
veri lovingly acsepted and agreed with us to ther execution
and saied so thay wear abell to satesfie ther subjects when thay
knew an indian sufered duly, but saied in what was only betwen
ther indians and not in towneshipes that we had purchased,
thay wold not have us prosecute and that thay had a great
fear to have[2] ani of ther indians should be Caled or forsed to
be Christian indians.[3] thay saied that such wer in everi
thing more mischivous, only disemblers, and then the English
made them not subject to ther kings, and by ther lying to
rong their kings. we knew it to be true, and we promising
them that how ever in government to indians all should be
alicke and that we knew it was our kings will it should be so,
that altho we wear wecker then other Colonies, thay having
submited to our king to protect them others dared not otherwise to molest them, so thay expresed thay tooke that to be
well, that we had litell Case to doute but that to us under the
king thay wold have yelded to our determenations in what
ani should have Cumplained to us against them, but Philop
Charged it to be disonesty in us to put of the hering the
complaints therfore we Consented to here them. thay saied
thay had bine the first in doing good to the English, and the
English the first in doing rong, saied when the English first
Came their kings father was as a great man and the English
as a litell Child, he Constraened other indians from ronging
the English and gave them Coren and shewed them how to
plant and was free to do them ani good and had let them have
a 100 times more land, then now the king had for his own
peopell, but ther kings brother when he was king Came miser-

---

[1] In so far as. [2] Lest.
[3] Neither Roger Williams nor any other religious leader appears to have tried
to Christianize the Narragansetts so persistently as John Eliot worked in Massachusetts.

abely to dy by being forsed to Court as thay judged poysoned,[1]
and another greavanc was if 20 of there onest indians testefied
that a Englishman had dun them rong, it was as nothing,
and if but one of ther worst indians testefied against ani
indian or ther king when it plesed the English that was sufitiant.
a nother grivanc was when ther kings sold land the English
wold say it was more than thay agred to and a writing must
be prove[2] against all them, and sum of ther kings had dun
rong to sell so much   he left his peopell none and sum being
given to drunknes the English made them drunk and then
cheted them in bargens, but now ther kings wear forewarned
not for to part with land for nothing in Cumpareson to the
valew therof. now home[3] the English had owned for king
or queen thay[4] wold disinheret, and make a nother king that
wold give or seell them there land, that now thay had no
hopes left to kepe ani land. a nother grivanc the English
Catell and horses still incresed that when thay removed 30
mill from wher English had anithing to do, thay Could not
kepe ther coren from being spoyled, thay never being iused
to fence, and thoft when the English boft[5] land of them that
thay wold have kept ther Catell upone ther owne land. a
nother grevanc the English wear so eger to sell the indians
lickers that most of the indians spent all in drunknes and then
ravened upone the sober indians and thay did belive often did
hurt the English Catell, and ther kings Could not prevent it.
we knew before these were ther grand Cumplaints, but then
we only indevered to perswaid that all Cumplaints might be
righted without war, but Could have no other answer but that
thay had not herd of that way for the Governer of yorke and
a indian king to have the hering of it. we had Case to thinke
in[6] that had bine tendred it wold have bine acsepted. we
indevered that however thay should lay doune ther arems for
the English wear to strong for them. thay saied then the
English should do to them as thay did when thay wear to
strong for the english. so we departed without ani discurtious-
nes, and sudingly had leter from Plimoth Governer thay intended in arems to Conforem[7] philop, but no information
what that was thay required or what termes he refused to

---

[1] See *post*, p. 26, note 2.   [2] **Proof.**   [3] Whom.   [4] The English.
[5] Thought; bought.   [6] It.   [7] Conform, subdue.

have ther quarell desided, and in a weckes time after we had bine with the indians the war thus begun. Plimoth soldiers were Cum to have ther head quarters within 10 mile of philop. then most of the English therabout left ther houses and we had leter from Plimoth governer to desier our help with sum boats if thay had such ocation and for us to looke to our selefs and from the genarall[1] at the quarters we had leter of the day thay intended to Cum upon the indians and desier for sum of our bots to atend, so we tooke it to be of nesesety for our Ieslanders one halef one day and night to atend and the other halef the next, so by turens for our oune safty. in this time sum indians fell a pilfering sum houses that the English had left, and a old man and a lad going to one of those houses did see 3[2] indians run out therof. the old man bid the young man shoote so he did and a indian fell doune but got away againe. it is reported that then sum indians Came to the gareson asked why thay shot the indian. thay asked whether he was dead. the indians saied yea. a English lad saied it was no mater. the men indevered to inforem them it was but an idell lads words but the indians in hast went away and did not harken to them. the next day[3] the lad that shot the indian and his father and fief[4] English more wear killed so the war begun with philop. but ther was a queen[5] that i knew was not a party with philop and Plimoth Governer recumended her that if shee wold cum to our Iesland it wold be well and shee desiered shee might if it wear but with six of hir men. I Can sufitiantly prove, but it is to large here to relate, that shee had practised much the quarell might be desided without war, but sum of our English allso in fury against all indians wold not Consent shee should be reseved to our Iesland alltho I profered to be at all the Charg to secuer

[1] Better known as Major James Cudworth. He was commander-in-chief by virtue of his command of the Plymouth forces representing the colony most interested.

[2] The reading is probably 3, possibly 30.

[3] June 24. See *post*, p. 28. On this same day an attack was made upon an Englishman at Rehoboth and upon June 25 two Englishmen were killed at Fall River.

[4] Five.

[5] The queen referred to was Weetamoo, queen of Pocasset, widow of Alexander the elder brother and predecessor of Philip.

hir and those shee desiered to Cum with hir, so at length prevailed we might send for hir, but one day acsedentaly we wear
prevented, and then our men had seased sum Cannos on hir
side suposing they wear Philops and the next day a English
house was there burned and mischif of ether side indevered
to the other and much dun, hir houses burned, so we wear prevented of ani menes to atain hir. the English army Cam not
doune as informed thay wold[1] so Philop got over and thay
could not find him. 3 days after thay came doune had a veri
stormy night, that in the morning the foote wear disabled to
returen before thay had refreshment. thay wear free to acsept
as we wear willing to relive them, but [boston] trupers Sayed
[by][2] thear Captaine[3] thay despised it and so left the foote.
after the foote had refreshed themselefs thay allso returned
to ther head quarters, and after hunt[ing] Philop from all sea
shors that thay Could not tell what was becum of him, the
naroganset kings informed us that the queen aforesaied must
be in a thicket a starving or conformed to Philop, but thay
knew shee wold be glad to be from them, so from us had in-
curedgment to get hir and as mani as thay Could from Philop.
after the English army with out our Consent or informing us
came into our coleny,[4] broft the naroganset indians to artickels
of agreement to them philop being flead about a 150 indians
Came in to a Plimoth gareson volentarely. Plimoth authority
sould all for slafes (but about six of them) to be Caried out of
the Cuntry.[5]—it is true the indians genaraly ar very barbarus
peopell but in this war I have not herd of ther tormenting ani

[1] The "English army" refers probably to the troops from Boston. Massachusetts at first thought that trouble would be averted by mediation, but on
June 26 troops were sent to aid the Plymouth forces. They reached Swansey
two days later, delayed by bad weather and some small engagements.

[2] The words in brackets are conjectural; the manuscript seems to read
"bonton."

[3] Probably Captain Thomas Prentice is meant.

[4] The troops from Plymouth and Boston seem to have aroused the jealousy
of the Rhode Islanders by their independent action. The treaty referred to is
the so-called treaty of July 15, 1675. "Broft" means brought.

[5] After the destruction of Dartmouth or New Bedford in July, 1675, Indians
who had no part in the attack were persuaded to surrender by promises of protection from the whites. They were then taken to Plymouth where, as stated
in the text, the whole party to the number of about 160 were ordered to be sold
as slaves. It was not the only instance of the treatment here mentioned.

but that the English army Cote an old indian and tormented him. he was well knone to have bine a long time a veri decreped and haremless indian of the queens. as Philop flead the fore said queen got to the narogansets and as mani of hir men as shee could get, but one part of the narogansets agreement to bostun was to kill or deliver as mani as they Could of philops peopell, therfore bostun men demanded the fore said queene and others that thay had so reseved for which the indians wear unfree and made mani excuses as that the queen was none of them and sum others wear but sudieners[1] with philop becase removed by the English having got ther land and wear of ther kindred which we kno is true. not but we think thay did shelter mani thay should not, and that thay did kno sum of ther men did asist Philop, but acording to ther barbarus ruells thay acounted so was no rong or thay could not help it, but sum enemis heds thay did send in and told us thay wear informed that however when winter Came thay might be suer the English wold be ther enemies, and so thay stood doutful for about 5 months. the English wear jelous that ther was a genarall plot of all indians against English and the indians wear in like maner jelous of the english. I think it was genarall that thay wear unwilling to be ronged and that the indians do judg the English partiall against them and among all a philthy Crue that did desier and indever for war and those of ani solidety wear against it and indevered to prevent the war,[2] for conserning Philop we have good intelegenc that he advised sum English to be gon from ther out plases wher thay lived or thay wear in danger to be killed, but whether it wear to prevent a war, or by ther prests informed if thay begun thay should be beaten and otherwise not so we have good intelegenc for I do think most of them had a desier the English wold begin, and if the English be not carefull to manefest the indians mai expect equity from them, thay mai have more enemies then thay wold and more Case of Jelosy. the report is that to the estward the war thus began, by suposing that sum of those indians wear at a fight in thes parts and that thear thay sa a man wonded, so authority sent sum forth to discufer, having before disarmed those indians

[1] Sojourners.
[2] War against the Narragansetts was not declared until November.

and confined them to a place, which the indians wear not
ofended at, but those men Coming upon them in a warlike
postuer thay fled that the men Cote but 3 of them. those in
authority sent out againe to excuse them selefs, but thay could
only cum to the spech with one man as he kept out of ther
reach. thay excused them selefs and saied his father was not
hurt, one of them thay had taken. he saied he could not belive them, for if it wer so thay wold have broft him, thay had
bin desaitfull to disarem them and so wold have killed them
all, and so he run away, and then English wear killed, and the
report is that up in the cuntri here away thay had demanded
the indians arems and went againe to parell[1] with them and
the indians by ambushcade tretcherously killed 8 that wear
going to treat with them. when winter was Cum we had
leter from bostun of the iunited Comitioners that thay wear
resolved to reduce the narogansets to Conformity not to be
trubled with them ani more and desiered sum help of botes and
otherwise if we sa Case and that we should kepe secret conserning it. our governer sent them word we wear satesfied nara-
gansets wear tretcherous, and had ayded Philop, and as we
had asisted to relive ther army before so we should be redy to
asist them still, and advised that terems might be tendered
that such might expect Cumpation[2] that wold acsept not to
ingag in war and that ther might be a seperation betwene the
gilty and the inosent which in war Could not be expected, we
not in the lest expecting thay wold have begun the war and
not before proclaimed it or not give them Defianc,[3] I having
often informed the indians that English men wold not begin
a war otherwise it was brutish so to do. i am sory so the
indians have Case to think me desaitfull for the English thus
began the war with the narogansets we having sent ofe our
Iesland mani indians and informed them if thay kept by the
water sides and did not medell that how ever the English

[1] Parley. The lines following are considered by some as an unjust statement of the case of Wonolancet and the Indians in the Merrimac country, and
the claim is made that the offense was on the side of the whites.

[2] Compensation.

[3] War was declared by the Commissioners at Boston on September 9, 1675.
In October the size of the war force was increased and Josiah Winslow of Plymouth
placed in command.

wold do them no harem alltho it was not save for us to let
them live here. the army first take all those prisoners then
fell upone indian houses burned them and killed sum men.
the war [began] without proclemation and sum of our peopell
did not kno the English had begun mischif to the indians   and
being Confedent and had Case therfore, that the indians wold
not hurt them before the English begun, so did not kepe ther
gareson exactly, but the indians having reseved that mischif
Came unexpected upone them destroyed 145 ¹ of them beside other gret lose, but the English army say thay suposed
coneticot forses had bine there. thay solde the indians that
thay had taken as aforesaied, for slafes, but one old man that
was Caried of our Iesland upone his suns back. he was so
decriped Could not go and when the army tooke them upone
his back Caried him to the garison, sum wold have had him
devouered by doges but the tendernes of sum of them prevailed to Cut ofe his head, and after Came sudingly upone the
indians whear the indians had prepared to defend themselefs
and so reseved and did much mischif and for aboute six wecks
sinc hath bine spent as for both parties to recruet, and now
the English army is out to seecke after the indians but it is
most lickly that such most abell to do mischif will escape and
women and children and impotent mai be destroyed and so
the most abell will have the les incumbranc to do mischif.²

but I am confident it wold be best for English and indians
that a peas wear made upone onest terems for each to have a
dew propriety and to injoy it without opretion or iusurpation
by one to the other. but the English dear not trust the indians promises nether the indians to the Englishes promises
and each have gret Case therfore. I see no way lickly but
if a sesation from arems might be procured untill it might be
knone what terems King Charels wold propound, for we have
gret Case to think the naroganset kings wold trust our king
and that thay wold have acsepted him to be umpier if it had
bine tendered about ani diferanc, for we do kno the English
have had much contention against those indians to invaled
the kings determenation for naroganset to be in our colony,

¹ Or perhaps the reading is 14.
² Compare this account of the proceedings of the summer of 1675 with that
given in *The Present State, post*, pp. 29–31.

and we have Case to think it was the greatest Case of the war against them. I see no menes lickly to procuer a sesation from arems exept the governer of new york can find a way so to intersete and so it will be lickly a pease mai be made without trubling our king. not but it allwais hath bine a prinsipell in our Colony that ther should be but one supreme to English men and in our natief Cuntry wher ever English have jurisdiction and so we know no English should begin a war and not first tender for the king to be umpier and not persecute such that will not Conforem to ther worship, and ther worship be what is not owned by the king. the king not to mind to have such things redresed, sum mai take it that he hath not pouer, and that ther mai be a wai for them to take pouer in oposition to him. I am so perswaided of new England prists thay ar so blinded by the spiret of persecution and to maintaine to have hyer, and to have rume to be mere hyerlings that thay have bine the Case that the law of nations and the law of arems have bine voiolated in this war, and that the war had not bine if ther had not bine a hyerling that for his maneging what he Caleth the gospell, by voiolenc to have it Chargabell for his gaine from his quarters and if ani in magestrasy be not so as ther pack horses thay will be trumpating for inovation or war.

5th : 12m : 1675. *Roadiesland.*

JOHN EASTON

THE PRESENT STATE OF NEW-ENGLAND WITH RESPECT TO THE INDIAN WAR, BY N. S., 1675

NOTE:

It is necessary to explain that, although it is customary in these reprints to preserve exactly the spelling and capitalization of the originals (though punctuation is often amended if it is misleading), this cannot be predicated of the pieces which stand second, third, fourth, and fifth in the present volume. The text of them presented in Drake's *Old Indian Chronicles,* which has all the appearance of close conformity to the originals, was taken as printer's copy. Collation with the rare originals was not practicable at the time when the book was prepared. When the opportunity for it was secured, it was discovered too late that Drake's text differed very widely from his originals in capitalization, and sometimes varied from them in spelling. But though correction of all these differences had become impracticable, all significant errors have been corrected.

J. F. J.

INTRODUCTION

IF it was fitting that the first narrative in this series dealing with our early Indian wars should come from Rhode Island it is equally important that Massachusetts should give us our account of the main features of King Philip's war. Massachusetts was the natural leader of New England at this time, and she suffered and fought for the preservation of New England from destruction at the hands of the Indians. The three following accounts of the state of New England at successive stages of the war, together with an equally vivid narration of the war's conclusion, detail the most important events of its beginning, progress, and end. They are well placed between the statements of a Rhode Island Friend as to the origin of the trouble and the experience of a clergyman's wife during its continuance.

The three letters of "N. S.," presumed to be Nathaniel Saltonstall, were "composed by a merchant in Boston and communicated to his friend in London." They were written in 1675 and 1676 when Saltonstall was about thirty-six years of age, and had been about sixteen years out of college. These narratives were "printed for Dorman Newman" at London during 1676, and with the addition of a short account by Richard Hutchinson of *The War in New England Visibly Ended* gave England a record of a most fierce struggle with the Indians, during which New England asked no military aid from Old England lest she be unable to free herself from the soldiers once they were received. Thus she gave proof of her desire for freedom and her willingness to protect herself

21

even if she could not do away with the inevitable control
from across the sea. The resources of Massachusetts were so
strained by this struggle with the Indians that she was unable
to resist successfully England's effort to take away her charters
in 1684, thus losing her much-prized local independence for
nearly a century.

The tracts here printed are four out of a larger number,
at least eight, which their writers in Boston sent over to
friends in London, and which were there printed in 1675–1677
as bulletins of the struggle. They are now very rare. Several
were reprinted by Samuel G. Drake in 1836 and 1850, and the
present four, with three others, appeared in 1867 in the second
edition of his work called *The Old Indian Chronicle*. The
four here selected give a continuous account of the war, which
the others would duplicate in part, and to which they would
add little.

Longer narratives exist, written by William Hubbard,
Increase Mather, and Thomas Church. That of Hubbard,
minister of Ipswich, entitled *Narrative of the Troubles with the
Indians* (Boston, 1677, and several times reprinted), appeared
in 1865 in an excellent edition with notes by Samuel G. Drake.
Selections from Hubbard's relation have been published in the
Old South Historical Leaflets (no. 88). The experiences of
Colonel Benjamin Church, the military hero of the war from
the colonial point of view, were detailed by his son Thomas
Church in a work entitled *Entertaining Passages Relating to
Philip's War* (Boston, 1716, reprinted in 1865–1867, with
elaborate notes by Dr. Henry M. Dexter), but they furnish
no such comprehensive record as is here given. The account
by Increase Mather in his *Brief History of the War* is well
known. It is that of a clergyman primarily interested in
religious history and treating events chiefly if not exclusively
as regards their effect upon the New England Church. For
this reason it is more appropriate that the record as given by

Saltonstall and Hutchinson, having neither military nor religious bias, should be given the central place in this volume. The influence of King Philip's war was primarily on the people as constituting a state and it should be described by a man of the people and of the state. Such a man was Saltonstall. Richard Hutchinson, nephew of Anne Hutchinson, and a member of the family which later gave Massachusetts a worthy historian and a notable governor in the person of Thomas Hutchinson, his relative, was a man of the same type. His father, of the same name, was a wealthy ironmonger in London, and it is possible that this letter was addressed to him. Hutchinson the younger returned to London shortly after the death of Philip; his subsequent history is unknown to the present editor.

THE PRESENT STATE OF NEW-ENGLAND
WITH RESPECT TO THE INDIAN WAR

The Present State of New-England With Respect to the Indian War,
Wherein is an Account of the true Reason thereof, (as far as can be judged by Men), Together with most of the Remarkable Passages that have happened from the 20th of June, till the 10th of November, 1675.
Faithfully Composed by a Merchant of Boston and Communicated to his Friend in London. Licensed Decemb. 13, 1675. Roger L'Estrange.
London: Printed for Dorman Newman, at the Kings-Arms in the Poultry, and at the Ship and Anchor at the Bridg-foot on Southwark side, 1675.[1]

The Present State of New-England with respect to the Indian War.[2]

THERE being many and various Reports concerning the Causes of the present War amongst us, it may not be amiss in the First Place, to give you a true Account of the Reasons thereof; which probably may add Something to the Satisfaction of our Christian Friends in Old England, Which is thus:

About five or six Years since, there was brought up (amongst others) an Indian in the Colledg at Cambridg, named Sosoman,[3] who after some Time he had spent in Preaching the Gospel to Unkus,[4] a Sagamore Christian in his Territories, was by the Authority of New-Plimouth sent to Preach in like Manner to King Philip, and his Indians: But King Philip (Heathen-

[1] Title-page of the original print.

[2] This narrative should not be confused with the edition of Rev. William Hubbard's *Narrative*, published in London in 1677 under the title *The Present State of New England being A Narrative of the Troubles with the Indians*, etc.

[3] See *ante*, p. 7, note 2, and *post*, p. 54.

[4] More commonly Uncas, the most famous of the Mohegan chiefs, who gave that tribe the Indian supremacy from the Connecticut River to the Thames.

like) instead of receiving the Gospel, would immediately have killed this Sosomon, but by the Perswasion of some about him did not do it, but sent him by the Hands of three of his Men to Prison; who as he was going to Prison, Exhorted and Taught them in the Christian Religion; they not liking his Discourse, immediately Murthered him after a most Barbarous Manner; They returning to King Philip, acquainted him what they had done. About two or three Months after, this Murther being Discovered to the Authority of New-Plimouth, Josiah Winslow being then Governour of that Colony, care was taken to find out the Murtherers; who upon Search were found and apprehended, and after a fair Trial were all Hanged.[1]

This so Exasperated King Philip, that from that Day after, he studied to be Revenged on the English, judging that the English Authority have Nothing to do to Hang any of his Indians for killing another.

In order thereunto, his first Errand is to a Squaw Sachem[2] (*i. e.* a Woman Prince, or Queen) who is the Widow of a Brother to King Philip, deceased, he promising her great Rewards if she would joyn with him in this Conspiracy, (for she is as Potent a Prince as any round about her, and hath as much Corn, Land, and Men, at her Command) she willingly consented, and was much more forward in the Design, and had greater Success than King Philip himself. The Place where this King Philip doth dwell, is on a Parcel of Land, called in English, Mount Hope,[3] about twelve Miles long, and judged to be the best Land in New England: And it was about thirty five Miles off of this Place, to the Northward, that the first English that ever came there, Landed; and by Degrees built Houses, and called the Name of the Place New-Plimouth,[4]

---

[1] Three were sentenced but one was reprieved for a month and then shot.

[2] Increase Mather considers Philip's first preparations as precautionary in case he be called to account for the death of Sausimun. The Squaw Sachem was Weetamoo, "queen of Pocasset," widow of Philip's elder brother Alexander. " N. S." confuses her with Awashonks, a sister of Ninigret.

[3] Mount Hope, or Montop, the Indian Pokanoket in the southern part of the present Bristol, Rhode Island, was the headquarters of Philip during the first part of the war. Pocasset was in the present Tiverton.

[4] This locality, called by the Indians Accomacke, was named Plymouth by Captain John Smith in 1614 and is so noted on his map of New England presented to Prince Charles.

(because Plimouth in Old England was the last Place they were at there.) The English took not a Foot of Land from the Indians, but Bought all, and although they bought for an inconsiderable Value; yet they did Buy it. And it may be judged that now King Philip repents himself, seeing what Product the English have made of a Wilderness, through their Labour, and the Blessing of God thereon; All the Land of the Colony of New Plimouth, was at first Bought of this King Philip's Grandfather,[1] Massasoit, by Name, except some few Parcels he hath Sold to some of the Inhabitants of Swanzy, not far from Mount Hope. Thereupon about five Years since, took an Occasion to Quarrel with the Town, partly because he was vexed he had Sold his Land, and partly because his Brother died five or six Years before, and he thought the English had Poysoned him,[2] and thereupon he troubled them, but killed none; but the Governour by timely Preparation hindred them of doing any hurt.

Thus after King Philip had secured his Interest in Squaw Sachem, (whom he perswaded that the English had Poysoned her Husband and thereupon she was the more willing to joyn with him)[3] he privately sent Messengers to most of the Indian Sagamores and Sachems round about him, telling them that the English had a Design to cut off all the Indians round about them, and that if they did not Joyn together, they should lose their Lives and Lands; whereupon several Sachems became his Confederates. And having now five Years Time, had Opportunity enough to furnish themselves with Ammunition and Arms, which they did plentifully at Canada, amongst the French; and it is judged that some English have also Sold them some Arms through Ignorance of their Design.

In the mean Time King Philip Mustered up about Five Hundred of his Men, and Arms them compleat; and had

[1] Philip, although second in succession, was the son and not the grandson of Massasoit or Woosamequen.

[2] There is no authority for the statement that Alexander was poisoned. The fact that he was entertained by Josiah Winslow at Marshfield shortly before his death may have caused the suspicion here noted.

[3] Philip seems to have married a sister of the Squaw Sachem, and Alexander's widow had trouble with Petananuet or Petownonowit, her second husband. These may be reasons why she sided with Philip rather than with the English whom her husband favored.

gotten about Eight or Nine Hundred of his Neighbouring Indians, and likewise Arms them compleat;[1] (*i. e.* Guns, Powder, and Bullets,) but how many he hath engaged to be of his Party, is unknown to any among us. The last Spring several Indians were seen in small Parties, about Rehoboth and Swansey, which not a little affrighted the Inhabitants.[2] Who demanding the Reason of them, wherefore it was so? Answer was made, That they were only on their own Defence, for they understood that the English intended to Cut them off. About the 20th of June last, Seven or Eight of King Philip's Men came to Swansey on the Lords Day, and would grind a Hatchet at an Inhabitants House there; the Master told them, it was the Sabbath Day, and their God would be very angry if he should let them do it. They returned this Answer, They knew not who his God was, and that they would do it for all him, or his God either. From thence they went to another House, and took away some Victuals, but hurt no Man. Immediately they met a Man travelling on the Road, kept him in Custody a short Time, then dismist him quietly; giving him this Caution, that he should not work on his God's Day, and that he should tell no Lies.

These Things happening, with many others of the like Nature, gave the Rehoboth and Swansey Men great Cause of Jealousies; which occasioned them to send to Plimouth, and to the Bay (*i. e.* Boston) for some Assistance, in Case they should need it. But before any came to them, they of both Towns were gathered together into three Houses, Men, Women, and Children, and there had all Provisions in common, so that they who had Nothing wanted not. Immediately after, Notice came hereof to the Governour of the Massachusets Colony, (Boston being Metropolis, and the Honourable John Leveret[3] Governour thereof.) Drums beat up for Volunteers, and in three Hours Time were Mustered up about an Hundred

---

[1] Great efforts had been made to obtain arms and ammunition from the Indians, *e. g.*, at Taunton in 1671, and communication between Indians and French was not intimate at this time. It is doubtful therefore if anything like the number of Indians here mentioned were armed "compleat."

[2] Swansey (or Swansea), "the next town to Philip's country," and Rehoboth (or Seaconke), six miles away, might well be alarmed. The former was said to consist "of forty dwelling houses, most of them very fair buildings."

[3] Leverett is the more usual spelling.

and ten Men, Captain Samuel Mosely being their Commander.[1] This Captain Mosely hath been an old Privateer at Jamaica, an excellent Souldier, and an undaunted Spirit, one whose Memory will be Honourable in New-England, for his many eminent Services he hath done the Publick. There were also among these Men, about Ten or Twelve Privateers, that had been there sometime before: They carried with them several Dogs, that proved serviceable to them, in finding out the Enemy in their Swamps; one whereof, would for several Days together, go out and bring to them six, eight, or ten young Pigs of King Philip's Herds. There went out also amongst these Men, one Cornellis[2] a Dutchman, who had lately been Condemned to die for Piracy, but afterwards received a Pardon; he willing to shew his Gratitude therefore, went out and did several good Services abroad against the Enemy.

Plimouth also sent out several Men at the same Time, both Horse and Foot: Also most Towns in all the United Colonies thereabout sent out some more, some less, as they were in Number. By this Time the Indians have killed several of our Men, but the first that was killed was June 23, a Man at Swansey, that he and his Family had left his House amongst the Rest of the Inhabitants; and adventuring with his Wife and Son, (about twenty Years old) to go to his House to fetch them Corn, and such like Things: He having just before sent his Wife and Son away, as he was going out of the House, was set on and shot by Indians; his Wife being not far off, heard the Guns go off, went back: They took her, first defiled her, then skinned her Head, as also the Son, and dismist them both, who immediately died.[3] They also the next Day killed six or seven Men at Swansey, and two more at one of the Garri-

---

[1] Captain Moseley (or Mosley) was not the only aid from the East coming in reply to Rhode Island's appeal. Massachusetts sent Captains Daniel Henchman, Thomas Prentice, and Nicholas Paige on June 26, and the forces from Plymouth under Major James Cudworth, Captains Matthew Fuller and Benjamin Church reached Taunton June 21.

[2] The full name is Cornelius Consert.

[3] Hubbard mentions "one Jones" as among the first six persons killed in the war, but omits the incidents relating to the family. In the absence of corroborative evidence we shall do well to reject the details here given. The ravishing of captured white women was not the practice of the seventeenth-century Indian.

sons; and as two Men that went out of one of the Garrisons to draw a Bucket of Water, were shot and carried away, and afterwards found with their Fingers and Feet cut off, and the Skin of their Heads flayed off.

About fourteen Days after that, they sent for more Help; whereupon the Authority of Boston, made Captain Thomas Savage the Major General in that Expedition, who with sixty Horse, and as many Foot,[1] went out of Boston; having prest Horses for the Footmen, and six Carts to carry Provisions with them: Whereof Mr. John Morse was Commissary General abroad, and Mr. Nathaniel Williams Commissary at Home.[2] They Travelled Day and Night till they came to their Garrisons, and within three Days after, marched Horse and Foot (leaving Guards in the Garrisons) towards Mount Hope, where King Philip and his Wife was; they came on him at unawares, so that Philip was forced to rise from Dinner, and he and all with him fled out of that Land, called Mount Hope, up further into the Countrey; they pursued them as far as they could go for Swamps, and killed fifteen or sixteen in that Expedition, and returned, and took what he had that was worth taking, and spoiled the Rest, taking all his Cattel and Hogs they could find, and also took Possession of Mount Hope, which had then a thousand Acres under Corn, which is since cut down by the English, and disposed of according to their Discretion.

Cornellis was in this Exploit, and pursued Philip so hard, that he got his Cap off his Head, and now weareth it.

About three Days after, the General (finding Cornellis to be a Stout Man, and willing to venture his Life in the Cause of the English) sent him with twelve Men under his Command to Scout about, with Orders to return in three Hours on Pain of Death; in his Way he met sixty Indians that were halling their Cannoues a-shore, he set on them, killing thirteen, and took eight alive, pursues the Rest as far as he could go for the Swamps; then he returned and Burnt all those Cannoues, about forty in Number: By this Time Cornellis and his twelve Men (all being preserved) returned to the Camp, but

---

[1] The size of Captain Savage's force varies according to different accounts from that here given to 380.

[2] John Morse and Nathaniel Williams were both prominent citizens of Boston.

they were eight Hours absent: Whereupon a Council of War was called, who past the Sentence of Death on him, for exceeding the Order given him. Immediately was also Pardoned, and received thanks for his good Service done in that Expedition; and was in a short Time sent out on the like Design, and brought Home with him twelve Indians alive, and two Indians Heads (*i. e.*, the Skin with the Hair on it.)

About the 25th of July, the General[1] returned with twelve Men to guard his Person.

Captain Mosely being there, and plying about, found Eighty Indians, who surrendered themselves, and were secured in a House provided for them near Plimouth: Thereupon came to Boston, to know the Pleasure of the Authority about them, and in a Days Time returned with this Order; he should kill none that he took alive, but secure them in Order to a Transportation; Wherefore afterwards there were Shipt on board Captain Sprague[2] an Hundred seventy eight Indians, on the 28th of September, bound for Cales.[3]

In this Time, the Indians continued daily to commit many Acts of Hostility on the English; they Burnt Twenty three Houses at Swansey, and killed many People there, and took much Cattle, as also Burnt the Hay and Corn in great Quantities. They Burnt near thirty Houses in Dartmouth,[4] (a Place in New-Plimouth Colony) killing many People after a most Barbarous Manner; as skinning them all over alive, some only their Heads, cutting off their Hands and Feet; but any Woman they take alive, they Defile, afterwards putting her to Death by some of these or the like Ways. They have Burnt most of the Houses in Rehoboth, Taunton, and Swansey; a Party of Indians came to Mendham, which is Thirty-two Miles from Boston, and there killed five or six Persons, who being pursued, two were killed, the Rest fled.[5]

---

[1] This statement may refer to the return of Savage to Boston, but more probably alludes to that of Cudworth to Scituate.

[2] Probably Captain Richard Sprague of Charlestown, Massachusetts.

[3] The Indians may be the women and children left by Philip upon his escape from the swamp. Cales is Cadiz in Spain.

[4] Dartmouth, which included the present New Bedford. The part of the town suffering most is now known as South Dartmouth.

[5] Mendon was surprised on July 14, 1675, the first place in the Massachusetts Bay to be assaulted.

Some Part of our Forces afterwards set on about Five hundred Indians, not far from Pocassit, pursuing them into a large Swamp, not far from thence; how many they killed is not known, in regard the Indians adventured back and took their dead Men away with them: (as they commonly do if they can possibly.) But in this Fight were killed King Philip's Brother, his Privy Councellor, (being one formerly Educated at Cambridg) and one of his chief Captains; the Heads of which three were afterwards brought to Boston. There were killed in this Pursuit six Englishmen, and nine or ten wounded.[1]

This Pocassit Swamp, is judged about seven or eight Miles long, and so full of Bushes and Trees, that a Parcel of Indians may be within the Length of a Pike of a Man, and he cannot discover them; and besides, this as well as all other Swamps, is so soft Ground, that an Englishman can neither go nor stand thereon, and yet these bloody Savages will run along over it, holding their Guns cross their Arms (and if Occasion be) discharge in that Posture.

On the Lords Day, the   of July, an Indian came to Dorchester, (within half a Mile of Mother Georges House) to the House of Mr. Minor, in Sermon Time, and there were then at Home the Maid Servant and two young Children, she keeping the Door shut for Safety; the Indian when he saw he could not come in at the Door, went about to come in at the Window, she perceiving his Resolution, took two Brass Kettles, under which she put the two Children, she ran up Stairs and charged a Musket and fired at the Indian, (he having fired at her, once or twice and mist her, but struck the Top of one Kettle, under which a child was) and shot him into his Shoulder; then he let his Gun fall, and was just coming in at the Window, she made haste and got a Fire-shovel full of live Coles and applied them to his Face, which forced him to flie and escape: But one was found dead within five Miles of that Place afterwards, and was judged to be this by his scalded Face.

[1] No other contemporary writer gives these details and "N. S." unites several occurrences into one engagement. Philip had a brother Sonconewhew who signed a deed for him in 1668 and who may have been one of the Indians educated at Cambridge. Pocasset was in modern Tiverton and Little Compton, Rhode Island.

These Transactions may be computed to end with July. Before any further Progress be made in this Relation, it may not be amiss to give you some Account of what concerns our Neighbour Indians at Peace with us.

There are two Potent Sagamores, that are in Amity with us: The one is Ninnicroft,[1] his Territories border on Connecticot Colony; the other is Unkus, the only Christian Sagamore among them.

This Unkus, and all his Subjects professing Christianity, are called Praying Indians. In the first Week in August, the Authority of Boston sent an Express to him, to require him to come in and Surrender himself, Men, and Arms, to the English; Whereupon, he sent along with the Messenger his three Sons, and about Sixty of his Men, with his Arms, to be thus disposed of, *viz.* His two youngest Sons, (about thirty Years old) to remain as Hostages (as now they do at Cambridg) and his Eldest Son to go Captain of the Men as Assistants to the English against the Heathens, which accordingly they did. And the English not thinking themselves yet secure enough, because they cannot know a Heathen from a Christian by his Visage, nor Apparel: The Authority of Boston, at a Council held there the 30th of August, Published this following Order.

At a Council held in Boston, August 30, 1675.

The Council judging it of absolute Necessity for the Security of the English, and the Indians that are in Amity with us, that they be Restrained their usual Commerce with the English, and Hunting in the Woods, during the Time of Hostility with those that are our Enemies,

Do Order, that all those Indians that are desirous to Approve themselves Faithful to the English, be Confined to their several Plantations under-written, until the Council shall take further Order; and that they so order the setting of their Wigwams, that

[1] Ninnicroft or Ninigret was chief of the Eastern Niantic Indians, seated between the Pawcatuck River and Point Judith; their chief town was Wekapaug, now Westerly, Rhode Island. The Niantics are considered a division of the Narragansetts and Ninigret professed friendship for Rhode Island. For Unkus see *ante*, p. 24. His best-known sons were Oneko (Owaneco) and Attawamhood or Joshua.

they may stand Compact in some one Part of their Plantations respectively, where it may be best for their own Provision and Defence. And that none of them do presume to Travel above one Mile from the Center of such their Dwelling, unless in Company with some English, or in their Service near their Dwellings; and excepting for gathering and fetching in their Corn with one Englishman, on peril of being taken as our Enemies, or their Abettors: And in Case that any of them shall be taken without the Limits abovesaid, except as abovesaid, and do lose their Lives, or be otherwise damnified, by English or Indians; The Council do hereby Declare, that they shall account themselves wholly Innocent, and their Blood or other Dammage (by them sustained) will be upon their own Heads. Also it shall not be lawful for any Indians that are in Amity with us, to entertain any strange Indians, or receive any of our Enemies Plunder, but shall from Time to Time make Discovery thereof to some English, that shall be Appointed for that End to sojourn among them, on Penalty of being reputed our Enemies, and of being liable to be proceeded against as such.

Also, whereas it is the Manner of the Heathen that are now in Hostility with us, contrary to the Practice of all Civil Nations, to Execute their bloody Insolencies by Stealth, and Sculking in small Parties, declining all open Decision of their Controversie, either by Treaty or by the Sword,

The Council do therefore Order, That after the Publication of the Provision aforesaid, It shall be lawful for any Person, whether English or Indian, that shall find any Indians Travelling or Sculking in any of our Towns or Woods, contrary to the Limits above-named, to command them under their Guard and Examination, or to Kill and destroy them as they best may or can. The Council hereby declaring, That it will be most acceptable to them that none be Killed or Wounded that are Willing to surrender themselves into Custody.

The Places of the Indians Residencies are, Natick, Punquapaog, Nashoba, Wamesit, and Hassanemesit:[1] And if there be any that belong to any other Plantations, they are to Repair to some one of these.

By the Council.
EDWARD RAWSON. Secr.

---

[1] These "Indian Residences" correspond to the modern Natick (Natchick), "The First Praying Town"; Punkapog or Punquapaog, now Canton, called by Gookin "The Second Praying Town"; Nashoba, later Lancaster, now Littleton; Wamesit, included in old Chelmsford, now in Lowell, and Hassanemesit, now Grafton. All these refuges were in the Massachusetts Bay colony. See Mrs. Rowlandson on Praying Indians, *post*, pp. 140, 152.

Which Company of Praying Indians[1] marched out of Town, (having saluted the Governour with three Volleys) and were appointed to march in the Front, which they did, and met with several Skirmishes, in which they Killed some, and about Forty five more Surrendred themselves; which were shipt off amongst those Captain Sprague carried away.

Concerning the Narragansets, Ninnicroft is their Saga-more; his Grand-father, and Father, always kept Truce with the English, but he now gives sufficient Cause to think other-wise of him.

The Squaw Sachem, having ran very far in her Engage-ments with King Philip, and fearing lest she should be taken, she committed her Person to the Possession of this Ninnicroft, judging herself safe by Virtue of his Protection; where she hath continued ever since July last. Whereupon a certain Number of Men were sent by the Authority of Connecticot Colony (John Wenthrop Governour) to the Narragansets,[2] to require them to deliver the Queen, and withal to Ratifie that long Peace they had maintained with the English: Whereupon the Narragansets concluded a Peace with them, and sent a Hundred Men to Connecticot for the Assistance of the Eng-lish. The English made this Agreement with them, That for every Indians Head-Skin they brought, they should have a Coat, (i. e. two Yards of Trucking Cloth, worth five Shillings per Yard here) and for every one they bring alive two Coats; for King Philips Head, Twenty Coats, and if taken alive, Forty Coats: These went out, and returned in Fourteen Days Time, bringing with them about Eighteen Heads in all.

Several other Sachems of the Countries, called in Indian, Nipmoog,[3] came to an English Town called Brookfield (but in Indian, Quawbawg), during the Time our Garrison was there, and told them they were Praying Indians (i. e. Christians)

[1] Oneko and his following of Mohegans, by no means all Christian Indians.

[2] John Winthrop, jr., governor of Connecticut 1657, 1659–1676. I find no other contemporary account of this important movement by Connecticut unless it be identified with the treaty of July 15. There is however no record of spoils and captives in connection with that treaty.

[3] The Nipmoog or Nipmuck, i. e., Fresh Water, Indians had no clearly de-fined location. Roughly they extended in Massachusetts east of the Connecti-cut River down the Blackstone or Nipmoog River and over a section east of northern Rhode Island.

and that they would be quiet, and do no Harm to the English; but withal, told them, that for their own Safety they could not deliver up their Arms: But the Inhabitants of Brookfield thought they would be Faithful, in regard they were Praying Indians, took their Words and dismist them.

The Authority of Boston, with the Advice of the Gover-nour of Connecticut, as also of Plimouth Colonies, then sit-ting in Council for several Days together at Boston,[1] For their better Satisfaction, sent a Party of thirty Horse under the Command of Captain Hutchison and Captain Wheeler;[2] when they were come to Quawbawg, they sent a Party of Horse to the Nipmoog Sachems to treat with them. (For you must understand that Captain Hutchison had a very consid-erable Farm therabouts, and had Occasion to employ several of those Sachems there, in Tilling and Plowing his Ground, and thereby he was known by Face to many of them.) The Sachems sent this Word, they would speak with none but Captain Hutchison himself; Whereupon Captain Hutchison and Cap-tain Wheeler sent them Word they would come to them themselves: Accordingly the Indians appointed the Meeting at such a Tree, and at such a Time. The Time being come Captain Hutchison, Captain Wheeler, and his Company, (with some of the Inhabitants of Brookfield, who thought them to be very Honest, therefore took no Arms with them) went to the Places, but the Nipmoog Indians were not there. Whereupon the Guide[3] that conducted them through the Woods, brought them to a Swamp not far off the appointed Place; out of which these Indians ran all at once and killed Sixteen Men, and Wounded Several others, of which Wounds three Weeks after, Captain Hutchison died, when his Wife and Son[4] were within twelve Miles of him in their Journey to see him; whose Death is the more lamented, in that his

---

[1] This was a meeting of the Commissioners of the United Colonies begin-ning October 2, 1675.

[2] Captains Edward Hutchinson and Thomas Wheeler. Perhaps the best contemporary account of the battle and defence of Brookfield is in Captain Wheeler's *True Narrative of the Lord's Providences* (Cambridge, 1676); see *post*, p. 38.

[3] The guides were Christian Indians.

[4] Presumably Elisha Hutchinson, grandfather of Thomas Hutchinson the governor and historian.

Mother and several others of his Relations, died by the Hands of the Indians, now near forty Years since.[1]

The rest that escaped, made what Haste they could to the Town of Brookfield, they made Choice of the Strongest House there, resolved to make a Garrison of it; in Order thereunto, as soon as they could, got all the People (about eighty in Number) into this House. The Indians pursued them close, and in four Hours Time had Burnt twenty and odd Houses in Brookfield, and abode there about three or four Days, shooting Day and Night, with most dreadful Screechings and Yellings, which Signified their Triumph. They in this Time endeavoured to set the Garrison on Fire divers Times, but by the Providence of God were prevented; once by a Shower of Rain, another Time by their Diligence within. One from within stept out to drink some Water and was killed, and one more killed within. The Bruits had contrived an Engine with many Wheels to fire the Garrison ten or twelve Rod off, and had loaded it with Combustibles therefore, (and News was brought to Boston that they were all Burnt, but it was not so) and had assuredly done it, had not Major Willard[2] come to their Relief with a flying Army of Sixty Horse, at nine or ten a Clock at Night; They forced their Way through the Body of the Indians, and fired Apace on them and in two Hours Time wholly Routed the Indians thence, killing several. Thus Deliverance was wrought by a mighty Hand for them, when they had no outward Reason to expect any.

During the Time these People kept themselves in that House, two Women were safely delivered of two Sons apiece, who in a Months Time brought them all themselves on Foot to Boston, where they were plentifully relieved out of the Church Stock there.

There are also another Sort of Indians, best known to the Commonalty of Boston by the name of Mr. Elliots Indians, or Captain Guggins Indians.[3] This Mr. Elliot, you must

[1] The celebrated Mrs. Anne Hutchinson, murdered by the Indians at Pelham Neck, New York, in 1643.

[2] Simon Willard, father of Rev. Samuel Willard, minister of the Old South Church in Boston and president of Harvard College.

[3] Rev. John Eliot, minister of Roxbury, and Apostle to the Indians; and Daniel Gookin, later major-general, who cared diligently for the Indians, and whose writings furnish our best description of those of Massachusetts.

understand, is the Man that hath by his own great Labour and Study, invented the Way of Printing the Indian Language, and hath also perfectly translated the whole Bible, with the Singing Psalms in Meeter; the Assemblies Catechism; the Practice of Piety, into the Indian Language; as also Written Several Books, very profitable for understanding the Grounds of Christian Religion; For which Pains and Labour, he deserves Honour from all such who are well-wishers to Things of the like Nature, whose Name will never Die in New-England.

A Specimen of his Translation of the Bible into the Indian Language, is as followeth.

Isaiah, Chap. 23, Ver. 1, 2, 3.

O O Weanun Tyre. O Onook kenaau Tarshishe kuht oonogquog, newutche mahchimoo, newaj matta wetuwomunoog, wanne petutteaun: wutch Chittimme ohkeit nag wehteduwahuoneau.

The burden of Tyre. Howl ye Ships of Tarshish; for it is laid waste, so that there is no house, no entering into it: from the Land of Chittim is it revealed to them.

2 Chequnappek wadohkeogish munóhhanébtu, ken, Zidone anaquishaenuog neg quoshkod teacheg keitoh, kenumwame chumuhkonukquog.

2 Be still, ye Inhabitants of the Isle; thou whom the Merchants of Zidon that pass over the Sea, have replenished.

3 Kah nashpe mishe nippeash, wuskannem Sihor, sepue kepenumoonk ne wutteashegenoom, kah noh wutohtimoinne ahhut kod tauwompasimuk.[1]

3 And by great Waters the Seed of Sihor, the Harvest of the River, is her Revenue, and she is a Mart of Nations.

This Captain Guggins is a Captain and Justice of Peace at Cambridg: He receives Thirty Pound *per annum* from the English, to sit as Judg among the Indians, to Judg any Difference (not Capital) among themselves, or between them and the English.

Of these Indians, thus distinguished, it may not be amiss to give a brief Account, in its proper Place.

Now it falls in Course, to think on what is done in the Field on both Sides.

---

[1] Corrected into accord with the edition of 1663.

On Thursday, the 5th of August, being Lecture Day at
Boston, was ordered by the Old Church[1] (of which the Governour is a Member) to be observed as a Fast by that Church,
which accordingly was done: And at the Contribution was
then collected Sixty Nine Pound, which was for the distressed
Families Relief. And on that very Day was Captain Hutchinson's Company so defeated: Which Thing was taken especial
Notice of, by all those who desire to see the Hand of God in
such sad Providences, which did occasion another Fast to be
kept by Mr. Mathers Church, at the North Meetinghouse the
Wednesday following.[2]

On Wednesday, the 12th of August, was appointed a Fast
for Mr. Mathers Church, which was duly observed; that Day
being a Court Day for the Council, no Magistrate was there,
yet notwithstanding there were gathered at the Contribution
sixty eight Pound.

Mr. Mather in his Sermon, took Occasion too in speaking
of the Benefit of Communion with God, to tell us that there
are in this Colony seventy nine gathered Churches, and that
to this Day the Indians had not done any Dammage to any
Thing that belonged to any of the Places where these Churches
were.

August coming on, we have now from all Parts raised more
Men, so that there are now in the Field in several Places, six
hundred Horse and Foot: Most of the Army were not far
from the Swamp wherein King Philip with all his People were,
they resolved to compass it, which they did once: And in
their second Encounter, forced King Philip with all his Retinue
out of the Swamp, and pursued them; in their Pursuit they
killed his Lieutenant General, with about twenty (that they
saw) of his Men, and the English had not the Loss of one
Man, but two wounded.   We having all this while a Party of
Unkus's Indians in the Field on our Side.[3]

[1] The "Old Church" was the First Church, James Allen, minister. Increase
Mather and his son Cotton officiated at the Second or North Church.

[2] The defeat mentioned was at Quaboag (Quabaog or Wickabaug) Pond,
Brookfield, Massachusetts, on Monday, August 2. The news reached Boston
later, which may have caused the confusion in dates given by "N. S." in the text.
Wednesday, the fast day, fell on August 11.

[3] An incorrect impression of Philip's escape is here given. Philip had been
driven from Mount Hope June 28-29, and had fled to Pocasset swamp. The

About the 15th of August, Captain Moseley with sixty Men, met with a Company, judged about three hundred Indians, in a plain Place where few Trees were, and on both Sides Preparations were making for a Battle; all being ready on both Sides to fight, Captain Moseley plucked off his Periwig, and put it into his Breeches, because it should not hinder him in fighting. As soon as the Indians saw that, they fell a Howling and Yelling most hideously, and said, *Umh, Umh me no stawmerre fight Engismon, Engismon got two Hed, Engismon got two Hed; if me cut off un Hed, he got noder, a put on beder as dis;* with such like Words in broken English, and away they all fled and could not be overtaken, nor seen any more afterwards. About a Week after this, Capt. Moseley took two Indians, the Father and his Son, and willing to examine them both apart, proceeded thus: Took the old Man and bound him to a Tree, after he was so bound, he sent away the Son by a File of Men out of Sight; the old Man there confessed he was a Praying Indian, and that he was only hunting for Deer thereabouts, but said that his Son was one of those Men that wounded Capt. Hutchinson: So then, after they had pumped him as much as they could, they fired a Gun with no Bullet in it over his Head, untied him, and sent him another Way with a File out Sight; then brought they his Son, bound in like Manner, they telling him that they had shot his Father, and would shoot him also, if he would not confess what he was, and what he knew: He fairly told them, that he was a Praying Indian, but his Father made him go with him to the Nipmoog Indians, and that there they shot three or four Times a Piece; whereupon they then brought the old Man and tied him to his Son, and Examined them together, at Length they confest they were both among the Nipmoogs, and that the Son did wound Captain Hutchison; after their Examination, they were both shot to Death.

In this same Week, King Philips Men had taken a Young

Nipmucks had attacked Mendon July 14, one day prior to the peace with the Narragansetts made by Massachusetts and Connecticut. A union of Philip and the Nipmucks was the one thing to be prevented, but he escaped on Sunday, August 1. The death of Woonashum or Nimrod, his lieutenant, and the scarcity of provisions in the camps, were insufficient compensation for this misfortune. See p. 63, *post.*

Lad alive about fourteen Years old, and bound him to a Tree two Nights and two Days, intending to be Merry with him the next Day, and that they would Roast him alive to make Sport with him; but God over Night, touched the Heart of one Indian so that he came and loosed him, and bid him *run Grande*, (*i. e.* run Apace) and by that Means he escaped.

Towards the latter End of August, Captain Moseley took eight Indians alive, and sent them Prisoners to Boston, who were put in Prison there; these were of the Number of Mr. Elliot's Indians; (as also many of those Indians that were shipt off by Captain Sprague, for the Straits and Cales). These Men were at several Times tried for their Lives, and condemned to die: Mean Time Mr. Elliot and Captain Guggins,[1] pleaded so very hard for the Indians, that the whole Council knew not what to do about them. They hearkened to Mr. Elliot for his Gravity, Age, and Wisdom, and also for that he hath been the chief Instrument that the Lord hath made use of, in Propagating the Gospel among the Heathen; And was their Teacher, till the Time that some Indians were brought up in the University to supply his place. But for Captain Guggins, why such a wise Council as they, should be so overborne by him cannot be judged otherwise than because of his daily troubling them with his Impertinences and multitudinous Speeches, in so much that it was told him on the Bench, by a very worthy Person (Capt. Oliver[2]) there present, that he ought rather to be confined among his Indians, than to sit on the Bench; his taking the Indians Part so much hath made him a Byword both among Men and Boys. But so it was, that by one and two at a Time most of these eight Indians (and four more sent afterwards on the same Account) were let loose by Night, which so Exasperated the Commonalty, that about the 10th of September, at nine O'clock at Night, there gathered together about forty Men (some of Note) and came to the House of Captain James Oliver; two or three of them went into the Entry to desire to speak with him, which was to desire him to be their Leader, and they should joyn together and go break open the Prison, and take one Indian out thence and Hang him: Captain Oliver hearing their Request, took his Cane and cudgelled them stoutly, and so for that Time

---

[1] See *ante*, p. 36, note 3.   [2] James, son of Thomas Oliver of Boston.

dismist the Company; which had he but in the least countenanced, it might have been accompanied with ill Events in the End. Immediately Captain Oliver went and acquainted Mr. Ting[1] his Neighbor, (a Justice of Peace) and they both went next Morning and acquainted the Governour, who thank'd Captain Oliver for what he had done last Night, but this rested not here; For the Commonalty were so enraged against Mr. Elliot, and Captain Guggins especially, that Captain Guggins said on the Bench, that he was afraid to go along the Streets; the Answer was made, you may thank yourself; however an Order was issued out for the Execution of that one (notorious above the rest) Indian, and accordingly he was led by a Rope about his Neck to the Gallows; when he came there, the Executioners (for there were many) flung one End over the Post, and so hoised him up like a Dog, three or four Times, he being yet half alive and half dead; then came an Indian, a Friend of his, and with his Knife made a Hole in his Breast to his Heart, and sucked out his Heart-Blood: Being asked his Reason therefore, his Answer, *Umh, Umh nu,* Me stronger as I was before, me be so strong as me and he too, he be ver strong Man fore he die.

Thus with the Dog-like Death (good enough) of one poor Heathen, was the Peoples Rage laid in some Measure, but in a short Time it began to work (not without Cause enough). About the beginning of September, Captain Hinksman[2] was sent out Commander of one hundred Men, and were to meet together at Roxbury Meeting-House-Yard; when they were there, ready to March, they all unanimously resolved not to go with him, but if Captain Oliver would go, they would go gladly; whereupon the Council sent for him Home, and sent Captain Lake in his Room.

On Wednesday August 25, was observed a Fast at Charles-Town whereto several of Boston went, there was gathered that Day Seventy eight Pound.

---

[1] Edward Tyng. The Indian mentioned appears to have been "Little John," who had been accused of a murder at Taunton.

[2] Captain Daniel Henchman of Worcester. He was not sufficiently bloodthirsty to satisfy the popular clamor against the Indians. The change in commanders appears to have prevented the expedition. Captain Thomas Lake was killed by Indians a little later at Arrowsick Island in the Kennebec.

King Philip now beginning to want Money (having a Coat made all of Wampampeag, (*i. e.* Indian Money) cuts his Coat to Pieces, and distributes it Plentifully among the Nipmoog Sachems and others, as well as to the Eastward as Southward, and all round about. This gives Occasion to suspect that the Narragansets may also be Bribed, who are out on our Side, in that they follow not Orders to pursue King Philip effectually.

Captain Lathrop, and Captain Beers,[1] being at Hadly, and there hearing of an Indian Castle not far thence, they marched with an Hundred and eighty Souldiers thither, who required the Indians to surrender their Arms; the Indians told Captain Beers, that they would the next Morning. But the Captains with their Men soon made themselves Masters thereof, forcing them into a Swamp, having killed nine or ten, they retreated.

By this Time the Town of Deerfield begins to be in Danger; Whereupon Captain Beers with eighty Men went to bring away the People, the Inhabitants thereof, the Indians having Burnt twenty five Houses; in their Way, they were met with by a Parcel of Indians of about a hundred and Sixty, which the English got the better of, killing near Forty Indians, having lost but four or five Englishmen:[2] But immediately there did appear the greatest Body that hath at one Time been seen by the English, and fell upon Captain Beers, immediately killing him and sixty five of his Men, and fifteen escaped;[3] these fifteen ran to Captain Moseley, who then was about nine or ten Miles off, he came with his sixty Men and gave the whole Body of the Indians Battel (judged about one thousand two hundred), for three Hours; whereupon after having killed

[1] Thomas Lathrop and Richard Beers.

[2] This "Sugar Loaf Hill" fight was at Deerfield, Massachusetts, August 26, 1675. Hadley, near the Connecticut, had been selected as English head-quarters soon after the affair at Brookfield. Located on a bend of the river, Hadley was readily defended against the Indians, easy of access for friends and had good facilities for protecting the adjacent country. " N. S." has pressed into small compass and confused events covering several days. More correct details are in Hubbard, Mather, and the Massachusetts Archives.

[3] The whole account is exaggerated. Hubbard states that but 19 men were killed with Captain Beers, and the number of Indians is overestimated. The person in Captain Mosely's company preserved so wonderfully was Robert Dutch, a townsman of Hubbard, but the latter does not mention the agency of an In-dian in this preservation.

several of the Indians, he was forced to Retreat, and continued Fighting for all the Time that he and his Men were Retreating nine Miles; Captain Moseley lost out of his Company nine, and thirteen wounded. The next Day they came up again, the Indians were gone, they had stript the dead Men of all their Clothes and Arms, and Horses; amongst which dead, was one who had Life in him, and was found by a Friend Indian, he took him up and said, *Umh, umh poo Ingismon, mee save yow Life, mee take yow to Captain Mosee;* he carries him fifteen Miles the Day after to Captain Moseley, and now this Man is well again and in good Health.

Immediately Orders were taken at Boston for the sending out new Relief; as many as to make up Captain Moselys Company an Hundred compleat, were forthwith sent away: They are fitting out an Hundred more from Connecticot, under the Command of Major Treat, and Captain Whiting[1] the Minister of Hartford.

September 10, Eight Indians came to Boston from Ninnicroft, in an Embassy, having a Certificate from Captain Smith an Englishman,[2] that hath a large Estate thereabouts. They dispatched their Business, and had another Pass, tied at the End of a Stick, that Englishmen may see it afar off. They were going out of Town a back Way, two Men met them and seized on him that had the Pass; these two Men were Brothers, and this Indian had been among King Philip's Indians, and these two Men Swore in Court that that was the Man that killed their Brother, they knew him; whereupon two Days after his Trial and Confession, he was Hanged like the other.

September 23. About ten at Night we had an Allarm given us, and before eleven we had one Thousand two Hundred Men in Arms, and dismist by twelve that Night: The Occasion was, one of the Watch was Drunk about thirty Miles off at Mendham, and he fired a Gun, so it came to Boston; the next Morning he paid ten Shillings, and sate Hours in the

[1] Robert Treat and John Whiting. The Commissioners of the United Colonies met at Boston September 9, 1675, declared war against the Indians, and agreed to raise 1,000 soldiers, one-half to be dragoons.

[2] Richard Smith, of Wickford, Rhode Island, long a resident of the Narragansett country.

Stocks for his being Drunk, and afterwards had twenty Lashes
for giving a false Allarm.

On the 28th Day of August, happened here at eleven a
Clock at Night, a most violent Storm of Wind and Rain, the
Like was never known before; it blew up many Ships together
that they Bulged one another, some up towards Cambridge,
some to Muddy-River, doing much Hurt to very many; also
it broke down many Wharffs, and blew down some Houses
thereupon. The Indians afterwards reported that they had
caused it by their *Pawwaw*, (*i. e.* worshipping the Devil).
They farther say, that as many Englishmen shall die, as the
Trees have by this Wind been blown down in the Woods:
But these Heathenish Stories are consonant to their Barbarous
Crueltie, and ought to be valued accordingly, by all who own
any Thing superiour to it or them.

Several Men, some whereof are Quakers, will not go out
on Command, and for their Disobedience thereunto, are
forced to run the Gantelop.[1]

About the 15th of September, the Authority of Boston
sent a Party to Ninnicroft, to require him to come to Boston,
to treat concerning the delivery [of the] Squaw Sachem.[2] He
sent word he would come, provided he might be safely returned back; Captain Smith living near him, offered himself,
Wife and Children, and Estate, as Hostages therefor.

Ninnicroft seeing this, resolved to send his eldest Son[3]
thither (he himself being very aged.) So away they came,
bringing Captain Smith with them; when they came to Roxbury, they sent Word to Boston they were come, and desired
to know if they might have Admittance into Boston: Word
was sent them, that they should be very welcome. In Order
thereto, Captain James Oliver, and Captain Clarke,[4] were or-

[1] "Gantelop," or gauntlet: a common punishment among the Indians. It
sometimes cost the runner his life, as he ran between two rows of men equipped
with switches, clubs, or even stones, and little mercy was shown.

[2] Weetamoo, who was reported as having gone to Ninigret (see *ante*, p. 12,
note 5, and p. 34), and who married his son Quinnapin.

[3] Quinnapin was the eldest son of Ninnicroft or Ninigret, but he did not
sign the treaty of October 18 at Boston. "N. S." confuses him with Canonchet
(Nanunteno), the "Great Chief" of the Narragansetts, who signed in behalf of
Quinnapin and others.

[4] Captain Thomas Clarke.

dered with six Files of Musquets a piece to meet on the Neck, to conduct them into Town. The Indians meeting these Captains, thought that they were all to die immediately; some were for running away, and some not, but Captain Smith being with them, endeavoured to pacifie them as well as he could. When they met, they opened to the Right and Left, and gave them three Volleys, and so Guarded them to the Governours House. The next Morning this Sagamore with all his Retinue, went to Captain Oliver's House, to give him hearty Thanks for Yesterday's Kindness, in his conducting them safe to Town.

The Council sat every Day during their Abode in Boston, until they came to an Agreement. The Narragansets[1] by Degrees, came to this Agreement, That they were to deliver the Squaw Sachem within so many Days at Boston; and the League of Peace was then by them Confirmed, which was much to the general Satisfaction; but yet many had hard Thoughts of them, fearing they will at last prove Treacherous: They were dismist out of the Town in Safety, according to their Desire.

The Governour and Council seeing, and seriously considering the Misery that many had already undergone, and that the Country was like to be in, Issued out this following Order for a solemn Fast all over the Colony; which was performed with a very great Show of outward Penitence, and (no Question) with much inward Affection by very many: The Governour himself beginning the Duty of the Day, with a most heavenly Prayer.

At a Council held in Boston, Sept. 17, 1675.

It pleased the Holy God (all whose Works are Truth and his Ways Judgment) for our Sins whereby he hath been provoked, in special by the undervaluation of our pleasant Things; great unthankfulness for, and manifold Abuses of our wonderful Peace, and the Blessings of it in this good Land, which the Lord hath given us;

---

[1] In this record the writer includes the Niantics among the Narragansetts, possibly because the Squaw Sachem had gone to Ninigret for protection. The two tribes were distinct, although Canonchet of the Narragansetts signed the treaty for the Niantic leader.

ill Entertainment of the Ministry of the precious Gospel of Peace;
Leaving our first-Love, dealing falsly in the Covenant of the Lord
our God: The Apostacy of many from the Truth unto Heresies,
and pernicious Errours; Great Formality, inordinate Affection,
and sinful Conformity to this present evil vain World:[1] And (beside many horrid and scandalous Sins breaking forth among us,
for which we have Cause to be greatly humbled before the Lord)
our great Unsensibleness of the Displeasure of the Lord in suffering
these Abominations to be perpetrated, together with our Carnal
Security, and Unquietness under the Judgments of God upon us;
our abiding very much unreformed, notwithstanding all Warnings,
and Chastisements, whereby the Lord hath been, and is still debating
with us; we having greatly incensed him to stir up many Adversaries
against us, not only Abroad, but also at our own Doors, (causing the
Heathen in this Wilderness to be as Thorns in our Sides, who have
formerly been, and might still be, a Wall unto us therein;[2] and others
also to become a Scourge unto us) the Lord himself also more immediately Afflicting us by Diseases, whereof so many Children in some
of our Towns have died this Summer, His not going forth with our
Armies as in former Times, but giving up many of our Brethren to
the Mouth of the devouring Sword, yea, shewing himself Angry
with the Prayers of his People, Threatning us also with Scarcity of
Provision and other Calamities, especially if this present War with
the barbarous Heathen should continue: And that the Lord of Hosts
himself withdraw not the Commission he hath given to the Sword,
and other Judgments to prevail against us.

The Governour and Council of this Jurisdiction therefore (being under the Sense of these Evils, and also of the distressed State
of the rest of the Colonies Confederate with our selves, and of the
Churches of Christ in other Parts of the Christian World, in this
Day of Trouble, Rebukes, and Blasphemy; and fearing the sad
Issue, unless the Lord help us with our whole Heart, and not feignedly,
to turn unto himself) Do Appoint, and Order the seventh Day of the
next Month, to be a Day of Publick Humiliation, with Fasting and
Prayer, throughout this whole Colony; that we may set ourselves
sincerely to seek the Lord rending our Hearts, and not our Garments
before Him, and pursue the same with a thorough Reformation of

[1] These accusations refer to the neglect at Plymouth to provide for the
adequate support of the established ministry and to the growth of the Baptists,
Episcopalians, and Friends, as well as to the lukewarmness of church members.

[2] It is interesting to see the idea of the Indians forming a neutral or protecting zone between the colonists and the French set forth thus early in American
history.

whatever hath been, or is an Image of Jealousie before the Lord, to offend the Eyes of his Glory; if so be the Lord may turn from his fierce Anger, that we perish not. We do therefore require all the Inhabitants of this Jurisdiction to forbear Servile Labour upon that Day, and that they apply themselves respectively to observe the same, as is Appointed,

By the Council,

EDWARD RAWSON, *Secr.*

On the 1st of October, News came to Boston, that the Indians had Burnt the Farmhouse of Major Pinchon, scituate near Springfield, and killed much Cattle, and Burnt much Corn, which occasioned his Son to abide Still in Boston (he being before provided to go for London, with Captain John Walley in the *John's Adventure*, Mr. Pinchons own Ship). It is judged that Major Pinchons Dammage may amount to eleven or twelve hundred Pound Sterling. This Day also came the News to Mr. Purchas that his House and Goods were Burnt, his Wife and Children killed; the Latter proved false: He was also bound in Capt. Walley for London, but remained at Boston for Sometime, in order to the settling his Family there. His Loss likewise amounted to above a thousand Pound Sterling.[1]

On the 12th of October, a Body of Indians came to Springfield, who immediately fired the Town, and consumed thirty-two Houses, and almost as many Barns, with their Corn and Hay.

The Indians that did this Mischief, were a Company of those Sort called Praying Indians,[2] about forty in Number, that always dwelt near to Springfield, and at that Time were confined to their Town and about a Mile about it; but for

---

[1] Important correspondence of John Pynchon from September 30 to October 17, 1675 (Massachusetts Archives, vol. 67) throws much light on these events near Springfield. Pynchon's house was on Stony Brook, now in Connecticut, but then a part of the Springfield district. Thomas Purchase lived near the mouth of the Androscoggin River in the district of Maine. Captain Walley was later a distinguished colonel in Sir William Phips's expedition of 1690 against Canada.

[2] Certain writers speak of this mischief as due to colonial neglect and done by preying rather than by Praying Indians. Hubbard places a part of the blame upon the English, and the closing words of this narrative illustrate one view of the Indians in which "N. S." may have shared.

their usual Civility Sake, were permitted daily to have Converse with the Town about what Business they had, and at Mid-night they did their Exploit. The Neighbouring Towns hearing it, and that it was done by them, Rose without any Commander or Leader, and slew all of them they could find, which was about thirty.

Likewise Tidings came this Day from the Eastward, that they have killed twenty Men within this ten Days; wherefore here is this 20th of October, marched forty Men out of Boston, for their Relief.

The Narragansets, we fear more and more every Day, will be perfidious to us, the Time being past that they should have delivered Squaw Sachem at Boston.[1] Our Fears are the more increased, as well in that we understand several of them appear up and down in Arms; however here is a Levie now coming out for a thousand Englishmen to wait on them, which we hope may reduce them to good Order, as well as recover Squaw Sachem out of their Hands; which if she be but taken by the English, her Lands will more than pay all the Charge we have been at in this unhappy War.

October 28, This Day by Advice from Hatfield, we have this particular Account of what happened there.

On Wednesday the 19th of October, a Party of Indians about seven Miles off Hatfield in the Woods, made several great Fires, to make the English think they were there, but as soon as ever they had set Fire to the Wood, they came directly towards Hatfield, and about two Miles from Hatfield they lay in Bushes by the Way Side undiscoverable, thinking to cut off the English in their Way to the Fires: About Noon, they of Hatfield sent ten Horsemen well armed, to scout out and see what is the Matter in the Woods; and in their Way the Indians at once shot down nine of them, and the other returned to Hatfield to carry the News: Capt. Samuel Moseley (being then not far from thence, with sixty Men,) was immediately sent for, who presently came. By four a Clock, there were come into the Town above seven hundred Indians armed, and immediately set Fire in three Places to the Town, but by Care were soon quenched; Capt. Moseley presently engaged

---

[1] As already noted, the Squaw Sachem was with the Niantics and not with the Narragansetts.

five hundred of these Indians, whilst two hundred and more other Indians were at the other End of the Town endeavouring to Fire it.[1] There was also another Captain, with about sixty Men not far off, who hearing the Guns, came immediately thither and set on the other Party of two hundred and odd; but the two English Captains soon joyned together, and they had a Fight with those seven hundred and odd Indians, for near two Hours Time, till they could see no longer. In this Fight we lost only three Men, and we judg we may have killed above an hundred Indians. we forced the Rest in great disorder to run away. We forced them over a large River, who in their Swimming over, lost all their Arms and Ammunition, and several were Drowned, as was seen the next Day. This Fight doth much discourage them, and encourage our English: there were ten Men wounded of ours in the Fight, but none Mortally we hope.[2]

Care now is taken to satisfie the (reasonable) desires of the Commonalty, concerning Mr. Elliot's Indians, and Capt. Guggin's Indians. They that wear the Name of Praying Indians, but rather (as Mr. Hezekiah Ushur[3] termed Preying Indians) they have made Preys of much English Blood, but now they are all reduced to their several Confinements; which is much to a general Satisfaction in that Respect.

Dated from Boston Novemb. 10, 1675.

Postscript.

Sir,

I have here enclosed you as large an Account as I can at Present of the State of this Wilderness, in Respect to the Heathens: I must confess, I was the willinger to take a little the more Pains in the collecting thereof, for the Sakes of those with you, who wish us well. Which if it may answer its

---

[1] Captain Samuel Mosely and Captain Jonathan Poole were the two officers in charge at the different ends of the town. Hatfield is opposite Hadley on the Connecticut River.

[2] Freegrace Norton, one of Major Appleton's sergeants, was shot at the side of his superior officer, the wound proving mortal. Major Appleton barely escaped a like fate.

[3] Hezekiah Usher, bookseller in Boston.

intended End therein, the Labour in Writing will be well
bestowed. You may expect more from me as there is Occasion, meanwhile I am,

Sir,
Your Friend and Servant.

Psal. 80, 7, 8, 9, 10, 11, 12, 13, 14.

Finis.

A CONTINUATION OF THE STATE OF NEW-ENGLAND, BY N. S., 1676

A CONTINUATION OF THE STATE OF NEW-ENGLAND, 1676

A Continuation of the State of New-England; Being a Farther Account of the Indian Warr, And of the Engagement betwixt the Joynt Forces of the United English Collonies and the Indians, on the 19th of December, 1675, With the true Number of the Slain and Wounded, and the Transactions of the English Army since the said Fight. With all other Passages that have there Hapned from the 10th of November, 1675, to the 8th of February 167⅞. Together with an Account of the Intended Rebellion of the Negroes in the Barbadoes.
Licensed March 27, 1676. Henry Oldenburg.
London: Printed by T. M. for Dorman Newman, at the Kings Armes in the Poultry, 1676.[1]

Boston, February the 9th, 1675.[2]

Sir,

My Last to you was of the 10th of November past,[3] (which in regard we have had much Westerly Winds since) I hope ere this Time you have received; according to the best Information I had or could procure, I made bold to acquaint you with Sundry Passages, that before the Date thereof, came to pass amongst us; I also sent you two of our Orders in Print by Order of the Council here; The one for the Confinement of our Neetop (*i. e.* Friend) Indians, the other for a general Fast throughout this Collony;[4] By the one you may see the

---

[1] Title-page of the original.

[2] This (meaning February 9, 1676, N. S.) is an erroneous date prefixed by the printer. The proper date is apparently December 21, 1675; see the beginning of the next letter.

[3] The date here given connects this piece with the preceding narrative. See *ante*, p. 49.

[4] See Proclamation for Fast, *ante*, pp. 45–47. *Neetop* is Indian for "friend." The confinement of the friendly Indians was on islands in Boston harbor.

great Care our Authority hath, as well to make a Distinction visible, betwixt our Friends the Christian Indians, and our Enemies the Heathens, as also, to secure the one from Injuries, and to lay the other open, and make them liable to the Hand of Justice: By the other you may see what Fear of the immediate Hand of God upon us our Majistrates have; and truly Sir, we have great Cause to bless the Lord for that we have such Magistrates and Councellors that we are so well assured do aime at the Glory of God, and the Peace and Welfare of his People in this Wilderness, that however the mighty Hand of God is lifted up upon us, and he hath given Commission to the Sword to destroy, yet we are well satisfied there is Nothing wanting that lyeth within the reach of their Wisdom or Strength: Wherefore in the midst of our Troubles we comfort ourselves in this, that we are satisfied they do what in them lyeth: I hope in some short Time I may hear of your receipt thereof.

Sir, In my Last I also gave you (at First) an Account of the Reasons of the Rise and Original of these unhappy Wars, in which, my Information was not so Perfect, but that there was somewhat amiss; although, at that Time, the Account thereof was generally receiv'd, and the Alteration is not much, only in some few particular Circumstances: Wherefore, that you might be the more Certain thereof, I shall give you an Account wherein I missed, Thus: About six Years since one Sosoman[1] (an Indian Schollar and Minister) having spent some Years in the Study of Divinity, being by that Time judged capable of Preaching the Gospel, was by the Authority of Plymouth[2] sent to Preach to King Philip; he with some seeming-kind of Devotion, heard him for a while at several Times; and however his Zeal was in outward Appearance, yet all that Time, and a good while before, he with several of his own Men, had a Conspiracy to cut off the English thereabouts, and scrupled not to make the Business known to Sosoman, as supposing he might be of great use to him, in carrying on that bloody Design; Whereupon this Sosoman soon after makes this Thing known to the Governor of New Plymouth Collony, Josiah Winslow Esq. King Philip suspecting he either would

[1] See p. 7, note 2, *ante*.
[2] A doubtful statement as to the action of Plymouth.

divulge, or had already made known this Secret to the English, took Councel to kill this Sosoman, wherefore in Order there-unto, one Day, as he sat fishing by a Riverside, two or three Indians came and barbarously Murthered him in the Place; Whereupon as soon as the Governor and Councel of Plymouth heard thereof, sent and took the said Murtherers; as also a small Party went to King Philip and brought him and most of his chief Men [1] to Plymouth, and there Examined them, and had several Meetings in Consultation about the Business; but King Philip behaved himself very uncivilly (like a Heathen) however due Proof could not be produced against him, and he nor his Men not having yet shed any English Blood, after his entring into a League of Peace with the English, was dismist; only the Murtherers after a legal Condemnation were Hanged.[2] Here lies the Occasion of our present Difference, which I have made bold to acquaint you of. Sir, towards the close of my Last to you, I gave you an Account of what was done at Hat-field the 19th of October last; in which Fight the Heathens were so put to it, that they were forced to go to their last Refuge, that is, the Narragansets, who I wrote you Word we feared every Day more and more would Prove perfidious to us; wherefore the Authority of the United Collonies having In-telligence that King Philip with his whole Retinue, as well Women and Children, etc., did Harbour themselves under the Protection of Ninicroft, who is the King of the Narragansets, as also hearing that that same Sachem, that came to Boston about the End of September last, (being Ninicroft's Eldest Son) is since Marryed to the Squaw Sachem; which Marriage doth signifie a near Alliance; and also seeing that what that Sachem did agree unto with our Authority, when in Boston, is not at all regarded by them, (for that Sachem sent Word when he came Home into his own Country, that Ninicroft would not agree to what he had done.)[3]

---

[1] By another account Philip "came downe of his own accord" to Plymouth.

[2] See p. 8, note 3, *ante*, and p. 25.

[3] The writer confuses Ninnicroft (Ninigret) with Canonchet, the leading chief of the Narragansetts and the brains of the war on the Indian side. It was the latter who came to Boston and signed for himself and others the treaty of October 18, 1675, and who later refused to keep the treaty, which led to the prac-tical declaration of war by the United Commissioners on November 2. So also

These Things so falling out near the same Time, put our Authority then in Councel upon some Necessity of finding out a speedy Way to Remedy the same, But notwithstanding their Perfidiousness hitherto, yet about three Weeks after, five Sachems came together from Ninicroft to Boston, and engaged[1] that our Enemies, entertained by them, should be delivered up Instantly; but Nothing being done of what they promised, the Commissioners of the United Collonies, sitting in Councel here, (the several Considerations here exprest, with Others moving them thereto) in the first Place published this following Remonstrance (here inserted verbatim)[2] and ordered a Body of Souldiers, Horse and Foot to march hence; in order thereunto, on the 10th of this Instant December, six Companies of Foot and Horse marched hence unto Seaconck: The Number of the Soulders were thus; Of Massachusetts and Plimouth Collonies 700 Foot and 200 Horse, and Connecticot Collony having 300 Foot and 100 Horse ready to meet them at New London,[3]—whereof Governour Josiah Winslow is gone out General: From Massachusetts Collony is gone out in Command, Major Appleton of Ipswich, Captain James Oliver, Captain Samuel Moseley, and Captain Nath. Davenport of Boston, Captain Johnson of Roxbury, Captain Gardner of Salem, and Captain Thomas Prentice, Captain of the Horse. These were commanders of those seven Companies that marched hence.

The 16th Instant we had Advice from them, that the Enemy had burnt Mr. Jeremiah Ball's[4] House at Narragansett, and killed 18 Men, Women, and Children that were in it, and that they had taken 55 Indians, and killed ten more and

it was Quanopin or Quinnapin who married the Squaw Sachem, as will appear in Mrs. Rowlandson's *Narrative*, pp. 125, 150, *post*.

[1] Not a new treaty but an addition to that of October 18.

[2] See the document at the end of this piece.

[3] Over 150 Indians were with the Connecticut forces. As to Rhode Island, Callender says: "It must be observed that though the Colony was not, as they ought to have been, consulted, yet they not only afforded Shelter and Protection to the flying English . . . but they likewise furnished some of the Forces with Provisions and Transports."

[4] Jeriah or Jireh Bull who kept a garrison house on Tower Hill at Petta-quamscut, between the present Wakefield, Rhode Island, and Narragansett Pier, is probably the person meant. A better estimate reduces the loss to fifteen persons.

burnt 150 Wigwams with the Loss of four of our Men, and as many Wounded. This Exploit was performed by Captain Prentice, a Captain of the Horse. The Weather now being extream Cold, having both Frost and Snow in most Places two Foot, in many Places three Foot deep, we have as yet had Nothing like to a Field Battel with the Indians, save that Fight we had at Hatfield of which I gave you an Account in my Last, until these Soulders went out Last; since which Time, by several Posts coming Daily thence, as also by private Letters, I have this Account of this Fight in particular. On Saturday the 19th Instant, the General mustered up the whole Army in November, as before, having with them three Ministers, *viz.* Mr. Dudley, Mr. Buckley and Mr. Samuel Nowell, at Capt. Smith's[1] House, (the same Capt. Smith I told you in my Last that came to Boston with Ninnicroft's Eldest Son a Sachem) whose Dwelling is about four Miles off the Narragansetts Dwellings, and is now the strongest Garrison in those Parts) and having given Orders for a March, according to Discretion, marched towards the Narragansets Country (or Town) where finding no Indians, they were at a Stand, not knowing which Way to go in Pursuit of the Indians; but however during their Stay, their Capt. Prentice with his Company discovered some Place under Ground, wherein was Indian Corn laid up in Store by them; this encouraged them to look further; Whereupon in their Search they found several good Quantities of that Grain in like Manner, which afterwards was conveyed to the Garrison. In the Afternoon of that Saturday, some of the Souldiers accidently espied an Indian[2] alone, whom they took and carried to the General, who upon his Refusal to answer to those Questions demanded, was ordered to be Hanged forthwith; Whereupon the Indian to save his Life, told them where the whole Body of the Indians were together, as well King Philip, and all other Confederate Sagamores and Sachems with their whole Retinue, as also the whole Body of the Narragansets, being joyned all in a Body in November, about 4500 Indian Men, besides Wives and Children: Whereupon, keeping this Indian for their Guide,

[1] Samuel Dudley, Gershom Bulkley, Richard Smith.
[2] Known to the English as Peter. The ensuing battle is known in New England history as the Great Swamp Fight.

they having Provisions with them, marched all Night, the
Indians being then 16 Miles distant from them, and that
Night there fell a very hard Snow two or three Foot deep,
and withal an extream hard Frost, so that some of our Men
were frozen in their Hands and Feet, and thereby disabled for
Service. The next Day, about Noon, they come to a large
Swamp, which by Reasons of the Frost all the Night before,
they were capable of going over (which else they could not
have done). They forthwith in one Body entered the said
Swamp, and in the Midst thereof was a Piece of firm Land, of
about three or four Acres of Ground, whereon the Indians
had built a Kind of Fort,[1] being Palisado'd round, and within
that a Clay Wall, as also felled down Abundance of Trees to
lay quite round the said Fort, but they had not quite finished
the said Work. The General placed Capt. Moseley in the Front,
to enter the Fort, and the Rest of the Companies were placed
according to Discretion. In their March they met with three
Indians sent out as Scouts, whom they shot dead at Sight
thereof: as soon as ever the Indians saw our Army coming,
they shot as fast as ever they could, and so our Men did the
like. Before our Men could come up to take Possession of the
Fort, the Indians had shot three Bullets through Capt. Davenport, whereupon he bled extreamly, and immediately called
for his Lieutenant, Mr. Edward Ting, and committed the
Charge of the Company to him, and desired him to take care
of his Gun, and deliver it according to Order, and immediately
died in the Place; his Company were extreamly grieved at his
Death, in Regard he was so courteous to them; for he being
Commander of that Company, belonging to Cambridge and
Watertown etc. was a Stranger to most of them; and at the
same Time that he came to take Possession of his Company, he
made a very civil Speech to them, and also gave them free
Liberty to choose their Serjeants themselves, which pleased

---

[1] This fortress of the Narragansetts is in the present town of South Kingstown, Rhode Island. The fort stood upon an island between the present Charles
River and Usquepaug River, and is marked by a monument visible from the Shore
Line railroad near West Kingstown station. See *A Record of the Ceremony and
Oration*, etc., printed by the Society of Colonial Wars (1906). It was built under
the direction of "Stone-wall John," an Indian engineer, referred to later (p.
59) as a blacksmith, possibly aided by Joshua Tift or Teft, a renegade white
man.

them very well, and accordingly did so; and it is very probable
the Indians might think that Capt. Davenport was the General, because he had a very good Buff Suit on at that Time,
and therefore might shoot at him. In a short Time our
Forces entred the Fort, Captain Mosely being in the Front,
the Indians knowing him very well, many directed their shot
to him, as he afterwards told the General that he believed he
saw 50 aim at him: As soon as he and they had entred the
Fort, he espied a Heap of above 50 Indians lay dead in a
Corner, which the Indians had gathered together; as soon
as ever our Men had entred the Fort, the Indians fled, our
Men killed many of them, as also of their Wives and Children, amongst which an Indian Black-Smith[1] (the only Man
amongst them that fitted their Guns and Arrow-heads;) and
amongst many other Houses burnt his, as also demolished
his Forge, and carried away his Tools; they fought with the
Indians, and pursued them so long as was advantageous to
them; then the General gave Order to Sound a Retreat, which
was done according to Order. The Retreat was no sooner
beaten, and the Souldiers were in a Marching Posture, before
they were got all out of the Fort, a thousand fresh Indians set
on our Men, but in an Hour's Time the Indians were forced
to Retreat and Flie. Our Men as near as they can judge, may
have killed about 600 Indian Men, besides Women and Children. Many more Indians were killed which we could have
no Account of, by Reason that they would carry away as many
dead Indians as they could. Our Men before they had been
set on by the fresh Indians, had set fire to most of the Wigwams in and about the Fort (which were near 1000 in all,)
how many were burnt down they could not tell positively,
only thus; That they Marched above three Miles from the
Fort by the Light of the Fires.[2] Here is an Account of the
Number of English-Men slain by the Indians in this Engagement.

[1] If the reference is to "Stone-wall John," it may be stated that he was not
killed at this time but by Connecticut forces under Major John Talcott, July
2, 1676. See p. 96, *post.*

[2] Improbable under the weather conditions. Our writer gives round numbers in this account and probably does not underestimate the size of the Indian
forces. He was not on the field, and neither Mather nor Hubbard gives these
details nor places the numbers of men so high.

*A List of the Number of the English Slain and Wounded in the
Battel with the Indians, on the 19th of December, 1675.*

Of the Massuchusets.

	Slain.	Wounded.
In the Company of		
Major Appleton	2	22
Capt. Moseley's	9	10
Capt. Oliver's	5	10
Capt. Johnson's	3	11
Capt. Gardner's	7	11
Capt. Davenport's	4	15
	30	79

Wounded, whereof some are
since dead.
Of Connecticot.

Major Treat's Com'y	20
Capt. Sealey's	20
Capt. Marshal's	14
Capt. Waite's	17
	71

Of Plymouth.

Capt. Bradford ⎱ Capt. Corum[1] ⎰	20
Troopers	02
Lost in the Woods	05
	27

Captains Slain.

Capt. Davenport
Capt. Johnson
Capt. Gardner
Capt. Marshal
Capt. Gallop, who Commanded
Uncas's Indians.

Wounded.

Captain Bradford, shot in the
Eye.
Captain Sealy, Mortally as is
Feared.
Captain Mason.
Captain White.

Lieutenants Wounded.

Lieut. Savage,
Lieut. Ting,
Lieut. Swan,
Lieut. Upham.
Wounded and Slain in
all - - - - 207[2]

We wanting good Accommodation for our Wounded Men,
our General ordered them to be removed to Road-Island,
where they have good Quarters provided, and care taken for
their Recovery.   Ninigret, the old Sachem of the Narragansets,
hath lately, with a small Party of Indians seperated himself
from the Rest of his People, disowning their Actions, and all

---

[1] Captain John Gorham.

[2] Another estimate gives the English loss as 6 captains and 80 men killed,
and 150 men wounded.

that joyn with King Philip, and professes himself a true Friend to the English Interest.[1]

It may not be amiss to acquaint you that the Night before the Fight was, and all that Day, and the Night after, there fell such an extraordinary Snow that the like hath not been known for many Years; and in Regard that we had no Post come from our Army for four or five Days, many Fears arose amongst us that our Men were lost either by the Enemy, or the Snow, which made many an Heart ake amongst us. But so it was, that which we feared would spoil us, did very much disable the Enemy; for we having burnt down almost all their Wigwams, as also all their Corn that we could find, they thereby have less Shelter and less Subsistance left them, which Misery of theirs is much aggravated by that great Snow.

The Fight being over, our Men Retreated to Mr. Smith's House, where the Noble General gave Order that the Wounded and Sick should first of all be cared for, which was done accordingly; and that they might have the better Accomodation in the House the General himself lay in a Barn belonging to the said House. Care is now taken to raise a thousand Men more to attend the General, which will suddenly march; What the Issue will be the Lord knows. King Philip supposing that Hatfield, a Town on Conecticot River, was very thin of Men; he drew together seven or 800 of his Indians, among which they had several Horses, and suddenly entred the Town on the 19th of October, 1675, which after they had set on Fire in three Places, they divided themselves into two Bodies and began to act several Cruelties on the Inhabitants. The English by their Diligence soon quenched the Fires; and making up a Body of 200 Men, most of which were newly come into the Town, they fell on the Indians with a great Deal of Fury, and after two Hours Fight, compelled the Indians to leave the Town with more Hast than they entred; the English having slain about 100 Indians, with very little Loss to themselves,[2] pursued the Rest to the River-side,

[1] Captain Bradford remained at Newport over a month, writing to Plymouth on January 20, 1676, that Ninigret had buried the English dead and wished a reward in powder for his work. See p. 65, *post*.

[2] There are better accounts of this Hatfield raid by Mather, *Brief History*, and by Hubbard. The number of Indians killed as given by our author is at least fivefold the truth.

where many were drowned that could not swim to the farther
Side. After this Fight, Philip and his Indians fled to the
Narragansets, which caused the Counsel of the Massachusets
to publish in Print this Remonstrance before spoken of.[1]

To our Brethren and Friends, the Inhabitants of the Colony of the Massachusetts.

Although you cannot be Ignorant how studious this Government hath been to preserve Peace in this Colony, and hath taken up
and Compromised diverse Quarrels that have Risen between our
Selves, our Neighbours, and the Indians; And thereby at several
Times prevented those Calamities wherewith we are now Pressed,
Yet to satisfie you that the same Mind, and the same Endeavours
are continued in the present Government, we have thought it necessary to let you understand the Rise and Progress of our present
Troubles, with our Endeavours to have prevented the same.

In June last, we were Certified by our Friends and Confederates
of Plimouth, that Philip the Sachem of Mount Hope was in Arms,
and had solicited all the Indians to joyn with him against the English; and withal they desired our Assistance to Suppress him; Which
we by the Articles of Confederation could not deny, and therefore
applied ourselves to Raise some Force for their Assistance: but were
still desirous to prevent a War with the Indians; and therefore upon
a former Experience of a good Effect wrought upon the said Philip,
we resolved to use the same Means, *viz.* sending Messengers from
hence to Philip to Treat with him, hoping of the like Issue, which
upon the like Case about four Years since we by Gods good Hand
obtained.[2] But our Messengers arriving at Swanzy, in their Way
towards Philip, found divers English Murthered on the Road, and
were informed by the English there, of divers Hostilities of the
Indians, which rendered our Design and their Negotiation hopeless:
Upon which they returned, and informed us as abovesaid, whereupon
our Forces began their March in Aid of our Friends at Plymouth;
and having driven Philip from his Country, we being informed that
the Narragansets harboured his Women, and aided him with Men,

---

[1] Plymouth issued a Justification for taking up Arms similar to the one
here given (*Plymouth Colony Records*, X. 362–363). Massachusetts certainly was
not eager for war at this time, whatever may have been the wish of Plymouth.

[2] The reference is to the treaty of Taunton already described. A reference
to the so-called treaty of July 15 with the Narragansetts occurs a few lines later,
and this is followed by a mention of the treaty with the Commissioners entered
into at Boston by Canonchet on October 18, 1675.

we ordered our Souldiers to march to Narraganset, in order to keep
them quiet, and prevent their succouring or harbouring the Enemy:
Where, after some Delay, they were drawn to consent to our Demands, promising neither to Entertain nor assist our Enemies, which
they since confirmed in a Treaty with the Commissioners of the
Colonies: Further engaging that they would deliver all those of
Philip's Party, that upon his Rout near Scatoneck,[1] or since, were
fled to them; but have failed in every Particular. You may also
take notice, That before any of our Souldiers marched to Mount
Hope, we were very careful to understand the State of the Nipnet[2]
Indians, to prevent Philip's Design, and secure those Indians, and
therefore dispatched two Messengers well known to them, to certifie
them of Philip's Motion and of our Design to keep Amity and Friendship with them, according to the Covenants made with them long
since, no Ways Violated on our Part. And by the said Messengers
received fair Returns from the most of them, being in 10 or 12 Plantations. Some of these pretended Fear of us: For their further Satisfaction (when our Forces were sent out against Philip) we to satisfie
and secure them, sent them by Ephraim Curtice, a Declaration[3]
under the Publick Seal, that we had no Design or Intent to disturb
them, or any other Indians that would remain in their Plantations
peaceably: which Message and Messenger was evilly treated by
many of them there Assembled, and the Messenger much endangered
by the Younger Men and not with any Satisfaction by their Sachems,
as the Event shewed, though at that Present more moderately
received.

Soon after this Dispatch, and before Philips flying from Pocasset, and March up towards the Nipnet Country; Some of the said
Nipnet-Indians Assaulted and slew divers of our People at Mendam;[4]
whereupon Captain Hutchinson with a small Guard, was sent up
to the said Nipnet-Indians, (if possible to keep them quiet) who
arriving at Quabaog, whereabouts was a Randezvous of the Indians,
and having sent to them, they promised to meet him in a certain
Place, whither he at the Time repairing, found not the Indians, and
being incouraged by the English of Quabaog, that the Indians were
peaceable, etc. he advanced forward towards the Place of the Indians
Randezvous, to Treat with them: But in the Way, was by Ambus-

---

[1] Seekonk, August 1.

[2] Better known as the Nipmoogs or Nipmucks, although but a part of the
Indians so called are here intended.

[3] Ephraim Curtis was a young trader of Quamsigamug or Worcester, Massachusetts, and a noteworthy scout and hunter.

[4] For the conflicts at Mendon and Quabaog (Brookfield), see pp. 35, 36,
ante.

cado treacherously way-laid, by which himself, and several others were wounded and slain, the English of Quabaog immediately Assaulted, and the Town, except one House, totally destroyed; at which Time, as we understand, Philip also with his broken Party came up to the said Indians, and upon the first, or immediately before the arrival of the Forces, we sent up for the Relief of those of Quabaog, Philip and his whole Crew retreated (as we then feared, and afterwards were informed) towards Conecticot-River, from whence Recruiting himself with Ammunition from Albany,[1] and with Men, partly from the treacherous Indians about Hadly and Springfield, to have prosecuted his first Design to Ruine and destroy the English. And notwithstanding all the Opposition of our Forces, hath done much Mischief and spoil; and since the Repulse he received at Hatfield,[2] withdrew into the Nipnet-Country, and since that (as we understand) towards the Narragansets, who we do conclude, have favoured, abetted, and assisted him therein; and by entertaining and harbouring our Enemies, have dealt falsely and perfidiously with us; whereby we find our selves necessarily Ingaged, with the Consent, Advice and Assistance of the Rest of the Colonies, in a War with them, as well as with Philip, unless they prevent the same by a timely Complyance and Performance, and Security for the Future: for the managing and carrying on whereof, we hope for, and expect (as we have hitherto had) the Assistance of all his Majesties Subjects of this Colony in their respective Capacities, in the just Defence of the Glory of God, the Honour, Defence and Safety of our King, Country, and our Selves, from the Subtlety, Rage, and Treacherous Attempt of our Barbarous Enemies.

Dated in Boston, the 7th of December, Anno Christi, 1675, Annoque Domini Caroli Secundi Regis Angl. Scot. Fran. et Hiber. Defensoris Fidei, etc. 27th.[3]

By the Council

EDWARD RAWSON, *Secret.*

[1] The New York Council on January 17, 1675/6, resolved "to write to the Governor of Boston to vindicate this Government from an Aspersion in a printed Paper of Decemr. the 7th last past, wherein was set forth that Philip in his Flight was supplyde with Ammunition from Albany whereby he was enabled to prosecute his bloody Designe against the English."

[2] For the encounters at Springfield and Hatfield, see pp. 47–49, *ante.*

[3] "And in the twenty-seventh year of our lord Charles the Second King of England, Scotland, France, and Ireland, Defender of the Faith."

Boston in New England, February the 8th, 1675/6.

Sir

My last Letter to you beared Date the 21st of December, 1675,[1] wherein I gave you a true Account of the State of our Affairs in New England, particularly of the Engagement of our Forces with the Indians on the 19th of December, 1675, And the Number of the Slain and Wounded. I shall now continue my Intelligence according to your Request, and my Promise, and give you a true Account of all Transactions here (worth your Information) since the foresaid 19th of December.

Our wounded Men (thanks be to God) are most of them pretty well recovered, and only Captain Sealy is dead that I can hear of.[2] By some Indian-Prisoners, lately taken, we are certainly informed that they had 355 Men killed outright, besides several burnt in their Wigwams, with Women and Children and 180 wounded, many of which are since dead, particularly Sachem Quanepins Brother, who was a Man of great Command among the Indians. That Night the Indians left the Place where the fight was, and retreated five Miles farther into the Country. Ninecroft an old Sachem in that Country, who hath hitherto continued Neuter, and neither assisted the Indians nor us, sent some of his Men the next Day, and Buried the dead Indians, and as many of the English as were left behind dead.

On the 23. and 24. of December, the Indians sent some Commissioners to our General to Treat of Peace, which they had no Mind to conclude; but we soon perceived it was only to prevent our falling upon them, and to gain themselves more Time to remove their Army and Provisions twenty Miles farther into the Country, to some Rocks where we could not get at them without great Danger. Although our General knew this, he was desirous to keep the Treaty on Foot by Reason the Forces of the Collony of Connecticot had left our

---

[1] This plainly refers to the previous letter, of which December 21 is the proper date.

[2] Captain Robert Sealy of Stratford, Connecticut, died shortly after the fight. The estimates of the Indians' loss range from one thousand, as given by Hubbard, to forty, an Indian estimate.

Army,[1] and went Home to Recruit, and those Supplies from Boston, that are daily expected, not being yet arrived, our Army was not in a Condition to make any new Attempts on the Enemy; but had not the Connecticot Forces left our Army, we had Hopes that we might have compelled the Enemy to yield to our Mercy. During this Time our Forces foraged the Country, and brought in great Quantities of Indian Corn to the Army.

About the beginning of January, the Forces from Boston that were sent to reinforce our Army arrived at Narraganset, where our Army then lay: the extreme Coldness of the Season had mightily incommoded them in their March; they lost Eleven of their Men on their March, that were frozen to Death and brought many others sick and disheartened with the extreme Coldness of the Season. They were joyfully received by the Army; and soon after them the Connecticot Forces came to the Army, having reinforced their Companies with some fresh Men; and brought with them Unkus an old Sachem, who dwelt in the Connecticot Jurisdiction; he brought with him some Companies of his own Indians to the Assistance of the English.

The Winter being now broke up, and the Snow and Ice all gone, our Army consisting in all of 1600 Men[2] began their March to the Rocks, where the Indians were fled for Protection, but in their Way, they had Intelligence that 300 Indians had been at Patuxit, an English Plantation on the Narraganset Bay, where they had burnt Mr. Carpenters Corn and Hay, and all his Houses, except his dwelling House, which likewise they had set on Fire, but it was again quenched by some English that were in it. They likewise drove away with them 180 Sheep, 50 Head of large Cattle, and 15 Horses: Besides, they took much Cattel from young Mr. Harris,[3] and killed a Negro Servant of his; and having done this Mischief, returned Home with their Booty.

[1] Massachusetts complained that the abrupt leave-taking of the Connecticut troops created a very difficult situation, but the southern colony had suffered more severely than either of her New England neighbors. "Supplies," below, means reinforcements.

[2] This estimate is high, considering the losses of the campaign and the withdrawal of the Connecticut men.

[3] William Carpenter, jr., of Providence, and Andrew Harris.

Our Army being arrived in Bumham's Country, an Indian Sachem,[1] we burnt his Town, and had a small Reincounter with some of his Indians, where we wounded his chief Captain Quaqualh on the Knee, and killed five of his Men, and had four of our Connecticot Men wounded.

Our Scouts brought in Prisoner one Tift,[2] a Renegadoe English Man, who having received a deserved Punishment from our General, deserted our Army, and fled to the Enemy, where had good Entertainment, and was again sent out by them with some of their Forces; he was shot in the Knee by our Scouts, and then taken before he could discharge his Musket, which was taken from him and found deep charged, and laden with Slugs. He was brought to our Army, and tryed by a Counsel of War, where he pretended that he was taken Prisoner by the Indians, and by them compelled to bear Arms in their Service; but this being proved to be false, he was condemned to be hanged and Quartered, which was accordingly done.

Our Army beat the Indians from the foresaid Rocks, and pursued them almost as far as Quabog, in which Pursuit we killed about 60 or 70 of them, and found many of the Matts scattered in the Way, with which they cover their Houses, which we suppose they could not carry with them by Reason of our close Pursuit. Some Prisoners taken from them, inform us, that their Body consists of 4000, whereof 1800 were fighting Men, half of which wanted Arms, that they were in great Want of Powder, and greater want of Provisions.[3]

Provision growing scarce in our Army, and the Enemy having cleansed the Country of Things that might tend to our Relief, our General resolved to pursue them no farther, but to hasten homewards, which accordingly was done with what Speed we could; but the Scarcity of Victuals daily encreasing, we were forced to kill several of our Horses for our Sustenance. Our General dismist the Connecticot Men, and sent them

[1] The Indian "Bumham," or Pumham, had his headquarters on the site of the present Warwick, Rhode Island; his country was Warwick and West Warwick.

[2] The story of Joshua Tift is more fully detailed by Hubbard. See also p. 58, note 1, *ante*.

[3] The route taken was northwest from Wickford and Warwick, Rhode Island, to Woodstock, Connecticut, and thence to Quabaog or Brookfield, Massachusetts.

Home the nearest Way, and old Unkus and his Indians along with them. They proved very faithful in our Service,[1] and were well treated by us. Our General having left 60 Men in Garrison at Mr. Smiths House at Narraganset, where the Fight was on the 19th of December, came Home by the Way of Marlborough: Many of our Souldiers are troubled with the Flux, of which our General is one.

King Philip hath not yet been at Narraganset, as we feared, but is retired with his Men near Albany,[2] where he hath kept his Winter Quarters. We very much fear the Indians falling on our Out Towns this Spring, which if they should, would extremely damnify us.

Our Friend Mr. H. O.[3] went out again into the Army, before he was cured of his old Wound, and hath received another on his Elbow-joynt, which we fear will cause him to lose his Arm, if not his Life. Our Enemies are yet very unmerciful, sparing no Persons Life that they can Master.

I see no likelihood of any Peace, but much fear our Wars are far from an End. Our Trade to Virginia is quite decayed, not one Vessel having gone from here thither since the Wars began, but by a small Vessel arrived here from thence, we are informed that the Indians have fallen unexpected on the English, and destroyed many of them, and done much harm with very little Loss to themselves,[4] but this Report finds very little Credit with us; by the next shipping I shall (God willing) give you a farther Account of our Affairs, and in the mean Time shall neglect no Opportunity of informing myself of the Transactions of those Parts, being sensible how much you have obliged

Your Friend to his Power   N. S.

Post-script.

I Thought it needful to acquaint you that on the 21th day of March, Anno 1621, the English made a League of Peace

---

[1] There exists no adequate account of the services of Uncas and his men, to whom was due most of whatever success attended this expedition.

[2] Philip's winter quarters were at Scattacook (Schaghticoke), about twenty miles north of Albany. See p. 87, *post*.

[3] Humphrey Osland may be the person mentioned.

[4] Bacon's Rebellion, so called, and other disorders were giving Virginia trouble at this period, the outbreak of the Indians coming in 1675.

with Massasoiet,[1] who was Grand father to the present King Philip, on the following Terms and Conditions,

1. That neither he nor any of his should injure or do hurt to any of our people.

2. That if any of his did any harm to any of ours, that then he should send the Offender unto us for punishment.

3. That if any English took any Goods belonging to the said Massasoit, or any of his Indians, they should restore them again: and he obliged himself to do the like.

4. That if any of the Neighbours of the said Massasoiet should make war against him, the English should assist him: and he obliged himself to assist the English on the like occasion.

5. That he should inform his Neighbours and Confederates of these Covenants, that they might be careful of wronging either party.

6. That where any of his Indians came amongst the English, they should have no Bows or Arrows, or any other Arms with them.

7. That in so doing, our Soveraign Lord King James should esteem him as his Friend and Ally.

These Articles were agreed on to the good satisfaction and content of both Parties, and Massasoiet was content to become the Subject of our Soveraign Lord King James, his Heirs and Successors, and gave to the English all the Lands adjacent, and to their Heirs for ever.

On the 25th day of September, in the year 1639, this great Sachem Massasoiet, with Moanam his Son, came personally to the Court held at Plimouth in New-England, and desired that the League and Confederacy formerly made with the Government of Plimouth, might stand and remain inviolable, and the said Massasoiet and his Son Moanam did faithfully promise to keep and observe the Covenants and Conditions therein expressed and contained; and that neither of them should needlesly or unjustly raise any quarrel, or do any wrong to other Natives, or provoke them to War against them; and that neither of them should give, sell, or convey any of their Lands, Territories, or Possessions whatsoever, to any person or persons whomsoever, without the privity and consent of the Government of Plimouth: All which conditions the said

[1] Father, not grandfather.

Massasoiet and Moanam his Son, for themselves and their Successors, did then faithfully promise to observe and keep; and the whole Court, in the name of the whole Government for each Town respectively, did then ratifie and confirm the aforesaid ancient League and Confederacy; and also did further promise to the said Massasoiet and to Moanam his Son, that they shall and will from time to time defend them and their Successors when need and occasion shall require, against all such as shall rise up against them, to wrong or oppress them unjustly.

Anno 1662. There being occasion of some suspition of a Plot intended by the Indians against the English, Philip, the Son of the aforesaid Moanam, and Grandson of Massasoiet, and now the implacable Enemy of the English, made his personal appearance at the Court held at Plimouth, August the 6th; and did there earnestly desire the continuance of that amity and friendship that had formerly been between the Governours of Plimouth and his Deceased Father and Grandfather; and for that end the said Philip doth for himself and his Successors, desire that they might for ever remain subject to the King of England, his Heirs and Successors; and doth faithfully promise and engage that he and his will truly and exactly observe and keep inviolable such conditions as have formerly been by his Predecessors made; and particularly, that he will not at any time needlesly or unjustly provoke or raise war with any of the Natives, nor at any time give, sell, or any way dispose of any Lands to him or them appertaining, to any Strangers, or to any without our privity or appointment; but will in all things endeavour to carry it peaceably and inoffensively towards the English. And the said Court did then also express their willingness to continue with him and his the abovesaid Friendship; and do on their part promise that they will afford them such friendly assistance by advice and otherwise, as they justly may; and we will require our English at all times to carry it friendly towards them: in witness whereof, the said Philip the Sachem hath set to his hand; as also his Unkle, and witnessed unto by sundry other of his chief men.

Witness, { John Sousamen. The Mark of Philip,
The Mark of Francis the alias Metacom.
Sachem of Nauset.

Likewise in the year 1621 several of the Indian Sachems, besides Massasoiet before-named, came unto the Government of New Plimouth, and acknowledged themselves to be the Loyal Subjects of our Soveraign Lord King James, and subscribed unto a writing to that purpose with their own hands; the tenour of which said writing followeth, with their names annexed thereunto, some judicious persons conceive it may be of use in succeeding Ages, if not in ours; I think it convenient here to insert it.

September the 13*th,* 1621.

Know all men by these Presents, that we whose Names are under written, do acknowledge our selves to be the Loyal Subjects of King James, King of Great Brittain, France, and Ireland, Defender of the Faith, etc. In Witness whereof, and as a Testimonial of the same, we have Subscribed our Names or Marks as followeth.

OBQUAMEHUD.	NATTAWAHUNT.	QUADAQUINTA.
CAWNACOME.	COUNBATANT.	HUTTAMOIDEN.
OBBATINNA.	CHIKKITABAK.	APANNOW.

The Original Instruments signed with their own hands, and the chief of their men, still remain on Record in the Register of the Court of New Plimouth.

In the said year, 1621, the Narraganset Indians sent a Messenger to the Governour of Plimouth with a bundle of Arrows tyed together with a Snakes skin, which he understood was a threatning and a challenge. Upon which the Governour sent them this Answer; That if they loved War rather than Peace, they might begin when they would; he had done them no wrong, neither did he fear them, nor should they find him unprovided; and by another Messenger sent the Snakes skin back with Bullets in it, but they would not receive them, but sent them back again; but the Indians were better advised than to quarrel with the English at that time.

Barbadoes, Spickes-Bay,[1] *November the* 30*th,* 1675.

My Last to you was an Information of a bloody Tragedy intended against his Majestie's Subjects here in this Island, by

[1] Now called Speight's Bay, on the northwest side of this West Indian island.

the Heathen the Negroes, which was by the Providence of
God miraculously discovered eight Days before the intended
Murder should have been acted.   The Manner of the Discovery
was thus: A Negro Man belonging to Mr. Hall Senior, being
absented from his said Master, among several other Negroes
who had a Hand in the Plot: In a Council among them, they
did contrive that the Negroes belonging to each several Plantation, should in the Dead Time of the Night fall on at the
Sound of the Allarm, which was to be given in one Hour, and
at several Places through the Island, which Negroes so allotted
was to kill their Masters and Mistresses with their Overseers;
this foresaid Negroe of Mr. Halls (though one of the chief
Plotters) yet having a Respect to his Master, would by no
Means consent to the killing of his Master, and upon Refusal
was much threatened; and being afraid of his Life, makes his
Escape and returns Home; and one Day, which was a little
before the Prosecution of the Murder, was over-heard (telling
the Plot to his Countrymen) by a Negro Woman, who waited
and attended on her Mistress, which the Negro Woman immediately reveals.   The Negroe Man being taken to Examination, confessed the whole Truth, which was immediately told
the Governour, who appointed some Captains to raise their
Companies for depressing the Rebels, which accordingly was
done, and Abundance taken and apprehended and since put
to Death, and the Rest kept in a more stricter Manner; yet
Jethuran-like, we have kicked against God, and slighted the
Mercy of so great a Deliverance.[1]   The Manner of their
Proceedings I wrote to you more at large; and as the Lord
did deliver us from the Tyranny and barbarous Cruelty of
Savage Heathens, and we still remaining obstinate, and refusing to return to him by Repentance; the Lord hath taken
us into his own Hand to chastise us, which Chastisements
lyeth very heavy on the poorer Sort, and none of the Rich
excepted.

Sir, upon the last Day of August last, about six of the
Clock in the Afternoon, there did arise a Violent Storm of
Wind and Rain out of the North-west, and continuing between
the North and the South so violent, that before the Hour of
Twelve at Night, there was not twenty Houses standing in

[1] "But Jeshurun waxed fat and kicked." Deuteronomy xxxii. 15.

our Parish,[1] in which there is above three hundred Families, and those that did stand, much damnified; our Neighbouring Parishes tasting of the same Cup. There is killed outright, (by the falling of Houses) in this Parish, thirty-seven, and many more is since, with the Violence of the Wind and Cold, dead, and many lying in their Beds of Sickness; and as to our Ships, all drove Ashore to Pieces, except one of the Kings Men at War, which went to Sea, and returning next Day after the Storm was ceased, did protest to the Governour, that twenty Leagues off there was no Storm. for he carried his Top-sail half Mast high.

Our Fellow-subjects in New-England[2] have the 28th of the same Month, tasted of the same Cup, and was very hard put to it this last Summer by one King Philip an Indian King, who hath Revolted without Cause given him by the English, neither will he shew any Reason why; but being by an Embassador from the Governour of Boston, demanded why he would maintain the War, refused to Treat with the Embassador, telling him, The Governour was but a Subject, and that he would not Treat except his Brother King Charles of England were there. There is Abundance of Families destroyed, besides those kill'd in the War; but it is very much hoped this Winter they will be Routed; the Reason is, because they have no Woods or Bushes to shelter in, which is a great Help to a Flying Army, such as they are, for they will not bide any pitch Battel. Our Brethren in Virginia had been hard put to it this last Summer, if it had not been for the Relief of New-England and New-York, which makes it the harder with us here: pray God mend it.[3] By the tempestuous Wind, and the violent raging of the Sea, which hath much overflowed our Banks, and incroacht upon the Land, here are many Houses lost; among which mine was in Number, where I saved Nothing to cover us from the Violence of the Storm but what was on

[1] Speight's Town is in the parish of St. Peter.

[2] This is the only paragraph of the section referring to New England. Philip's classification of himself with King Charles was made in 1671 when the Indian chief was in Boston. Whether or not "G. W." had been in Boston at the time of the incident mentioned, or had learned of it by letter the editor is unable to say, as he is to state the person writing over the initials "G. W."

[3] The editor has found no statement as to the character of the aid to Virginia here mentioned.

our Backs. Pray God that I may make a sanctified Use of
the Chastisement, because the Lord hath not given over our
Life to Death. So having no more at Present, but my Service to your Self and good Lady, I rest your humble Servant,

G. W.

I forbear to tell or to write to you of the strange Accidents,
as the removing of whole Frames, great Timber Trees many
Yards from their proper Stations, by the Violence of the Storm;
if I should, it would be counted Ridiculous, but I leave it to
the Relation of others. Wind-mills down in this Parish 16,
much damnified 12, indeed none standing but stone Mills in
the Parish, but what must be pull'd down. Churches down
nine. Such another Blow will bring Barbadoes near the
Horizon.

Finis.

A NEW AND FURTHER NARRATIVE OF THE STATE OF NEW-ENGLAND, BY N. S., 1676.

A NEW AND FURTHER NARRATIVE OF THE STATE OF NEW-ENGLAND, BY N. S., 1676.

*A New and Further Narrative of the State of New-England;
being a Continued Account of the Bloudy Indian War.
From March till August 1676, Giving a Perfect Relation
of the Several Devastations, Engagements, and Transactions
there; As also the Great Successes Lately obtained against
the Barbarous Indians, The Reducing of King Philip, and
the Killing of one of the Queens, etc., Together with a Cata-
logue of the Losses in the whole, sustained on either Side
since the said War began, as near as can be collected.
Licensed October 13. Roger L'Estrange.
London: Printed by F. B. for Dorman Newman at the Kings
Arms in the Poultry, 1676.*[1]

For the better understanding some Indian Words, which
are necessarily used in the following Narrative, the Reader
is desired to take Notice,

That a *Swamp* signifies a Moorish Place, overgrown with
Woods and Bushes, but soft like a Quagmire or Irish Bogg,
over which Horse cannot at all, nor English Foot (without
great Difficulty) passe.

A *Sachem* is a King, Prince, or Chief of an ancient Family,
over whom he is an absolute Monarch.

A *Squaw Sachem* is a Princess or Queen.

Wigwams are Indian Huts or Houses.

Boston, July 22, 1676.

Sir,

Having presumed in Two former Letters to give you a
faithfull Account of the Original Occasion (as near as I could
Discover) and sad Progresse of the cruel Wars between us

[1] Title-page of the original.

77

and our Barbarous Enemies, the Indians; I thought (having this other Opportunity) your Curiosity might expect, at least (from that Knowledge I have for many Years had of your courteous Disposition) was assured your Good Nature would Pardon, the Trouble, of a Further Relation of material Occurrences which have since happened amongst us, the rather for that I remember my self under the voluntary Obligation of a Promise so to do.

My Last (which I hope you Received) was of the 9th of February, 167⅞: And seriously at that Time my Hand Trembled, and my Heart almost fainted, when my Mind reflected on our present Miseries, and revolved for the Future what might be the Issue of that Deluge of Calamity which threatned us. The Dispensation we lay under was Cloudy and Affrighting, Fresh Messengers (like Job's Servants) howrly arriving to bring the Doleful Tidings of New Massacres, Slaughters and Devastations committed by the Brutish Heathens; and certainly it cannot but deserve both Wonder and Commiseration, that these Parts which were not many Moneths since hardly to be Parrallel'd for Plenty and Security, are now almost destroyed and laid Waste by the savage Cruelties of a Bloody (and sometimes Despicable) Enemy; who are now become so well furnisht with Arms and Ammunition (by the base Treachery we fear of some of our Neighbours)[1] so instructed in Discipline by Experience, and heightened in Pride by unexpected Successe, That unlesse our God (whose tender Mercies are over all his Works) in Compassion to the English Nation in this Wildernesse, wonderfully appear for our Deliverance, Nothing could be expected but an utter Desolation; and of this his gracious Dealing towards us, we have lately had several Instances, our Forces being crowned with Successe, and the Enemy put to Flight, or so far divided and discouraged, that great Numbers have surrendered themselves when by our own Strength or outward Circumstances we could least expect it. But that I may set down Things in some Method, I shall reassume the Narritive of our Troubles, where I left off in my last Letter, and relate the most considerable Actions from that Time, in the same Order as they happened.

[1] The Dutch and French.

After that sharp Fight on the 19 of [December], whereof I
formerly gave you the Particulars, our wounded Men (in
Number about 150) being drest, were sent into Rhode Island,
as the best Place for their Accommodation, where accordingly
they were kindly received by the Governour and others, only
some churlish Quakers were not free to entertain them, until
compelled by the Governour.　Of so inhumane, peevish and
untoward a Disposition are these Nabals,[1] as not to Vouchsafe
Civility to those that had ventured their Lives, and received
dangerous Wounds in their Defence.[2]　As for the Indians
that survived the Battell, they forsook their New-built Fort,
and that Swamp where the Fight hapned, and posted themselves in a Swamp twenty Miles distant from thence; The
Weather being extreme cold, and the Snow so deep, that we
could not for some Time march in Pursuit of them: yet still
kept Scouts abroad daily to observe their Motions, and thereby
hindred them from coming to the Sea-side; killed and took
Prisoners divers of them, as they were found straggling; and
burnt great Numbers of their Wigwams (or Houses:) And
being reinforced with some Additionall Forces from Boston
and Plimouth, together with a Bark laden with Provision, we
resolved to set upon them again with the first Opportunity;
and in Order thereunto marched to Potuxit, where we understood, that two Nights before the Indians had assaulted a
Gentleman's House [3] about Break of Day with much Violence,
and wounded two Men in it, striving to Fire the House several
Times, by tying Pine-splinters [on] long Poles, in a Bunch fired,
and held upon the Shingles; but those within prevented that
Stratagem from taking Effect, beat off the Assailants, and
found one of them left dead upon the Place; But the Out-
Houses and Hay the Indians burnt, and drove away all the

---

[1] An allusion to the churlish Nabal of I Samuel xxv.

[2] The feeling between Massachusetts and Rhode Island needs no emphasis
after this passage.　It must be remembered that Rhode Island was not in the
New England Confederation; that she suspected Plymouth of desiring the
Narragansett lands; and that many thought the war unrighteous.　On the other
hand, Massachusetts had little use for men who would not fight for their rights,
and less for those who appeared to disregard the needs of men injured in such
warfare.

[3] The attack upon the Carpenter house has been mentioned before, p. 66,
ante, but not in so great detail.

Sheep and Cattell: we marched after them with all convenient
Expedition, and came to the Swamp where they had been,
but most of them were then fled, having by their Scouts discovered the Advance of our Men, yet our Horse killed, and
took many of them, following the Pursuit, till our Horses were
tired, our Men faint, and our Victuals spent: Insomuch that
several Horses were killed and eaten, whereof the General
(the worthy Josiah Winslow, Esquire, Governor of New
London),[1] eat his Part, and in all, as well hardships and
dangers, was not wanting to encourage his Men by his own
valiant Example: but finding it both vain and hazardous to
march farther after this flying Rabble of barbarous Heathens,
who we heard were then got together, about 5000 Men, Women
and Children, towards Quobage; our Army left the Chace,
and having placed a Garrison of about seventy Men, in Captain Smith's (a strong) House, within four Miles of the Narragansets Dwellings, marched homewards to Marleborough, and
from thence to Boston, where they were disbanded in December.[2]

But upon this, the Indians began to appear abroad again,
as mischievous as ever; For the very next Week[3] they set
upon Lancaster Town, killed several People, and carried away
many Prisoners; such Houses as were fortified, defended themselves, but the greatest Part of the Town they fired and plundered; and had destroyed the whole Place, had not Captain
Wadsworth, upon hearing of the Guns, come with great Expedition from Sudbury, with a Party to their Relief. After
this they cut off a Farm-house near Sudbury, killed seven
People in a barbarous Manner, and carried some away captive. Three hundred of them set upon the Town of Maides-
field,[4] and burnt at least fifty Houses, killed and took divers

---

[1] Plymouth.

[2] In the account on p. 67, *ante*, the total number of Indians was given
as 4,000, of whom 1,800 were fighting men. The reader of to-day knows also
that the Indians were as destitute of provisions as the whites. Finally the troops
were disbanded in Boston in February and not in December.

[3] Although warning of this attack was given by James Wiser, an Indian,
Lancaster was surprised on February 10. The house of Rev. Joseph Rowland-
son was burned and his wife and children, except one, were carried away by the
Indians. Mrs. Rowlandson's story is given on pp. 112–167, *post*.

[4] Medfield, February 21. The attack at Sudbury, February 1, was upon the
family of Thomas Eames.

of the Inhabitants, being all surprised before they were aware:
For the subtle Indians near Daybreak, came about the Houses
privately and lay close in the Fences; And as People came
out of their Houses shot them down.   Upon this the Governour
of Massachuset sent out about Five hundred or six hundred
Men under the Conduct of Major Thomas Savadge and Captain Mosely, as next in command to him, who, having Intelligence by a Girl that had made her Escape,[1] that the Indians
were in three Towns beyond Quoboge, marched thither, where
they joyned Major Treat[2] with the Connecticot Forces; but
the Enemy were fled: only, skulkingly out of the Woods, they
shot one of Capt. Mosely's Men and wounded one or two
more.   But their main Body being closely pursued, dispersed
and ran into Woods and Swamps, so that it was impossible
for our Men to come up with them, and therefore marched
away for Hadley and Northampton, to secure them and the
other Towns in those Parts, and by a special Providence came
very seasonably; for within two Days after his Arrival,
Northampton (though fortified round) was assaulted, the Centinel Surprised and slain, and the Enemy entred the Fortifications: Being ignorant (as it is supposed) of any Recruits
newly come thither, but found such warm Entertainment, that
though they had kindled their Fire, they durst not stay to
roast their Breakfast, but were forced to fly with great Confusion; we having lost only three Men, and the Enemy above
twenty, as was judged, though the Number could not be certainly known; it being their Custome to carry off their Dead
always with them, if possible.   The next Day they appeared
about a thousand strong, whereupon the Major drew out his
Forces, and pursued them to their usual Place of Rendevouz
near Deerfield; But they would not abide his coming up with
them, but fled dispersedly into the Woods, where he was able
to do little or no Execution upon them.

   The Councill of Boston (to the great Surprise of many
People) refusing to maintain the Narraganset Garrison raised
by the United Colonies, lodged as aforesaid in Mr. Smith's
House, they having eat and destroyed what they could,
quitted the said House, those of the Soldiers that belonged

---

[1] Mary Sheppard, who had been taken prisoner February 12.
[2] Major Robert Treat, mentioned *ante*, pp. 43 and 60.

to Connecticot hiring a Boat to transport them to Pawcatucke, fearing to march through the Narraganset Country and those of the Massachusets and Plimmouth went to Seacunicke. But the very next Day after their Departure, the Indians came and burnt the said Garrison-house (one of the most delightful Seats in New England) and another House of the said Capt. Smiths at Sawgaw, together with all the Houses at Narraganset;[1] and the Day following assaulted Warwick with so unhappy a Successe, that they burnt most of the Houses there, and indeed ruined all but four, which during the present Danger were kept by their Owners with their Friends and Servants as Garrisons; out of which there was a Sally made with twenty Men, who with the Losse of one of their Number, killed ten of the Indians, yet could not preserve the Rest of the Town, nor hinder them from carrying from thence a considerable Booty of Cattel.

The 14th of March, the savage Enemy set upon a considerable Town called Groughton,[2] and burnt Major Wilberds House first (who with his Family removed to Charls Town) and afterwards destroyed sixty-five Dwelling-houses more there, leaving but six Houses standing in the whole Town, which they likewise furiously attempted to set on Fire; But being fortified with Arms and Men as Garrisons, they with their Shot, killed several of the Enemy, and prevented so much of their Designe; Nor do we hear that any Person on our Side was here either slain or taken Captive; But the very next Day two Men coming from Malbury[3] to Sudbury, were set upon in the Woods by a great Number of Indian Women armed with Clubs, Pieces of Swords, and the like, who by their Numbers having over-mastered the two poor Travellers, that had Nothing but small Sticks to defend themselves with, beat out their Brains, and cut off their privy Members, which they carried away with them in Triumph; so vain it is to expect any Thing but the most barbarous Usage from such a People amongst whom the most milde and gentle Sex delight in

---

[1] Pawcatucke or Paugatuck is Westerly, Rhode Island; Seacunicke is Seekonk, Massachusetts, and Sawgaw is near Wickford, Rhode Island.

[2] The date of this attack upon Major Simon Willard at Groton is usually given March 13. One writer makes it March 7.

[3] Marlborough.

Cruelties, and have utterly abandoned at once the two proper Virtues of Womankinde, Pity and Modesty.

Their next Attempt (I mean of any considerable Body of the Indians) was upon a Town called Nashaway,[1] which they set Fire to, and burnt down to the Ground; there was little Resistance made here, People endeavoring rather to escape their Fury by Flight than Opposition; and yet they killed many, burnt the Town down to the Ground, and took no lesse than five and fifty Persons into their merciless Captivity. And that you may perceive the malicious Hatred these Infidels have to Religion and Piety, it may be observed, how they endeavored to signalize their Cruelty, and gratifie their enraged Spleen, chiefly on the Promoters of it; For of these 55 Captives, the Minister of the Towns Relations made up no lesse than seventeen, viz: Mrs. Rowlinson[2] the Minister's Wife, and his three Children, and two Sisters of her own, with seven, and the other with four Children. As they were leading them away in this lamentable Condition, one of the Sisters being big with Childe, going into the Woods to be privately delivered, the Indians followed and in a jeering Manner, they would help her, and be her Midwives, and thereupon they barbarously ript up her Body, and burnt the Child before her Face, and then in a merciful Cruelty, to put her out of her Pain, knockt her o'th Head. There was a Report that they had forced Mrs. Rowlinson to marry the one eyed Sachem, but it was soon contradicted; for being a very pious Woman and of great Faith, the Lord wonderfully supported her under this Affliction, so that she appeared and behaved her self amongst them with so much Courage and majestick Gravity, that none durst offer any Violence to her, but on the contrary (in their rude Manner) seemed to show her great Respect; But who can expresse the Sorrows of her Husband, the Minister and his Brother, when returning from Boston, presently after the Engagement, they found all their Goods destroyed, their Houses laid in Ashes, and their dear Wives and Children thus miserably captivated: this was a fit Scene for Faith and Patience to be exercised in. In such a Junction of Affairs a Man had need have a God to go to for Support, and an Interest

---

[1] Lancaster; see p. 80, ante, and pp. 118–121, post.

[2] Mrs. Joseph Rowlandson.

in Christ to yield him Consolation. Mr. Rowlinson, after much Pains and Trouble ransomed his Wife for Twenty Pounds, and got her out of their Hands, but his Children and the Rest (if living) remain still in that most wretched Slavery.

About the same Time one Mr. Clarke's Wife, Children, and all his Family at his Farm House two Miles from Plimouth were surprized and killed, except one Boy, who was knockt down, and left for Dead, but afterwards taken up and revived. The House they plundered of ·Provisions and Goods to a great Value. Eight compleate Arms, 30 *l.* of Powder, with an answerable Quantity of Lead for Bullets, and 150 *l.* in ready Money; the said Mr. Clark himself narrowly escaping their Cruelty by being at that Instant at a Meeting.[1]

Sunday the 26th of March was sadly remarkable to us for the Tidings of a very deplorable Disaster brought unto Boston about 5 a Cloak that Afternoon, by a Post from Dedham, *viz.*, that Captain Peirce [of] Scituate,[2] in Plimmouth Colony, having Intelligence in his Garrison at Seaconicke, that a Party of the Enemy lay near Mr. Blackstones,[3] went forth with 63 English and twenty of the Cape Indians, (who had all along continued faithful, and joyned with them;) and upon their March, discovered rambling in an obscure woody Place, four or five Indians, who, in getting away from us, halted, as if they had been lame or wounded. But our Men had pursued them but a little Way into the Woods, before they found them to be only Decoys to draw them into their Ambuscade: for on a Sudden, they discovered above 500 Indians, who in very good Order, furiously attacqued them, being as readily received by ours. So that the Fight began to be very fierce and

[1] The massacre at William Clarke's house was on March 12.

[2] Captain Michael Pierce. The Indians declared later that Pierce had attacked them on their way to Plymouth and that no injury to Rhode Island had been intended.

[3] William Blackstone was a clergyman of the Church of England, who had come out to Massachusetts Bay in 1623, and is famous as the first white inhabitant of Boston, and the sole occupant of that peninsula when Winthrop arrived. In 1634 he removed with his library to a place he called Study Hill, now Lonsdale, Rhode Island, on Blackstone River, continued there his recluse life, and died there May 26, 1675. A few weeks later his house, library, and papers were destroyed by the Indians.

dubious, and our Men had made the Enemy begin to retreat; but so slowly that it scarce deserved that Name, when a fresh Company of about 400 Indians came in; so that the English and their few Indian Friends were quite surrounded, and beset on every Side. Yet they made a brave Resistance, for above two Hours: during all which Time they did great Execution upon the Enemy, whom they kept at a Distance, and themselves in Order. For Captain Pierce cast his 63 English and 20 Indians into a Ring, and fought Back to Back, and were double-double Distance, all in one Ring, whilst the Indians were as thick as they could stand, thirty deep. Overpowered with whose Numbers, the said Captain, and 55 of his English, and ten of their Indian Friends were slain upon the Place; which, in such a Cause, and upon such Disadvantages, may certainly be stiled *The Bed of Honour*. However, they sold their worthy Lives at a gallant Rate; it being affirmed by those few that (not without wonderful Difficulty, and many Wounds,) made their Escape, that the Indians lost as many Fighting Men, (not counting Women and Children,) in this Engagement, as were killed at the Battle in the Swamp, near Narraganset, mentioned in our last Letter, which were generally computed to be above three Hundred.

The same Day, some Christians going to a Meeting at Springfield, with a small Guard, were ambuscaded by eight Indians, and a Man and Woman slain; and the Rest, supposing the Enemies Number to have been greater than it was, for in Truth, our Men were twice as many, yet struck with Terror, fled,[1] and left two Women and two Children to the Enemies Mercy, whom they carried away Captive, greatly insulting [exulting] that so few of them should make so many English fly. Of this Accident Major Savage of Hadley, being immediately advertised by a Post sent specially on that Occasion, dispatcht a Party of Horse to pursue the Enemy, and the next Morning found their Track, and soon after discovered them; who, seeing our Men approach, took the two poor Infants, and in the Sight both of their Mothers and our Men, tossed them up in the Air, and dasht their Brains out against the Rocks, and with their Hackets [Hatchets] knockt down the Women,

---

[1] A rumor that Philip himself with over a thousand warriors was in the neighborhood may have caused the terror here mentioned.

and forthwith fled. The Place being exceeding rocky, and a Swamp just by, our Horse could not follow them, and on Foot were not able to overtake them; so that the bloudy Villains, for the Present, escaped deserved Vengeance; yet it pleased God, that both the Women revived, and being come again to their Understanding, one of them declared that she knew every Particular Person of these eight Indians, and that they advised them to put all the Men they could light upon to Death but to save as many Women and Houses as they could, for them.

On Tuesday following, the barbarous Infidels destroied sixty and six Houses, besides Barns and Buildings in Seaconicke,[1] but we do not hear of any Person there slain. On Wednesday, they stormed Providence, and consumed the greatest Part of the Houses; but without taking away the Life of any Person, except one Wright, of whom it is reported, that he was a Man of a singular and sordid Humour; of great Knowledge in the Scriptures, but of no particular professed Sect or Perswasion; one that derided Watches, Fortifications, and all publick Endeavours and Administrations for the common Safety; insomuch, that after all Alarms round about, he refused to bring in any of his Goods, (which were of considerable Value,) or to shelter himself in any Garrison, but presumed he should be safe in his own House, where the Enemy found and butchered him. It is further credibly related concerning him, that he had a strange Confidence, or rather Conceit, that whilst he held his Bible in his Hand, he looked upon himself as secure from all kinde of Violence; and, that the Enemy, finding him in that Posture, deriding his groundless Apprehension, or Folly therein, ripped him open and put his Bible in his Belly.

But indeed the Reason that the Inhabitants of the Town of Seaconicke and Providence generally escaped with their Lives, is not to be attributed to any Compassion or Good Nature of the Indians, (whose very Mercies are inhumane Cruelties,) but, (next to God's Providence,) to their own Prudence in avoiding their Fury, when they found themselves too weak and unable to resist it, by a timely Flight into Rhode

[1] That part of Seekonk constituting Rehoboth, Massachusetts, burned apparently March 28, 1676. Providence suffered further on June 29.

Island,[1] which now became the common Zoar,[2] or Place of Refuge for the Distressed; yet some remained till their coming to distroy the said Towns; as, in particular, Mr. Williams, at Providence,[3] who knowing several of the Chief Indians that came to Fire that Town, discoursed with them a considerable Time, who pretended their greatest Quarrel was against Plimmouth; and as for what they attempted against the other Colonies, they were constrained to it, by the Spoil that was done them at Narraganset. They told him that when Capt. Pierce engaged them near Mr. Blackstone's they were bound for Plimouth. They gloried much in their Success, promising themselves the Conquest of the whole Country, and rooting out of all the English. Mr. Williams reproved their Confidence; minded them of their Cruelties, and told them that the Bay, viz., Boston, could yet spare ten thousand Men; and if they should destroy all them, yet, it was not to be doubted, our King would send as many every Year from Old England, rather than they should share the Countrey. They answered proudly, that they should be ready for them, or to that Effect; but told Mr. Williams that he was a good Man, and had been kinde to them formerly, and therefore would not hurt him.[4]

About the latter End of March came Advice from New York, that the Indians, in a Bravado, had released two English Captives, and sent them down thither to give Information of what they had seen, which was, that being carried with a Party three Days Journey towards the North-East, from the Place where King Philip lay, (which was between thirty and fourty English Miles from Albany),[5] He came up to an Indian Rendevouz, made by a mighty Sachem near Hossicke-River,[6] towards Canada, where one of them told one and

---

[1] "Rhode Island" means specifically, as it usually means in writings of that period, the island of that name, on which Newport is situated, as distinguished from Providence Plantations.

[2] Gen. xix. 20–22.   [3] Roger Williams.

[4] A somewhat different account of the meeting between Williams and the Indians given by Backus, the historian of the Baptists, states that the elder Indians warned Williams against venturing among the younger warriors, upon which he returned to the garrison.

[5] Philip's place of retreat during the preceding winter—Schaghticoke.

[6] Hoosic.

twenty hundred Men, compleat; and the Indians themselves
drawing out into three Ranks, (that he might view them
the Better,) made him tell them over three Times; who,
he said, were generally well armed, with good Firearms,
and most of them young Men; few so old as forty. And,
that amongst them there were about 500 of those with
Straws about their Noses, commonly called French Indians.
That neither King Philip nor that Party, consisting of about
four Hundred, were then with them and that the said Philip's
own Men were not above one Hundred; himself being very
sickly, and having but little Esteem or Authority amongst
them.

One of the said released Prisoners declared further, that
from that Rendevouz he returned with the Rest towards
Albany, being afterwards given by the North Indians to the
Mahicanders[1] or River Indians, (who have been always sus-
pected to be too kinde to those bloody Ones of the North.)
And also affirms that the said North Indians, at the said
Rendevouz, in a vapouring Manner, declared, that their In-
tent was, first to destroy Connecticot this Spring, then Boston
in the Harvest, and afterwards the Dutch, (meaning what the
Dutch had here.)

About the same Time also, there was much Discourse and
Consultation about a Project for giving these Northern Indians that thus infested and harassed New England, a Diversion, by engaging the Mohucks[2] (another Sort of Indians,
inhabiting towards New-York, and formerly inveterate Enemies to these,) against them on the other Side. And it was
certainly reported, that the Governour of New York would,
upon request, and reasonable Proposalls, freely make use of
his Interest amongst that People, (which is very great,) for
effecting so good a Design. Yea, the Pequod Sachem, who
always has continued friendly and faithful to the English, venturing his Men on all Occasions, (who have done very good
Service,) seemed much to wonder that we did not carry it
on; affirming that the said Mohucks were the only Persons
likely to put an End to the War, by hindering the Enemy
from Planting; and forcing them down upon us. But this
Counsell, (for I know not what good Reasons of Some amongst

---

[1] Mohegans.   [2] Mohawks.

as,) was not thought fit,[1] (at least for the Present,) to be so vigourously pursued, as Some expected: But to proceed with the Narrative.

On the second of April, Maj. Savage, Capt. Mosely, Capt. William Turner, and Capt. Whitpoll[2] with 300 Men, marched from Marleborow to Quoboge, where they had ordered the Connecticot Forces to attend their coming. And accordingly the Parties being joined, endeavoured to finde out the Enemy, and give them Battel; but these Heathens being like Wolves, and other Beasts of Prey, that commonly do their Mischiefs in the Night, or by Stealth, durst not come forth out of the Woods and Swamps, where they lay skulking in small Companies, being so light of Foot that they can run away when they list, and pass Boggs, rocky Mountains and Thickets, where we could by no Means pursue them. Only now and then we met with some Straglers before they were aware. And one Time marching towards Northampton, had a brisk Dispute with a small Party who fell upon our Rear; but we quickly repelled them, and killed about 20, in a hot Pursuit after them, without the Losse of one Man on our Side, and but one wounded.

About the same Time, Maj. Palmer,[3] having been scouring the Narragansets Country, brought in 30 of the Enemy, and 60 of Ninnicrofts People, which were about 30 fighting Men, who delivered up themselves to our Protection. We kept their Wives and Children safely, as Hostages, and made the Men go abroad with our Parties, who did us great Service in clearing the Woods. Likewise the Pequods and Mohegins, (who proved a good Guard to New London, Norwich, and the River's Mouth,) brought in 27 of the Enemy and much Plunder.

April the 6 John Winthrope, Esq. a Member of the Royal Society, and Governour of Connecticot Colony, having like a faithful Patriot, served his Country, dyed at Boston, of a natural Distemper, after about eight Days Sickness, and was

---

[1] The correspondence between the governments of Connecticut and New York regarding this proposed stirring up of the Indians against each other reflects little credit on either party. Little wonder the plan "was not thought fit."

[2] Captain John Whipple. Further information as to Captain Turner is on p. 95, *post.*

[3] Major Edward Palmes, according to Hubbard.

there interred in his Fathers Tomb, with an universal Lamentation, and all the Honours that our Distresses and Distractions would allow. And, though it be usually said *Inter arma silent Musæ*, yet could not all our martial Confusions wholly strike our Muses dumb, upon so worthy an Occasion, (enough to make our Country bathe itself in Tears, as it hath lately done in Bloud,) but they appeared in Publique to pay a Funeral Tribute to his honourable Dust, in a no lesse ingenious than passionate and mournfull Elegy upon him, printed here at Boston.[1]

The next Day the Governour intended to have marched out with about three hundred English of his own Colony, and 50 Cape-Indians,[2] and all Things were in a Readiness accordingly; but not being supplied with any Assistance from us, he wanted Soldiers to secure his own Towns, if they should be attacqued suddenly by the Indians, (who lie in Wait for such Opportunities,) during his Absence, and therefore was forced to let fall his Designe, and continue at Home.

The 11 of April, Capt. Denison,[3] with an 100 English Volunteers, belonging to Connecticot Colony, and as many Indians, of whom some were Mohegins, some Pequods, and some of Ninnicrofts Men, that had revolted from him; the said friendly Indians being commanded by the young Sachem Unkus, whose Father, (the only Christian Sagamore,) hath during all this War continued faithful; upon their March, ranging the Narraganset Countrey near Potuxit, they fell upon a Party of the Enemy, commanded by that famous but very bloudy and cruel Sachem, Quononshot, otherwise called Myantonomy, whom the English formerly presented with a rich Lac't Coat.[4] They fought very obstinately a considerable

---

[1] Benjamin Thompson's *A Funeral Tribute to the Honourable Dust of that Most Charitable Christian, Unbiassed Politician, and unimitable Pyrotechnist John Winthrope esq.*, a broadside (Boston, John Foster, 1676), of which only one copy is known. The elegy was included in Thompson's *New England's Tears for her present Miseries*, and is prefixed to the 1677 edition of Hubbard's *Indian Wars*.

[2] Indians from Cape Cod.

[3] Captain George Denison. For Ninnicroft (Ninigret) and Uncas see pp. 24, 32, *ante*.

[4] Quononshot or Canonchet is identified by "N. S." with Myantonomy (Miantonomo), but the former was the son of the latter, who had been killed by Uncas, at the instance of the English, in 1643. The "Lac't Coat" had been given at the treaty in Boston the preceding October.

Time, but at last, our Men, with very small Losse, obtained the Victory; killed above 50 of the Enemy on the Place, and took 40 more alive; and amongst the Rest that insolent Sachem, Myantonomy himself, together with another Sachem, and several other of his chief Counsellors and Friends. The said Myantonomys Carriage was strangely proud and lofty, after he was taken. Being examined why he did foment that War, which would certainly be the Destruction of him and all the Heathen Indians in the Country, etc. He would make no other Reply to any Interrogatories, but this;—That he was born a Prince, and if Princes came to speak with him he would answer, but none present being such, he thought himself obliged in Honour to hold his Tongue, and not hold Discourse with such Persons, below his Birth and Quallity. He told them he wisht rather to die than to continue under Confinement;[1] that all he desired was not to be tortured, but presently be put to Death; which he requested might be done by young Unkus, that aided us; as acknowledging him his fellow Prince; yet, withall, threatned, he had 2,000 Men would revenge his Death severely. Wherefore, our Forces, fearing an Escape, put the stoutest Men to the Sword, but preserved Myantonomy till they returned to Stonington, where our Indian Friends and most of the English Soldiers, declaring to the Commanders their Fear, that the English should, upon Conditions, release him, and that then he would, (though the English might have Peace with him,) be very pernicious to those Indians that now assisted us, The said Indians, (on these Considerations, and the Mischiefs, and Murthers he had done, during this War,) [were] permitted to put him to Death. And, that all might share in the Glory of destroying so great a Prince, and come under the Obligation of Fidelity each to other, the Pequods shot him, the Mohegins cut off his Head and quartered his Body, and the Ninnicrofts Men made the Fire and burned his Quarters; and as a Token of their Love and Fidelity to the English, presented his Head to the Council at Hartford.

About the same Time we had Information from an Indian Spy, taken by our Army, that the Enemy had a Designe, on the next Day, to fall upon the Garrison, and some few Houses

---

[1] Canonchet was offered his life "upon condition of compliance with the English," but refused the terms.

that remained at Marlborough, to revenge the Death of one
of their eminent Men that was slain when they were last there:
(His Name being concealed.) Upon which, our Major General, who was sent to meet Major Savage, and accompany
him and his Forces to Boston, commanded Capt. Moseley and
another Captain, with their Companies, thither, to abide and
expect the Enemy, 24 Hours; but they not coming in that
Time, our said Forces were called Home and disbanded, to
the Dissatisfaction of some People, who thereupon feared the
like fatall Consequences, that but a little before attended the
like Occasion. Nor were such their Apprehensions vain, for
within four Days afterwards News arrived at Boston that all
the Houses at the said Town of Marleborough (except the
Garrison) were destroied.

April 20. Capt. Wadsworth[1] of Dorchester, being designed
with an 100 Men to repair to Marlborough, to strengthen the
Garrison, and remove the Goods, etc., there; did accordingly
this Evening march with about 70 Men from Sudbury the
Rest of his Men not appearing. The Enemy who were about
a 1000 strong lay near his Passage, but kept themselves undiscovered, and permitted him to passe them in the Night,
but in the Morning assaulted and burned most of the Houses
in Sudbury (save those that were ingarrisoned:) Upon which
the Town of Concord receiving the Alarm, 12 resolute young
Men hastened from thence to their Neighbour's Relief, but
were waylaid, and 11 of them cut off; But by the Time Capt.
Wadsworth was come to Marlborough, the Alarm and News of
this Disaster overtook him, and although he had marched all
the Day and Night before, and his Men much wearied, yet he
hastened back againe and was accompanied by Capt. Brocklebank,[2] Commander of the Garrison at Marleborough, with
what small Number he durst spare out of his Garrison. When
they arrived within a Mile and a half of Sudbury, the Enemy,
having hid themselves behind the Hills, sent forth two or three
to cross the March of our Forces, and being seen, to counterfeit themselves affrighted and fly, thereby to trapan our Men
into their Ambuscade, which mischievous Designe succeeded

---

[1] Captain Samuel Wadsworth of Milton, a town created from Dorchester
in 1662.

[2] Captain Samuel Brocklebank of Rowley.

according to their Wishes, for our Men pursuing them, and
being not above 80 in Number, and those miserably tired as
well with tedious Marches as for want of Sleep, were suddenly
set upon, and on every Side encompassed with the Enemy,
being about a 1000 strong; yet not at all dismaied with their
Numbers, nor dismal Shouts, and horrid Yellings, ours made
a most couragious Resistance; and having gained the Top of
a Hill, they from thence gallantly defended themselves with
the Loss of five Men near four Hours; the cowardly Savages
disheartened with the Sight of so many of their Fellows slain
in the first Attacque, not daring to venture close upon them,
yet (that we may not think these Barbarians altogether un-
acquainted with Stratagems, nor so Silly as to neglect any
Advantages,) at last they set the Woods on Fire to the Wind-
ward of our Men, which by Reason of the Winde blowing very
hard and the Grass being exceeding dry, burnt with a terrible
Fierceness, and with the Smoak and Heat was like to choak
them; so that being no longer able at once to resist the approaching Fire, and the cruel Enemy, they were forced to quit
that advantagious Post in Disorder; which the Indians taking
Advantage of came on upon them like so many Tigers, and
dulling their active Swords with excessive Numbers, obtained
the Dishonour of a Victory; our two Captains after incomparable Proofs of their Resolution and Gallantry, being slain upon
the Place; together with most of their Men; but those few
that remained, escaped to a Mill, which they defended till
Night, when they were hapily rescued by Capt. Prentice, who
coming in the Day hastily, though somewhat too late to the
Relief of Capt. Wadsworth, having not above Six Troopers
that were able to keep Way with him, fell into a Pound or
Place near Sudbury Towns End, where all Passages were
stopt by the Indians; and had not Captain Cowell [1] (who in
his Return from Quoboge had avoided the Common Rode
providentially), at that Instant come thither with about thirty
Dragoons (who were forced to fight their Way through) and two
Files of Men sent from a Garrison to secure another Passage,
which the Enemy hastned to stop against Capt. Cowell, both
the said Capt. Prentice and his Men, and the Remainder of
the said Captain Wadsworths Men in the Mill, had been all

[1] Captain Edward Cowell of Boston.

killed or taken alive: nor did Captain Cowell lose above six or seven of his Men in this Engagement: but so insolent were the Indians grown upon their first Successe against Captain Wadsworth, that they sent us Word, to provide Store of good Chear, for they intended to dine with us upon the Election Day.[1]

But for preventing any Danger that might happen on that Occasion, the following Order was printed and published.

At a Council held at Boston, April 21 1676.

For the Prevention of such Mischiefs as may be designed by the common Enemy, and the Securing of the several Plantations upon the Day of Publike Election now drawing near:

It is Ordered, That the Committees of Militia in each Town, do take effectual Care that the Trained Soldiers be in Arms upon that Day, and keep Watch and Ward with all Diligence, under the Command of one Commission-Officer at least, or some other meet Person where no Commission-Officer is to be had. Which Commander so employed for that Day in every Town, is also strictly required to forbid and prevent all Rudeness by Playing, Drinking, or otherwise; and for the better Execution of this Order, The Committees of Militia aforesaid shall take some meet Course for the seasonable Publishing the same to their several Towns; that such of them as are Freemen, may (as many of them as may be) timely put in their Votes by Proxy, which for this extraordinary Season is most advisable, and hereby recommended to them to do: All Soldiers and Inhabitants being hereby enjoyned and Commanded in all Respects to yield Obedience accordingly.

By the Council,
EDWARD RAWSON, Sec'r.

April 26. Captain Hinskman[2] having received Commission and Instruction, did then march for Major Wilberds Funerall (who died in his Bed in Peace, though God had honoured him with severall signal Victories over our Enemys in War) to Charles-Town, and from thence to Concord, the Place of Rendevouz. From Mr. Woodcock's Garrison[3] we hear

---

[1] By the charter, election day was the last Wednesday in Easter term; this year, May 3, 1676.

[2] Captain Daniel Henchman of Worcester, Massachusetts.

[3] Woodcock's Garrison was on the old stage road from Providence to Boston, about 30 miles from the latter city. The attack mentioned was on April 27, and John Woodcock's son Nathaniel was killed.

that himself and two of his Sons, and some other Men being gone out to Labour in the Field, were, about this Time surprised; one of his Sons and another Man being killed, and himself and the other Son dangerously (though it pleased God, not mortally) wounded; so that there were only five sound Persons left to keep Garrison, besides the old Woman and three Daughters, and yet (through Mercy) it has always held out.

May the First, Captain Dennison with his Volunteers and Indians fell upon a Party of the Enemy, and killed Six and 20 of them, and took fifty Captives; Also we had Advice, that the Pequods and other friendly Indians, had carried many Prisoners to New-London; that some had voluntarily surrendered themselves to the Magistrates of Connecticot-Colony, and more came in from the Sachem of Penny-cook.[1]

About a Fortnight afterwards, the forementioned Captain Turner,[2] by Trade a Taylor, but one that for his Valour has left behind him an Honourable Memory, hearing of the Indians being about Twenty Miles above them at Connecticot River, drew out a Party at Hadly and Northampton, where there was a Garrison, and marching all Night, came upon them before Day-break, they having no Centinels or Scouts abroad, as thinking themselves secure, by Reason of their remote Distance from any of our Plantations: Ours taking this Advantage of their Negligence, fell in amongst them, and killed several hundreds of them upon the Place; they being out of any Posture or Order to make any formidable Resistance, though they were six Times superiour to us in Number: But that which was almost as much, nay in some respect more considerable than their Lives, We there destroied all their Ammunition and Provision, which we think they can hardly be so soon and easily recruited with, as possibly they may be with Men. We likewise here demolisht Two Forges they had to mend their Armes; took away all their Materialls and Tools, and drove many of them into the River, where they were

---

[1] The Pennacook tribe was a part of a group of Indians living along the Merrimac River and known as Pawtuckets. The Pennycook division were seated near Concord, New Hampshire, and their Sachem was Wanalancet.

[2] Captain William Turner; see p. 89, *ante*. The place of the conflict has ever since been called Turner's Falls, Massachusetts.

drowned, and threw two great Piggs of Lead of theirs (intended for making of Bullets) into the said River. But this great Success was not altogether without its Allay, as if Providence had designed to Checquer our Joys and Sorrows; and lest we should Sacrifice to our own Nets, and say, Our own Arms or Prowesse hath done this, to permit the Enemy presently after to take an advantage against us; For as our Men were returning to Hadly, in a dangerous Passe, which they were not sufficiently aware of, the skulking Indians (out of the Woods), killed at one Volley, the said Captain and Eight and Thirty of his Men; but immediately after they had discharged, they fled.

In *June* Major Talkot[1] slew and took Captive Four and Twenty of the Enemies in one Weeks Time, and also killed the Old Queen of Narraganset, and an arch Villain of their Party, that had been with them at the sacking of Providence, famously known by the Name of Stonewall, or Stone-Layer John,[2] for that being an active ingenious Fellow he had learnt the Mason's Trade, and was of great Use to the Indians in building their Forts, etc. Likewise Potucke, the Great Indian Counsellour, (a Man considering his Education of a wonderfull Subtlety) was brought Prisoner into Rhode Island.

In *July*, we had very considerable Forces abroad, who took and killed above 200 of the barbarous bloudy Indians, and that cruell Infidel Puncham[3] among the Rest.

The Squaw Sachem,[4] King Philip's Sister, who at First so much promoted this Warr, and was since by Treaty with Ninnicroft, Sachem of the Narragansetts, to be delivered up,

[1] Major John Talcott.

[2] "Stone-wall, or Stone-Layer John," mentioned *ante*, p. 59. The "Old Queen of Narraganset" was sister to Ninigret and married a son of Canonicus. She is known by other names, the most common being Quaiapen.

[3] Potucke (Potuck, Potok) lived near the present Point Judith. He was sent to Boston later and is said to have been shot. For Puncham (Pumham), see p. 67, *ante*.

[4] The Squaw Sachem of Pocasset, Weetamoo (p. 25, *ante*), never surrendered. The person confused with her is Awashonks, sometimes called the "Squaw Sachem of Saconet," whom Captain Benjamin Church persuaded to surrender in July, 1676. Weetamoo was found August 3, drowned in Taunton River, when on her way to rejoin Philip at Mount Hope.

hath lately surrendered herself, and is come into the Plimmouth Army, having submitted to the Mercy of Major Bradford, who[1] with a small Party some Time since separated himself from the Rest of his Narragansets, pretending (when he found they could not Prosper) that he disapproved of their Doings, in breaking their Treaty with the English, hath likewise taken Shelter under our Forces at Stonington, to secure his Life at present: For not only those of his Men that continue in Rebellion still, but likewise those that formerly surrendered themselves to us, threaten to cut off his Head; the First pretending that by his treacherous Councils he drew them into this Warr, and then basely deserted them: and the Second, charging him as a Traytor and Truce-breaker to the English. Thus abominable is Treachery and Violation of ones Faith, even amongst the most barbarous and savage Infidels.

King Philip and some of these Northern Indians being wandered up towards Albany, the Mohucks marched out very strong, in a warlike Posture upon them, putting them to Flight, and pursuing them as far as Hossicke River, which is about two Days March from the East Side of Hudson's River to the N. E., killing divers, and bringing away some Prisoners with great Pride and Triumph; which ill Successe on that Side where they did not expect any Enemy, having lately endeavoured to make up the ancient Animosities, did very much daunt and discourage the said Northern Indians; so that some hundreds came in and submitted themselves to the English at Plimmouth-Colony; and Philip himself is run skulking away into some Swamp, with not above ten Men attending him; Nor doubt we shortly to have a good Account given of that Prime Incendiary; there being severall of our Troops daily abroad in Quest of him.[2]

It is computed by most judicious Men, That the Indians that were killed, taken, sent away, and now of Late come in by Way of Submission, cannot in all, (Men, Women and Children,) amount to fewer than Six Thousand, besides vast Quantities of their Corn, Houses, Ammunition, and other

---

[1] "Who," *i. e.*, Ninnicroft or Ninigret. The charges made against him by our writer are unjust, considering the circumstances of the time and the position of the Indian leader.

[2] Until July, 1676, Philip had never been seen by the colonists in any battle.

Necessaries, without which they cannot long Subsist, in Hostility, taken and destroyed.

A True but Brief Account of our Losses sustained since this Cruel and Mischievous War began, take as follows:

In Narraganset not one House left standing.
At Warwick, but one.
At Providence, not above three.
At Potuxit, none left.
Very few at Seaconicke.
At Swansey, two, at most.
Marlborough, wholy laid in Ashes, except two or three Houses.
Grantham and Nashaway,[1] all ruined but one House or two.
Many Houses burnt at Springfield, Scituate, Lancaster, Brookefield and Northampton.
The greatest Part of Rehoboth and Taunton destroyed.
Great Spoil made at Hadley, Hatfield and Chelmsford.
Deerfield wholly, and Westfield much ruined.
At Sudbury, many Houses burnt, and some at Hingham, Weymouth, and Braintree.
Besides particular Farms and Plantations, a great Number not be reckoned up, wholly laid waste, or very much damnified.
And as to Persons, it is generally thought, that of the English there hath been lost, in all, Men Women and Children, above Eight Hundred,[2] since the War began: Of whom many have been destroyed with exquisite Torments, and most inhumane Barbarities; the Heathen rarely giving Quarter to those that they take, but if they were Women, they first forced them to satisfie their filthy Lusts and then murdered them; either cutting off the Head, ripping open the Belly, or skulping the Head of Skin and Hair, and hanging them up as Trophies; wearing Men's Fingers as Bracelets about their Necks, and Stripes of their Skins which they dresse for Belts. They

---

[1] Groton and Lancaster.

[2] Another estimate (*News from New England*, 1676) gives the loss as 444 killed and 55 taken prisoners for the colonists, and 910 for the Indians. Trumbull in his *History of Connecticut* gives the total loss of the colonists as about 600.

knockt one Youth of the Head, and laying him for dead, they flead (or skulp'd) his Head of Skin and Hair. After which the Boy wonderfully revived, and is now recovered, only he hath Nothing but the dry Skull, neither Skin nor Hair on his Head. Nor have our Cattle escaped the Cruelty of these worse than Brute and Savage Beasts: For what Cattle they took they seldom killed outright: or if they did, would eat but little of the Flesh, but rather cut their Bellies, and letting them go several Days, trailing their Guts after them, putting out their Eyes, or cutting off one Leg, etc.

But to reckon up all their Cruelties, would be no lesse burthensome to compassionate Christians Ears, than too tedious for a Letter, which is already swelled too big; and therefore I think it now high Time to conclude, with hearty Thanks to Almighty God for our late Successes against this bloudy Enemy, whereby though not wholly freed from Apprehensions of future Dangers; yet we have Grounds to hope, that their Fury is much quasht and abated; so that (if our Sins obstruct not so great a Blessing) we may shortly once again see Peace and Safety restored to our (lately disconsolate) Habitations in this Wilderness, For which, as I doubt not of the Concurrence of yours and all good Christians Prayers: so I shall not fail to recommend you and yours to the same Almighty Protection, and with my hearty Respects presented, remain,

Your affectionate Friend and Servant,

N. S.

Finis.

THE WARR IN NEW-ENGLAND VISIBLY ENDED, BY R. H., 1677

THE WARR IN NEW-ENGLAND VISIBLY ENDED, BY R. H., 1677

The Warr in New-England Visibly Ended. King Philip that barbarous Indian now Beheaded, and most of his Bloudy Adherents submitted to Mercy, the Rest fled far up into the Countrey, which hath given the Inhabitants Encouragement to prepare for their Settlement, Being a True and Perfect Account brought in by Caleb More, Master of a Vessel newly Arrived from Rhode Island, And Published for general Satisfaction.
Licensed November 4. Roger L'Estrange.
London: Printed by F. B. for Dorman Newman at the King's Arms, in the Poultry, 1677.[1]

New-Englands Warr Visibly Ended.

Sir,

In my last, which I hope you received, I must acknowledge what I writ (though Truth) yet I had not that comfortable Satisfaction in my Spirit, to give me Hopes, that our publique Calamities were so near an End as now I have, which God in Mercy sanctify to us, that we may see the Rod, and wherefore it is come.

We have been, and still are ready to put different Reflections upon the Murders and Spoils that have been made upon us by this Destructive War: Various are Men's Thoughts why God hath suffered it, all acknowledge it was for Sin; many wish there hath not been some Leaven of that Spirit in the Provocation for which we left Old England. I am in great Pain while I write, to remember how severe some of us have been to Dissenters,[2] making Spoil without Pity, but God is teaching us Moderation.

---

[1] Title-page of original.

[2] Doubtless the reference is partly to Anne Hutchinson, the aunt of the author of this tract.

That black Cloud (God be thanked) begins to waste almost to Nothing, which may not only give us an hopeful Opportunity of repairing the Spoils made by our barbarous Neighbors, but also, deliberating upon the true Causes of these great Distractions: for now we have no visible Appearance of an Enemy: Terrour is fallen upon very many, who come in dayly with Submission, and the Rest withdraw into Places remote, hiding their Weapons of War, and flying from Justice in small Numbers.

King Philip, who hath been a pestilent Ringleader, that had once three hundred Men (Barbarously inclined) as I told you in my last,[1] was reduced to ten, but now is killed, in this Manner. He being hid in a Swamp on Mount Hope Neck, with his little Party, one of his Indians being discontented with him made an Escape from him, and came to Rhode-Island, and informed Capt. Church a Plimouth Captain of a Company that was in Search after this said King Philip, (the Captain being at this Time on the said Island, refreshing his Men with Necessary Provisions) but understanding where King Philip was, and that he intended very speedily to remove far off, to provide his Winter-quarter, retaining still the same Barbarous Spirit and Purposes, without the least Appearance of Reluctancy or Offers of Mediation, towards his Surrender to Mercy; whereupon the said Captain and his Company with some Rhode-Island Men went in Pursuit and Search after him, taking an Indian Guide with them, and beset a Swamp where they heard he was, which was very miry, and the Ground so loose, that our Men sunk to the Middle in their Attempts to come at this sculking Company; but all in vain, the Passage was too difficult.

While we were thus beset with Difficulties in this Attempt, the Providence of God wonderfully appeared, for by Chance[2]

---

[1] The tract, or unprinted letter, to which the author refers is unknown, but the general feeling in New England regarding King Philip is well expressed in these and the following lines. Captain (later Colonel) Benjamin Church who captured Philip became from that circumstance the hero of the war. His memoirs, written down by his son Thomas Church, *Entertaining Passages*, etc., are among the most valuable sources for a history of the period covered by them.

[2] The "Plimouth Man" and the guide named Alderman had been stationed by Captain Church at a point where the latter thought Philip likely to appear, and according to the Church narrative it was the guide whose shots took effect.

the Indian Guide and the Plimouth Man being together, the Guide espied an Indian and bids the Plimouth-man shoot, whose Gun went not off, only flashed in the Pan; with that the Indian looked about, and was going to shoot, but the Plimouth-man prevented him, and shot the Enemy through the Body, dead, with a Brace of Bullets; and approaching the Place where he lay, upon Search, it appeared to be King Philip, to their no small Amazement and great Joy.[1] This seasonable Prey was soon divided, they cut off his Head and Hands, and conveyed them to Rhode-Island, and quartered his Body, and hung it upon four Trees. One Indian more of King Philip's Company they then killed, and some of the Rest they wounded, but the Swamp being so thick and miry, they made their Escape.

This is the Substance of this Enterprize, and the small Remnant we left as inconsiderable, who must either fly up into the Countrey, or perish in the Place.

There is one Potuck, a mischievous Engine, and a Counsellour, taken formerly, said to be in Goal[2] at Rhode-Island, is now sent to Boston, and there shot to Death. One Quonepin a young lusty Sachem, and a very Rogue is now in Goal at Rhode-Island, who was there some Years ago for his Misdemeanours, but broke Goal, and run away, and could never till now be laid hold on.

God be thanked, many Indians come in daily, and submit themselves with much Dejection, crying out against King Philip, and other ill Counsellors, as the Causes of their Misfortunes.[3]

The English go many of them now to their Old Habitations, and Mow down their Ground, and make Hay, and do other Occasions necessary for their resettling: All which gives us

causing Philip to fall "upon his face in the mud and water, with his gun under him."

[1] The next morning, August 12, 1676, "Captain Church gave them the news of Philip's death upon which the whole army gave three loud huzzas."

[2] Gaol, jail.

[3] With the capture of Potuck, p. 96, *ante*, Quinnapin, the husband of Weetamoo, and Annawon and Tishaquin, two able lieutenants of Philip, the war in southern New England virtually ended. In Maine there were minor conflicts until winter, when the Indians were compelled to look to the English for food.

comfortable Hope that God will graciously repair our Breaches,
and cause this Bloody War to End in a lasting Peace, so prays,
Your faithful Friend,

R. H.[1]

Finis.

[1] The initials stand for Richard Hutchinson, nephew of the well known
Anne Hutchinson. See the introduction to *The Present State of New England.*

NARRATIVE OF THE CAPTIVITY OF MRS. MARY ROWLANDSON, 1682

INTRODUCTION

In January, 1676, a Christian Indian, Quanapaug (James Wiser) of the Nashaway tribe, appears to have warned Governor John Leverett, of Massachusetts, of a probable attack upon Lancaster, but because of other points of danger and the uncertainty resulting from the Swamp Fight of the preceding December, this warning was not heeded. Lancaster was a frontier town of some fifty families, already organized into five or six garrisons. The colonial government thought its aid more needed elsewhere, and appears to have disregarded the pleas of Mr. Rowlandson, the minister, and of Lieutenant Henry Kerley for help, even when they came to the colonial capital to reinforce the written appeals. Not until the arrival of Job Kattenait, of Natick, at the house of Major Daniel Gookin at Cambridge about midnight of February 9–10 was anything done. Then Samuel Wadsworth and his forty men posted at Marlborough were sent as relief, but they were too late. It may be added in palliation of the seeming lethargy of the Massachusetts authorities, that Lancaster was fairly well fortified at this time and that in the attack upon the town described in the ensuing narrative the Rowlandson garrison was the only one of the six that succumbed to the Indians. The palisaded houses of Nathaniel Joslin, John Prescott, Thomas Sawyer, Cyprian Stevens, and Richard Wheeler were defended until the Indian warriors retired for fear of the mounted force from Concord, and the men under Wadsworth.

The following narrative gives a personal note, a story of individual experience, which serves to round out the more general history as told by our other writers. Mary White Rowlandson was the daughter of John and Joane White, settlers in Salem in 1638, and citizens of Lancaster in 1653. No detailed record of the date and place of her birth or death exists. She had six brothers and sisters. Married to Rev. Joseph Rowlandson in 1656, she had four children, one of whom died before the outbreak of this war and another during the period of captivity forming the subject of this narrative. After the ransom the Rowlandson family went to Boston, where they lived for a time in a house engaged for them by the Old South Church. Following this residence the Rowlandsons moved from Massachusetts to Wethersfield, Connecticut, in the spring of 1677.

Lancaster was incorporated in 1653. Rev. Joseph Rowlandson was the first ordained minister of the parish, and this narrative by his wife was the first literary work of a citizen of the town which appeared in print. The narrative gives not alone a clear exposition of the dangers to which the early settlers of New England were exposed, but a graphic picture of the life and character of the people themselves. No narrative illustrates more fully the confidence in a Providence which overrules every peril for the good of the sufferer than does this chronicle, and its wording shows plainly to what an extent the Bible had become incorporated into the daily life of the people of New England at the end of the seventeenth century. For these reasons, no less than because of the vividness with which the picture was drawn, this narrative of Mary Rowlandson became at once a marked book. No contemporary New England publication commanded more attention in Great Britain or in America. It became a favorite specimen of the class of writings known as Indian Captivities, now so eagerly collected.

The earliest edition of the *Narrative of Mary Rowlandson* was that printed by Samuel Green at Cambridge in 1682. No copy of this edition is known to exist. Of the second edition, or as the title-page has it "The second Addition Corrected and amended," printed at the same place, by the same publisher and in the same year, a copy once owned by the Reverend John Cotton is in the Prince Library at Boston. This edition has been followed accurately in the text of the following narrative. The only other edition of equal date is the London reprint, by Joseph Poole, in 1682, of which there are several copies in the United States, but these are less reliable than the copy followed in the text. A facsimile of the John Cotton volume was published in 1903 under the joint editorship of Henry S. Nourse and John E. Thayer, in an excellent annotated edition, limited to 250 copies, but for this latter reason has had a very restricted circulation. Various editions were issued during the eighteenth century, in many of which the text was emended and in some cases mutilated, the title-page itself being one of the most severe sufferers. To some of the later editions a copy of Joseph Rowlandson's last sermon has been added, but it has little connection with the narrative, and is omitted in this publication.

Mrs. Rowlandson's "removes" can be traced on the map which appears in this volume (opposite p. 121). A map is needful, for the journeyings of her captors between Wachusett Mountain and the Connecticut River were irregular, and their line of march was circuitous. They knew the ransom value of their captive, and were alert and watchful lest she escape or be retaken by her white friends.

NARRATIVE OF THE CAPTIVITY OF MRS. MARY ROWLANDSON, 1682

*The Soveraignty and Goodness of GOD, Together With the Faith-
fulness of His Promises Displayed; Being a Narrative Of
the Captivity and Restauration of Mrs. Mary Rowlandson.
Commended by her, to all that desires to know the Lords
doings to, and dealings with Her. Especially to her dear
Children and Relations. The second Addition Corrected
and amended.*

*Written by Her own Hand for Her private Use, and now made
Publick at the earnest Desire of some Friends, and for the
benefit of the Afflicted.*

*Deut. 32. 29.   See now that I, even I am he, and there is no God
with me; I kill and I make alive, I wound and I heal,
neither is there any can deliver out of my hand.*

Cambridge, Printed by Samuel Green, 1682.[1]

THE PREFACE TO THE READER.

IT was on Tuesday, Feb. 1, 1675,[2] in the afternoon, when
the Narrhagansets quarters (in or toward the Nipmug Country, whither they are now retyred for fear of the English Army
lying in their own Country) were the second time beaten up,
by the Forces of the united Colonies, who thereupon soon betook themselves to flight, and were all the next day pursued
by the English, some overtaken and destrcyed.   But on Thursday, Feb. 3d, The English having now been six dayes on their
march, from their head quarters, at Wickford, in the Narrhaganset Country, toward, and after the Enemy, and provision grown exceeding short, insomuch that they were fain
to kill some Horses for the supply, especially of their Indian
friends, they were necessitated to consider what was best to

[1] Title-page of the original.   [2] 1675/6.

be done. And about noon (having hitherto followed the chase as hard as they might) a Councill was called, and though some few were of another mind, yet it was concluded by far the greater part of the Councill of War, that the Army should desist the pursuit, and retire: the Forces of Plimouth and the Bay to the next Town of the Bay, and Connecticut Forces to their own next Towns; which determination was immediately put in execution. The consequent whereof, as it was not difficult to be foreseen by those that knew the causless enmity of these Barbarians, against the English, and the malicious and revengefull spirit of these Heathen: so it soon Proved dismall.

The Narrhagansets were now driven quite from their own Country, and all their provisions there hoarded up, to which they durst not at present return, and being so numerous as they were, soon devoured those to whom they went, whereby both the one and other were now reduced to extream straits, and so necessitated to take the first and best opportunity for supply, and very glad, no doubt, of such an opportunity as this, to provide for themselves, and make spoil of the English at once; and seeing themselves thus discharged of their pursuers, and a little refreshed after their flight, the very next week on Thursday, Feb. 10, they fell with mighty force and fury upon Lancaster: which small Town, remote from aid of others, and not being Garisoned as it might, the Army being now come in, and as the time indeed required (the design of the Indians against that place being known to the English some time before) was not able to make effectual resistance: but notwithstanding utmost endeavour of the Inhabitants, most of the buildings were turned into ashes; many People (Men, Women and Children) slain, and others captivated. The most solemn and remarkable part of this Trajedy, may that justly be reputed, which fell upon the Family of that reverend Servant of God, Mr. Joseph Rolandson, the faithfull Pastor of Christ in that place, who being gone down to the Councill of the Massachusets to seek aid for the defence of the place, at his return found the Town in flames, or smoke, his own house being set on fire by the Enemy, through the disadvantage of a defective Fortification, and all in it consumed: his precious yokefellow, and dear Children, wounded and captivated (as the issue evidenced, and following Narrative declares) by these cruel and barbarous Salvages. A sad Catestrophe! Thus all things come alike to all: None knows either love or hatred by all that is before him. It is no new thing for Gods precious ones to drink as deep as others, of the Cup of common Calamity: Take just Lot (yet captivated) for instance beside others. But it is not my business to dilate on these things, but only in few words introductively to preface to the following script, which is a Narrative of the wonderfully awfull, wise, holy, powerfull, and gracious providence of God, towards that worthy and precious Gentlewoman, the dear Consort of the said Reverend Mr. Rowlandson, and her Children with her, as in casting of her into such a waterless pit, so in preserving, supporting, and carrying thorow so many such extream hazards, unspeakable difficulties and disconsolateness, and at last delivering her out of them all, and her surviving Children also. It was a strange and amazing dispensation, that the Lord should so afflict his precious Servant, and Hand maid. It was as strange, if not more, that he should so bear up the spirits of his Servant under such bereavments and of his hand-maid under such captivity, travels and hardships (much too hard for flesh and blood) as he did, and at length deliver and restore. But he was their Saviour, who hath said, *When thou passest through the Waters, I will be with thee, and thorough the Rivers, they shall not overflow thee: When thou walkest through the fire, thou shall not be burnt, nor shall the flame kindle upon thee,* Isa. 43. ver. 2. and again, *He woundeth and his hands make whole. He shall deliver thee in six troubles, yea in seven there shall no evil touch thee. In Famine he shall redeem thee from Death, and in War from the power of the sword.* Job 5 : 18, 19, 20. Methinks this dispensation doth bear some resemblance to those of Joseph, David and Daniel; yea, and of the three Children too,[1] the stories whereof do represent us with the excellent textures of divine Providence, curious pieces of divine work: and truly so doth this, and therefore not to be forgotten, but worthy to be exhibited to, and viewed, and pondered by all, that disdain not to consider the operation of his hands.

The works of the Lord (not only of Creation, but of Providence also, especially those that do more peculiarly con-

[1] See Daniel iii.

cern his dear ones, that are as the Apple of his Eye, as the
Signet upon His Hand, the Delight of his Eyes, and the Object of his tenderest Care) [are] great, sought out of all those
that have pleasure therein. And of these verily this is none
of the least.

This Narrative was penned by the Gentlewoman her self,
to be to her a memorandum of Gods dealing with her, that she
might never forget, but remember the same, and the severall
circumstances thereof, all the dayes of her life. A pious
scope which deserves both commendation and imitation.
Some friends having obtained a sight of it, could not but be
so much affected with the many passages of working providence discovered therein, as to judge it worthy of publick
view, and altogether unmeet that such works of God should
be hid from present and future Generations: And therefore
though this Gentlewomans modesty would not thrust it into
the Press, yet her gratitude unto God made her not hardly
perswadable to let it pass, that God might have his due glory,
and others benefit by it as well as her self. I hope by this
time none will cast any reflection upon this Gentlewoman, on
the score of this publication of her affliction and deliverance.
If any should, doubtless they may be reckoned with the nine
lepers, of whom it is said, *Were there not ten cleansed, where
are the nine?* but one returning to give God thanks. Let
such further know that this was a dispensation of publick note,
and of universall concernment, and so much the more, by how
much the nearer this Gentlewoman stood related to that faithfull Servant of God, whose capacity and employment was publick in the house of God, and his name on that account of a
very sweet savour in the Churches of Christ, who is there of
a true Christian spirit, that did not look upon himself much
concerned in this bereavment, this Captivity in the time
thereof, and in his [this] deliverance when it came, yea
more then in many others; and how many are there, to
whom so concerned, it will doubtless be a very acceptable
thing to see the way of God with this Gentlewoman in the
aforesaid dispensation, thus laid out and pourtrayed before
their eyes.

To conclude: whatever any coy phantasies may deem, yet
it highly concerns those that have so deeply tasted, how good

the Lord is, to enquire with David, *What shall I render to the Lord for all his benefits to me.* Psal. 116. 12. He thinks nothing too great; yea, being sensible of his own disproportion to the due praises of God he calls in help. *Oh, magnifie the Lord with me, let us exalt his Name together,* Psal. 34. 3. And it is but reason, that our praises should hold proportion with our prayers: and that as many hath helped together by prayer for the obtaining of his Mercy, so praises should be returned by many on this behalf; And forasmuch as not the generall but particular knowledge of things makes deepest impression upon the affections, this Narrative particularizing the several passages of this providence will not a little conduce thereunto. And therefore holy David in order to the attainment of that end, accounts himself concerned to declare what God had done for his soul, Psal. 66. 16. *Come and hear, all ye that fear God, and I will declare what God hath done for my soul, i. e.* for his life, see v. 9, 10. *He holdeth our soul in life, and suffers not our feet to be moved, for thou our God hast proved us, thou hast tryed us, as silver is tryed.* Life-mercies, are heart-affecting mercies, of great impression and force, to enlarge pious hearts, in the praises of God, so that such know not how but to talk of Gods acts, and to speak of and publish his wonderfull works. Deep troubles, when the waters come in unto thy soul, are wont to produce vowes: vowes must be paid. It is better not vow, than vow and not to pay. I may say, that as none knows what it is to fight and pursue such an enemy as this, but they that have fought and pursued them: so none can imagine what it is to be captivated, and enslaved to such atheisticall, proud, wild, cruel, barbarous, bruitish (in one word) diabolicall creatures as these, the worst of the heathen; nor what difficulties, hardships, hazards, sorrows, anxieties and perplexities do unavoidably wait upon such a condition, but those that have tryed it. No serious spirit then (especially knowing any thing of this Gentle-womans piety) can imagine but that the vows of God are upon her. Excuse her then if she come thus into publick, to pay those vows, come and hear what she hath to say.

I am confident that no Friend of divine Providence will ever repent his time and pains spent in reading over these sheets, but will judg them worth perusing again and again.

Hear Reader, you may see an instance of the Soveraignty of God, who doth what he will with his own as well as others; and who may say to him, What dost thou? Here you may see an instance of the faith and patience of the Saints, under the most heart-sinking tryals; here you may see, the promises are breasts full of consolation, when all the world besides is empty, and gives nothing but sorrow. That God is indeed the supream Lord of the world, ruling the most unruly, weakening the most cruel and salvage, granting his People mercy in the sight of the unmercifull, curbing the lusts of the most filthy, holding the hands of the violent, delivering the prey from the mighty, and gathering together the out casts of Israel. Once and again you have heard, but hear you may see, that power belongeth unto God; that our God is the God of Salvation, and to him belong the issues from Death. That our God is in the Heavens, and doth whatever pleases him. Here you have Sampson Riddle [1] examplified, and that great promise, Rom. 8. 28, verified, *Out of the Eater comes forth meat, and sweetness out of the strong*; The worst of evils working together for the best good. How evident is it that the Lord hath made this Gentlewoman a gainer by all this affliction, that she can say, 'tis good for her yea better that she hath been, then that she should not have been thus afflicted.

Oh how doth God shine forth in such things as these!

Reader, if thou gettest no good by such a Declaration as this, the fault must needs be thine own. Read therefore, Peruse, Ponder, and from hence lay by something from the experience of another against thine own turn comes, that so thou also through patience and consolation of the Scripture mayest have hope.

TER AMICAM.

[1] For Samson's riddle, see Judges xiv.

A NARRATIVE OF THE CAPTIVITY AND RESTAURATION OF MRS. MARY ROWLANDSON

On the tenth of February 1675,[1] Came the Indians with great numbers upon Lancaster: Their first coming was about Sun-rising; hearing the noise of some Guns, we looked out; several Houses[2] were burning, and the Smoke ascending to Heaven. There were five persons[3] taken in one house, the Father, and the Mother and a sucking Child, they knockt on the head; the other two they took and carried away alive. Their were two others, who being out of their Garison upon some occasion were set upon; one was knockt on the head, the other escaped: Another their was who running along was shot and wounded, and fell down; he begged of them his life, promising them Money (as they told me) but they would not hearken to him but knockt him in head, and stript him naked, and split open his Bowels. Another seeing many of the Indians about his Barn, ventured and went out, but was quickly shot down. There were three others belonging to the same Garison[4] who were killed; the Indians getting up upon the roof of the Barn, had advantage to shoot down upon them over their Fortification. Thus these murtherous wretches went on, burning, and destroying before them.

At length they came and beset our own house, and quickly it was the dolefullest day that ever mine eyes saw. The House stood upon the edg of a hill; some of the Indians got behind the hill, others into the Barn, and others behind any thing that could shelter them; from all which places they shot against the House, so that the Bullets seemed to fly like hail; and

---

[1] Thursday, February 10, 1675/6.

[2] The houses mentioned were those of John White, Thomas Sawyer, John Prescott, and the Rowlandson and Wheeler garrisons. The site of the Rowlandson garrison is indicated on a picture in Ellis and Morris, *King Philip's War* (New York, 1906), opposite p. 171.

[3] The family of John Ball, the tailor.

[4] The garrison of Richard Wheeler, on the southern side of George Hill.

quickly they wounded one man among us, then another, and
then a third,   About two hours (according to my observation,
in that amazing time) they had been about the house before
they prevailed to fire it (which they did with Flax and Hemp,
which they brought out of the Barn, and there being no defence about the House, only two Flankers[1] at two opposite
corners and one of them not finished) they fired it once and
one ventured out and quenched it, but they quickly fired it
again, and that took.   Now is the dreadfull hour come, that
I have often heard of (in time of War, as it was the case of
others) but now mine eyes see it.   Some in our house were
fighting for their lives, others wallowing in their blood, the
House on fire over our heads, and the bloody Heathen ready
to knock us on the head, if we stirred out.   Now might we
hear Mothers and Children crying out for themselves, and
one another, Lord, What shall we do?   Then I took my Children (and one of my sisters, hers) to go forth and leave the
house: but as soon as we came to the dore and appeared, the
Indians shot so thick that the bulletts rattled against the
House, as if one had taken an handfull of stones and threw
them, so that we were fain to give back. We had six stout
Dogs belonging to our Garrison, but none of them would stir,
though another time, if any Indian had come to the door,
they were ready to fly upon him and tear him down.   The
Lord hereby would make us the more to acknowledge his hand,
and to see that our help is always in him.   But out we must
go, the fire increasing, and coming along behind us, roaring,
and the Indians gaping before us with their Guns, Spears and
Hatchets to devour us.   No sooner were we out of the House,
but my Brother in Law[2] (being before wounded, in defending
the house, in or near the throat) fell down dead, wherat the
Indians scornfully shouted, and hallowed, and were presently
upon him, stripping off his cloaths, the bulletts flying thick,
one went through my side, and the same (as would seem)
through the bowels and hand of my dear Child in my arms.
One of my elder Sisters Children, named William,[3] had then

---

[1] Flankers were projections from which blank walls (curtains) could be enfiladed.

[2] John Divoll had married Hannah, the youngest sister of Mrs. Rowlandson.

[3] William Kerley was the son of Mrs. Rowlandson's sister Elizabeth White,
who had married Henry Kerley.

his Leg broken, which the Indians perceiving, they knockt him
on head.   Thus were we butchered by those merciless Heathen,
standing amazed, with the blood running down to our heels.
My eldest Sister being yet in the House, and seeing those wofull
sights, the Infidels haling Mothers one way, and Children
another, and some wallowing in their blood: and her elder
Son telling her that her Son William was dead, and my self
was wounded, she said, And, Lord, let me dy with them;
which was no sooner said, but she was struck with a Bullet,
and fell down dead over the threshold.   I hope she is reaping
the fruit of her good labours, being faithfull to the service of
God in her place.   In her younger years she lay under much
trouble upon spiritual accounts, till it pleased God to make
that precious Scripture take hold of her heart, 2 Cor. 12. 9.
And he said unto me, my Grace is sufficient for thee.   More then
twenty years after I have heard her tell how sweet and comfortable that place was to her.   But to return: The Indians
laid hold of us, pulling me one way, and the Children another,
and said, Come go along with us; I told them they would kill
me: they answered, If I were willing to go along with them,
they would not hurt me.

Oh the dolefull sight that now was to behold at this House!
*Come, behold the works of the Lord, what dissolations he has made
in the Earth.*[1]   Of thirty seven persons who were in this one
House, none escaped either present death, or a bitter captivity,
save only one,[2] who might say as he, Job 1. 15, *And I only am
escaped alone to tell the News.*   There were twelve killed, some
shot, some stab'd with their Spears, some knock'd down with
their Hatchets.   When we are in prosperity, Oh the little that
we think of such dreadfull sights, and to see our dear Friends,
and Relations ly bleeding out their heart-blood upon the
ground.   There was one who was chopt into the head with
a Hatchet, and stript naked, and yet was crawling up and
down.   It is a solemn sight to see so many Christians lying in
their blood, some here, and some there, like a company of
Sheep torn by Wolves,   All of them stript naked by a company

---

[1] Psalm xlvi. 8.

[2] The person escaping was Ephraim Roper.   The size of the garrison as
given by contemporary writers varies from 37 to 55, of whom three Kettle children escaped in some way unknown to Mrs. Rowlandson.

of hell-hounds, roaring, singing, ranting and insulting, as if they would have torn our very hearts out; yet the Lord by his Almighty power preserved a number of us from death, for there were twenty-four of us taken alive and carried Captive. I had often before this said, that if the Indians should come, I should chuse rather to be killed by them then taken alive but when it came to the tryal my mind changed; their glittering weapons so daunted my spirit, that I chose rather to go along with those (as I may say) ravenous Beasts, then that moment to end my dayes; and that I may the better declare what happened to me during that grievous Captivity, I shall particularly speak of the severall Removes we had up and down the Wilderness.

The first Remove.

Now away we must go with those Barbarous Creatures, with our bodies wounded and bleeding, and our hearts no less than our bodies. About a mile we went that night, up upon a hill within sight of the Town,[1] where they intended to lodge. There was hard by a vacant house (deserted by the English before, for fear of the Indians). I asked them whither I might not lodge in the house that night to which they answered, what will you love English men still? this was the dolefullest night that ever my eyes saw. Oh the roaring, and singing and danceing, and yelling of those black creatures in the night, which made the place a lively resemblance of hell. And as miserable was the wast that was there made, of Horses. Cattle, Sheep, Swine, Calves, Lambs, Roasting Pigs, and Fowl (which they had plundered in the Town) some roasting, some lying and burning, and some boyling to feed our merciless Enemies; who were joyful enough though we were disconsolate. To add to the dolefulness of the former day, and the dismalness of the present night: my thoughts ran upon my losses and sad bereaved condition. All was gone, my Husband gone (at least separated from me, he being in the Bay;[2] and to add to

[1] George Hill.
[2] "In the Bay" means at Massachusetts Bay, *i. e.*, at or near Boston. If Joseph Rowlandson was in Boston he may have heard the summons for defence given at midnight of February 9 by Job Kattenait in Cambridge. The sum-

my grief, the Indians told me they would kill him as he came homeward) my Children gone, my Relations and Friends gone, our House and home and all our comforts within door, and without, all was gone, (except my life) and I knew not but the next moment that might go too.   There remained nothing to me but one poor wounded Babe, and it seemed at present worse than death that it was in such a pitiful condition, be-speaking Compassion, and I had no refreshing for it, nor suit-able things to revive it.   Little do many think what is the savageness and bruitishness of this barbarous Enemy, I[1] even those that seem to profess more than others among them, when the English have fallen into their hands.

Those seven that were killed at Lancaster the summer before upon a Sabbath day,[2] and the one that was afterward killed upon a week day, were slain and mangled in a barbarous manner, by one-ey'd John,[3] and Marlborough's Praying In-dians,[3] which Capt. Mosely brought to Boston, as the Indians told me.

The second Remove.[4]

But now, the next morning, I must turn my back upon the Town, and travel with them into the vast and desolate Wilder-

mons resulted in an appeal to Captain Wadsworth at Marlborough, but was too late.

[1] Ay.

[2] The seven victims of the defeat of August 22, 1675, were George Bennett, Jacob Farrar, jr., William Flagg, Mordecai McLoud, Mrs. McLoud, and two children.   Joseph Wheeler died later.

[3] One-eyed John was known also as Monoco and Apequinsah.   "Marl-borough's Praying Indians" means the settlement of Christianized Indians at Marlborough, Massachusetts.   On August 30, 1675, Captain Samuel Mosely, "being instigated thereunto by some people of those parts, no lovers of the Christian Indians, sent down to Boston with a guard of soldiers, pinioned and fastened with lines from neck to neck, fifteen of those Indians that lived with others of them upon their own lands, and in their own fort at Okonhomesitt near Marlborough, where they were orderly settled and were under the English conduct."   In Gookin's *Historical Account of the Doings and Sufferings of the Christian Indians of New England,* from which the above is quoted, the question of the guilt of the Marlborough Indians is discussed at length by that constant friend of the converts.   *Transactions of the American Antiquarian Society,* II. 454–461.

[4] The second remove was to Princeton, Massachusetts, near Mount Wachu-sett.

ness, I knew not whither. It is not my tongue, or pen can express the sorrows of my heart, and bitterness of my spirit, that I had at this departure: but God was with me, in a wonderfull manner, carrying me along, and bearing up my spirit, that it did not quite fail. One of the Indians carried my poor wounded Babe upon a horse, it went moaning all along, I shall dy, I shall dy. I went on foot after it, with sorrow that cannot be exprest. At length I took it off the horse, and carried it in my armes till my strength failed, and I fell down with it: Then they set me upon a horse with my wounded Child in my lap, and there being no furniture upon the horse back, as we were going down a steep hill, we both fell over the horses head, at which they like inhumane creatures laught, and rejoyced to see it, though I thought we should there have ended our dayes, as overcome with so many difficulties. But the Lord renewed my strength still, and carried me along, that I might see more of his Power; yea, so much that I could never have thought of, had I not experienced it.

After this it quickly began to snow, and when night came on, they stopt: and now down I must sit in the snow, by a little fire, and a few boughs behind me, with my sick Child in my lap; and calling much for water, being now (through the wound) fallen into a violent Fever. My own wound also growing so stiff, that I could scarce sit down or rise up; yet so it must be, that I must sit all this cold winter night upon the cold snowy ground, with my sick Child in my armes, looking that every hour would be the last of its life; and having no Christian friend near me, either to comfort or help me. Oh, I may see the wonderfull power of God, that my Spirit did not utterly sink under my affliction: still the Lord upheld me with his gracious and mercifull Spirit, and we were both alive to see the light of the next morning.

The third remove.[1]

The morning being come, they prepared to go on their way. One of the Indians got up upon a horse, and they set me up

[1] The third remove, February 12-27, ended at an Indian village, Menameset (Wenimesset), on the Ware River, in what is now New Braintree. Quabaug was Brookfield.

behind him, with my poor sick Babe in my lap. A very wearisome and tedious day I had of it; what with my own wound, and my Childs being so exceeding sick, and in a lamentable condition with her wound. It may be easily judged what a poor feeble condition we were in, there being not the least crumb of refreshing that came within either of our mouths, from Wednesday night to Saturday night, except only a little cold water. This day in the afternoon, about an hour by Sun, we came to the place where they intended, *viz.* an Indian Town, called Wenimesset, Norward of Quabaug. When we were come, Oh the number of Pagans (now merciless enemies) that there came about me, that I may say as David, Psal. 27. 13, *I had fainted, unless I had believed,* etc.[1] The next day was the Sabbath:[2] I then remembered how careless I had been of Gods holy time, how many Sabbaths I had lost and mispent, and how evily I had walked in Gods sight; which lay so close unto my spirit, that it was easie for me to see how righteous it was with God to cut off the thread of my life, and cast me out of his presence for ever. Yet the Lord still shewed mercy to me, and upheld me; and as he wounded me with one hand, so he healed me with the other. This day there came to me one Robbert Pepper (a man belonging to Roxbury) who was taken in Captain Beers his Fight,[3] and had been now a considerable time with the Indians; and up with them almost as far as Albany, to see king Philip, as he told me, and was now very lately come into these parts.[4] Hearing, I say, that I was in this Indian Town, he obtained leave to come and see me. He told me, he himself was wounded in the leg at Captain Beers his Fight; and was not able some time to go, but as they carried him, and as he took Oaken leaves and laid to his wound, and through the blessing of God he was able to travel again. Then I took Oaken leaves and laid to my side, and with the blessing of God it cured me also; yet before the cure

---

[1] "Unless I had believed to see the goodness of the Lord in the land of the living."

[2] Sunday, February 13.

[3] Captain Beers, attempting to relieve the garrison of Northfield, was slain with most of his men, September 4, 1675. See p. 42, *supra.*

[4] Philip's headquarters during the winter had been somewhat east of Albany in New York, as stated earlier, pp. 68, 87, *ante.*

was wrought, I may say, as it is in Psal. 38. 5, 6. *My wounds stink and are corrupt, I am troubled, I am bowed down greatly, I go mourning all the day long.* I sat much alone with a poor wounded Child in my lap, which moaned night and day, having nothing to revive the body, or cheer the spirits of her, but in stead of that, sometimes one Indian would come and tell me one hour, that your Master will knock your Child in the head, and then a second, and then a third, your Master will quickly knock your Child in the head.

This was the comfort I had from them, miserable comforters are ye all, as he said.[1] Thus nine dayes I sat upon my knees, with my Babe in my lap, till my flesh was raw again; my Child being even ready to depart this sorrowfull world, they bade me carry it out to another Wigwam (I suppose because they would not be troubled with such spectacles) Whither I went with a very heavy heart, and down I sat with the picture of death in my lap. About two houres in the night, my sweet Babe like a Lambe departed this life, on Feb. 18, 1675. It being about six yeares, and five months old. It was nine dayes from the first wounding, in this miserable condition, without any refreshing of one nature or other, except a little cold water. I cannot, but take notice, how at another time I could not bear to be in the room where any dead person was, but now the case is changed; I must and could ly down by my dead Babe, side by side all the night after. I have thought since of the wonderfull goodness of God to me, in preserving me in the use of my reason and senses, in that distressed time, that I did not use wicked and violent means to end my own miserable life. In the morning, when they understood that my child was dead they sent for me home to my Masters Wigwam: (by my Master in this writing, must be understood Quanopin,[2] who was a Saggamore, and married King Phillips wives Sister; not that he first took me, but I was sold to him by another Narrhaganset Indian, who took me when first I came out of the Garison). I went to take up my dead child in my arms to carry it with me, but they bid me let it alone: there was

---

[1] *I. e.*, as Job said. Job xvi. 2.

[2] Quinnapin was the husband of Weetamoo, the widow of Alexander, already referred to as the Queen of Pocasset. Mrs. Rowlandson became a servant to this wife. He had as well two other squaws. See p. 150, *post.*

no resisting, but goe I must and leave it. When I had been at my masters wigwam, I took the first opportunity I could get, to go look after my dead child: when I came I askt them what they had done with it? then they told me it was upon the hill: then they went and shewed me where it was, where I saw the ground was newly digged, and there they told me they had buried it: There I left that Child in the Wilderness, and must commit it, and my self also in this Wilderness-condition, to him who is above all. God having taken away this dear Child, I went to see my daughter Mary, who was at this same Indian Town, at a Wigwam not very far off, though we had little liberty or opportunity to see one another. She was about ten years old, and taken from the door at first by a Praying Ind and afterward sold for a gun. When I came in sight, she would fall a weeping; at which they were provoked, and would not let me come near her, but bade me be gone; which was a heart-cutting word to me. I had one Child dead, another in the Wilderness, I knew not where, the third they would not let me come near to: *Me* (as he said) *have ye bereaved of my Children, Joseph is not, and Simeon is not, and ye will take Benjamin also, all these things are against me.*[1] I could not sit still in this condition, but kept walking from one place to another. And as I was going along, my heart was even overwhelm'd with the thoughts of my condition, and that I should have Children, and a Nation which I knew not ruled over them. Whereupon I earnestly entreated the Lord, that he would consider my low estate, and shew me a token for good, and if it were his blessed will, some sign and hope of some relief. And indeed quickly the Lord answered, in some measure, my poor prayers: for as I was going up and down mourning and lamenting my condition, my Son came to me, and asked me how I did; I had not seen him before, since the destruction of the Town, and I knew not where he was, till I was informed by himself, that he was amongst a smaller percel of Indians, whose place was about six miles off; with tears in his eyes, he asked me whether his Sister Sarah was dead; and told me he had seen his Sister Mary; and prayed me, that I would not be troubled in reference to himself. The occasion of his coming to see me at this time, was this: There was, as I said, about

[1] The lament of Jacob in Genesis xlii. 36.

six miles from us, a smal Plantation of Indians, where it seems he had been during his Captivity: and at this time, there were some Forces of the Ind. gathered out of our company, and some also from them (among whom was my Sons master) to go to assault and burn Medfield: In this time of the absence of his master, his dame brought him to see me. I took this to be some gracious answer to my earnest and unfeigned desire. The next day, *viz.* to this, the Indians returned from Medfield,[1] all the company, for those that belonged to the other smal company, came thorough the Town that now we were at. But before they came to us, Oh! the outragious roaring and hooping that there was: They began their din about a mile before they came to us. By their noise and hooping they signified how many they had destroyed (which was at that time twenty three.) Those that were with us at home, were gathered together as soon as they heard the hooping, and every time that the other went over their number, these at home gave a shout, that the very Earth rung again: And thus they continued till those that had been upon the expedition were come up to the Sagamores Wigwam; and then, Oh, the hideous insulting and triumphing that there was over some Englishmens scalps that they had taken (as their manner is) and brought with them. I cannot but take notice of the wonderfull mercy of God to me in those afflictions, in sending me a Bible. One of the Indians that came from Medfield fight, had brought some plunder, came to me, and asked me, if I would have a Bible, he had got one in his Basket. I was glad of it, and asked him, whether he thought the Indians would let me read? he answered, yes: So I took the Bible, and in that melancholy time, it came into my mind to read first the 28. Chap. of Deut.,[2] which I did, and when I had read it, my dark heart wrought on this manner, That there was no mercy for me, that the blessings were gone, and the curses come in their room, and that I had lost my opportunity. But the Lord helped me still to go on reading till I came to Chap. 30 the seven first verses, where I found, There was mercy promised

---

[1] The Medfield fight has been recounted *ante*, pp. 80, 81. It occurred on February 21; fifty houses were burned.

[2] Ch. xxviii. of Deuteronomy is occupied with a recital of blessings for obedience to God and curses for disobedience.

again, if we would return to him by repentance; and though
we were scatered from one end of the Earth to the other, yet
the Lord would gather us together, and turn all those curses
upon our Enemies. I do not desire to live to forget this
Scripture, and what comfort it was to me.

Now the Ind. began to talk of removing from this place,
some one way, and some another. There were now besides
my self nine English Captives in this place (all of them Children, except one Woman). I got an opportunity to go and
take my leave of them; they being to go one way, and I another, I asked them whether they were earnest with God for
deliverance, they told me, they did as they were able, and it
was some comfort to me, that the Lord stirred up Children to
look to him. The Woman *viz.* Goodwife Joslin told me, she
should never see me again, and that she could find in her heart
to run away; I wisht her not to run away by any means, for
we were near thirty miles from any English Town, and she
very big with Child, and had but one week to reckon; and another Child in her Arms, two years old, and bad Rivers there
were to go over, and we were feeble, with our poor and course
entertainment. I had my Bible with me, I pulled it out, and
asked her whether she would read; we opened the Bible and
lighted on Psal. 27, in which Psalm we especially took notice
of that, *ver. ult.*, *Wait on the Lord, Be of good courage, and he
shall strengthen thine Heart, wait I say on the Lord.*[1]

The fourth Remove.[2]

And now I must part with that little Company I had.
Here I parted from my Daughter Mary, (whom I never saw
again till I saw her in Dorchester, returned from Captivity),
and from four little Cousins and Neighbours, some of which I
never saw afterward: the Lord only knows the end of them.
Amongst them also was that poor Woman before mentioned,
who came to a sad end, as some of the company told me in
my travel: She having much grief upon her Spirit, about her

[1] Psalm xxvii. 14.

[2] The fourth remove occupied February 28 to March 3. The camp was
between Ware River and Miller's River, at the Indian village of Nichewaug in
modern Petersham.

miserable condition, being so near her time, she would be often asking the Indians to let her go home; they not being willing to that, and yet vexed with her importunity, gathered a great company together about her, and stript her naked, and set her in the midst of them; and when they had sung and danced about her (in their hellish manner) as long as they pleased, they knockt her on head, and the child in her arms with her: when they had done that, they made a fire and put them both into it, and told the other Children that were with them, that if they attempted to go home, they would serve them in like manner: The Children said, she did not shed one tear, but prayed all the while. But to return to my own Journey; we travelled about half a day or little more, and came to a desolate place in the Wilderness, where there were no Wigwams or Inhabitants before; we came about the middle of the afternoon to this place, cold and wet, and snowy, and hungry, and weary, and no refreshing, for man, but the cold ground to sit on, and our poor Indian cheer.

Heart-aking thoughts here I had about my poor Children, who were scattered up and down among the wild beasts of the forrest: My head was light and dissey (either through hunger or hard lodging, or trouble or altogether) my knees feeble, my body raw by sitting double night and day, that I cannot express to man the affliction that lay upon my Spirit, but the Lord helped me at that time to express it to himself. I opened my Bible to read, and the Lord brought that precious Scripture to me, Jer. 31. 16. *Thus saith the Lord, refrain thy voice from weeping, and thine eyes from tears, for thy work shall be rewarded, and they shall come again from the land of the Enemy.* This was a sweet Cordial to me, when I was ready to faint, many and many a time have I sat down, and weept sweetly over this Scripture. At this place we continued about four dayes.

The fifth Remove.[1]

The occasion (as I thought) of their moving at this time, was, the English Army, it being near and following them:

[1] In the fifth remove, March 3–5, they crossed the Baquaug (Miller's) River in Orange. The "Army" following was composed of Massachusetts and Connecticut forces under Captain Thomas Savage. This troop was detained at

For they went, as if they had gone for their lives, for some considerable way, and then they made a stop, and chose some of their stoutest men, and sent them back to hold the English Army in play whilst the rest escaped: And then, like Jehu, they marched on furiously, with their old, and with their young: some carried their old decrepit mothers, some carried one, and some another.   Four of them carried a great Indian upon a Bier; but going through a thick Wood with him, they were hindered, and could make no hast; whereupon they took him upon their backs, and carried him, one at a time, till they came to Bacquaug River.   Upon a Friday, a little after noon we came to this River.   When all the company was come up, and were gathered together, I thought to count the number of them, but they were so many, and being somewhat in motion, it was beyond my skil.   In this travel, because of my wound, I was somewhat favoured in my load; I carried only my knitting work and two quarts of parched meal: Being very faint I asked my mistriss[1] to give me one spoonfull of the meal, but she would not give me a taste.   They quickly fell to cutting dry trees, to make Rafts to carry them over the river: and soon my turn came to go over: By the advantage of some brush which they had laid upon the Raft to sit upon, I did not wet my foot (which many of themselves at the other end were mid-leg deep) which cannot but be acknowledged as a favour of God to my weakned body, it being a very cold time.   I was not before acquainted with such kind of doings or dangers. *When thou passeth through the waters I will be with thee, and through the Rivers they shall not overflow thee*, Isai. 43. 2.   A certain number of us got over the River that night, but it was the night after the Sabbath before all the company was got over.   On the Saturday they boyled an old Horses leg which they had got, and so we drank of the broth, as soon as they thought it was ready, and when it was almost all gone, they filled it up again.

The first week of my being among them, I hardly ate any thing; the second week, I found my stomach grow very faint

Quabaug by the Indians sent back for that purpose, else some of the cavalry might have come up with the main party of Indians as it crossed the river. The difficulty of the colonists in crossing is told on p. 159, *post.*

[1] Weetamoo.

for want of something; and yet it was very hard to get down their filthy trash: but the third week, though I could think how formerly my stomach would turn against this or that, and I could starve and dy before I could eat such things, yet they were sweet and savoury to my taste. I was at this time knitting a pair of white cotton stockins for my mistriss; and had not yet wrought upon a Sabbath day; when the Sabbath came they bade me go to work; I told them it was the Sabbath-day, and desired them to let me rest, and told them I would do as much more to morrow; to which they answered me, they would break my face. And here I cannot but take notice of the strange providence of God in preserving the heathen: They were many hundreds, old and young, some sick, and some lame, many had Papooses at their backs, the greatest number at this time with us, were Squaws, and they travelled with all they had, bag and baggage, and yet they got over this River aforesaid; and on Munday they set their Wigwams on fire, and away they went: On that very day came the English Army after them to this River, and saw the smoak of their Wigwams, and yet this River put a stop to them. God did not give them courage or activity to go over after us; we were not ready for so great a mercy as victory and deliverance; if we had been, God would have found out a way for the English to have passed this River, as well as for the Indians with their Squaws and Children, and all their Luggage. *Oh that my People had hearkened to me, and Israel had walked in my ways, I should soon have subdued their Enemies, and turned my hand against their Adversaries*, Psal. 81: 13. 14.

The sixth Remove.[1]

On Munday (as I said) they set their Wigwams on fire, and went away. It was a cold morning, and before us there was a great Brook with ice on it; some waded through it, up to the knees and higher, but others went till they came to a Beaver-dam, and I amongst them, where through the good providence of God, I did not wet my foot. I went along that day mourning and lamenting, leaving farther my own Country,

[1] The sixth remove was on Monday, March 6, ending near a swamp in Northfield, Massachusetts.

and travelling into the vast and howling Wilderness, and I understood something of Lot's Wife's Temptation, when she looked back: we came that day to a great Swamp, by the side of which we took up our lodging that night.   When I came to the brow of the hil, that looked toward the Swamp, I thought we had been come to a great Indian Town (though there were none but our own Company)   The Indians were as thick as the trees: it seemed as if there had been a thousand Hatchets going at once: if one looked before one, there was nothing but Indians, and behind one, nothing but Indians, and so on either hand, I my self in the midst, and no Christian soul near me, and yet how hath the Lord preserved me in safety?   Oh the experience that I have had of the goodness of God, to me and mine!

The seventh Remove.[1]

After a restless and hungry night there, we had a wearisome time of it the next day.   The Swamp by which we lay, was, as it were, a deep Dungeon, and an exceeding high and steep hill before it.   Before I got to the top of the hill, I thought my heart and legs, and all would have broken, and failed me. What through faintness, and soreness of body, it was a grievous day of travel to me.   As we went along, I saw a place where English Cattle had been: that was comfort to me, such as it was: quickly after that we came to an English Path, which so took with me, that I thought I could have freely lyen down and dyed.   That day, a little after noon, we came to Squauk-heag, where the Indians quickly spread themselves over the deserted English Fields, gleaning what they could find; some pickt up ears of Wheat that were crickled down, some found ears of Indian Corn, some found Ground-nuts, and others sheaves of Wheat that were frozen together in the shock, and went to threshing of them out.   My self got two ears of Indian Corn, and whilst I did but turn my back, one of them was stolen from me, which much troubled me.   There came an Indian to them at that time, with a basket of Horse-liver. I asked him to give me a piece: What, sayes he, can you eat Horse-liver?   I told him, I would try, if he would give a piece,

[1] The seventh remove carried Mrs. Rowlandson to Squakeag near Beers's plain in Northfield.

which he did, and I laid it on the coals to rost; but before it was half ready they got half of it away from me, so that I was fain to take the rest and eat it as it was, with the blood about my mouth, and yet a savoury bit it was to me: *For to the hungry Soul every bitter thing is sweet.*[1] A solemn sight methought it was, to see Fields of wheat and Indian Corn forsaken and spoiled: and the remainders of them to be food for our merciless Enemies. That night we had a mess of wheat for our Supper.

The eight Remove.[2]

On the morrow morning we must go over the River, *i. e.* Connecticot, to meet with King Philip; two Cannoos full, they had carried over, the next Turn I my self was to go; but as my foot was upon the Cannoo to step in, there was a sudden out-cry among them, and I must step back; and instead of going over the River, I must go four or five miles up the River farther Northward. Some of the Indians ran one way, and some another. The cause of this rout was, as I thought, their espying some English Scouts, who were thereabout. In this travel up the River, about noon the Company made a stop, and sate down; some to eat, and others to rest them. As I sate amongst them, musing of things past, my Son Joseph unexpectedly came to me: we asked of each others welfare, bemoaning our dolefull condition, and the change that had come upon uss. We had Husband and Father, and Children, and Sisters, and Friends, and Relations, and House, and Home, and many Comforts of this Life: but now we may say, as Job, *Naked came I out of my Mothers Womb, and naked shall I return: The Lord gave, and the Lord hath taken away, Blessed be the Name of the Lord.*[3] I asked him whither he would read; he told me, he earnestly desired it, I gave him my Bible, and he lighted upon that comfortable Scripture, Psal. 118. 17, 18. *I shall not dy but live, and declare the works of the Lord: the Lord hath chastened me sore, yet he hath not given me over to*

[1] Proverbs xxvii. 7.

[2] The eighth remove was to Coasset in South Vernon, Vermont, where Mrs. Rowlandson seems to have met King Philip for the first time, as he was returning from New York to take up the campaign of 1676.

[3] Job i. 21.

death. Look here, Mother (sayes he) did you read this? And here I may take occasion to mention one principall ground of my setting forth these Lines: even as the Psalmist sayes, To declare the Works of the Lord, and his wonderfull Power in carrying us along, preserving us in the Wilderness, while under the Enemies hand, and returning of us in safety again, And His goodness in bringing to my hand so many comfortable and suitable Scriptures in my distress. But to Return, We travelled on till night; and in the morning, we must go over the River to Philip's Crew. When I was in the Cannoo, I could not but be amazed at the numerous crew of Pagans that were on the Bank on the other side. When I came ashore, they gathered all about me, I sitting alone in the midst: I observed they asked one another questions, and laughed, and rejoyced over their Gains and Victories. Then my heart began to fail: and I fell a weeping which was the first time to my remembrance, that I wept before them. Although I had met with so much Affliction, and my heart was many times ready to break, yet could I not shed one tear in their sight: but rather had been all this while in a maze, and like one astonished: but now I may say as, Psal. 137. 1. *By the Rivers of Babylon, there we sate down: yea, we wept when we remembered Zion.* There one of them asked me, why I wept, I could hardly tell what to say: yet I answered, they would kill me: No, said he, none will hurt you. Then came one of them and gave me two spoon-fulls of Meal to comfort me, and another gave me half a pint of Pease; which was more worth than many Bushels at another time. Then I went to see King Philip, he bade me come in and sit down, and asked me whether I woold smoke it (a usual Complement nowadayes amongst Saints and Sinners) but this no way suited me. For though I had formerly used Tobacco, yet I had left it ever since I was first taken. It seems to be a Bait, the Devil layes to make men loose their precious time: I remember with shame, how formerly, when I had taken two or three pipes, I was presently ready for another, such a bewitching thing it is: But I thank God, he has now given me power over it; surely there are many who may be better imployed than to ly sucking a stinking Tobacco-pipe.

Now the Indians gather their Forces to go against North-

Hampton:[1] over-night one went about yelling and hooting to give notice of the design. Whereupon they fell to boyling of Ground-nuts, and parching of Corn (as many as had it) for their Provision: and in the morning away they went. During my abode in this place, Philip spake to me to make a shirt for his boy, which I did, for which he gave me a shilling: I offered the mony to my master, but he bade me keep it: and with it I bought a piece of Horse flesh. Afterwards he asked me to make a Cap for his boy, for which he invited me to Dinner. I went, and he gave me a Pancake, about as big as two fingers; it was made of parched wheat, beaten, and fryed in Bears grease, but I thought I never tasted pleasanter meat in my life. There was a Squaw who spake to me to make a shirt for her *Sannup*,[2] for which she gave me a piece of Bear. Another asked me to knit a pair of Stockins, for which she gave me a quart of Pease: I boyled my Pease and Bear together, and invited my master and mistriss to dinner, but the proud Gossip,[3] because I served them both in one Dish, would eat nothing, except one bit that he gave her upon the point of his knife. Hearing that my son was come to this place, I went to see him, and found him lying flat upon the ground: I asked him how he could sleep so? he answered me, That he was not asleep, but at Prayer; and lay so, that they might not observe what he was doing. I pray God he may remember these things now he is returned in safety. At this Place (the Sun now getting higher) what with the beams and heat of the Sun, and the smoak of the Wigwams, I thought I should have been blind. I could scarce discern one Wigwam from another. There was here one Mary Thurston of Medfield, who seeing how it was with me, lent me a Hat to wear: but as soon as I was gone, the Squaw (who owned that Mary Thurston) came running after me, and got it away again. Here was the Squaw that gave me one spoonfull of Meal. I put it in my Pocket to keep it safe: yet notwithstanding some body stole it, but put five Indian Corns in the room of it: which Corns were the greatest Provisions I had in my travel for one day.

---

[1] The attack upon Northampton here referred to occurred on March 14, but the town had been defended by palisades and the Indians were repulsed. The colonists lost six men. See p. 8, *ante*.

[2] Husband.   [3] "Gossip" in the obsolete sense of fellow.

The Indians returning from North-Hampton, brought with
them some Horses, and Sheep, and other things which they
had taken: I desired them, that they would carry me to Albany,
upon one of those Horses, and sell me for Powder: for so they
had sometimes discoursed. I was utterly hopless of getting
home on foot, the way that I came. I could hardly bear to
think of the many weary steps I had taken, to come to this
place.

The ninth Remove.[1]

But in stead of going either to Albany or homeward, we
must go five miles up the River, and then go over it. Here we
abode a while. Here lived a sorry Indian, who spoke to me
to make him a shirt. When I had done it, he would pay me
nothing. But he living by the River side, where I often went
to fetch water, I would often be putting of him in mind, and
calling for my pay: at last he told me if I would make another
shirt, for a Papoos not yet born, he would give me a knife,
which he did when I had done it. I carried the knife in, and
my master asked me to give it him, and I was not a little glad
that I had any thing that they would accept of, and be pleased
with. When we were at this place, my Masters maid came
home, she had been gone three weeks into the Narrhaganset
Country, to fetch Corn, where they had stored up some in the
ground: she brought home about a peck and half of Corn. This
was about the time that their great Captain, Naananto,[2] was
killed in the Narrhaganset Countrey. My Son being now
about a mile from me, I asked liberty to go and see him, they
bade me go, and away I went: but quickly lost my self, travelling over Hills and thorough Swamps, and could not find the
way to him. And I cannot but admire at the wonderfull power
and goodness of God to me, in that, though I was gone from
home, and met with all sorts of Indians, and those I had no
knowledge of, and there being no Christian soul near me;
yet not one of them offered the least imaginable miscarriage
to me. I turned homeward again, and met with my master,

---

[1] To the Ashuelot valley in New Hampshire.

[2] Naananto is better known as Canonchet. He was the leading spirit of
the war rather than King Philip. Upon the death of Canonchet, April 3, 1676,
the war lost its vigor and soon ceased.

he shewed me the way to my Son: When I came to him I found him not well: and withall he had a boyl on his side, which much troubled him: We bemoaned one another awhile, as the Lord helped us, and then I returned again. When I was returned, I found my self as unsatisfied as I was before. I went up and down mourning and lamenting: and my spirit was ready to sink, with the thoughts of my poor Children: my Son was ill, and I could not but think of his mournfull looks, and no Christian Friend was near him, to do any office of love for him, either for Soul or Body. And my poor Girl, I knew not where she was, nor whither she was sick, or well, or alive, or dead. I repaired under these thoughts to my Bible (my great comfort in that time) and that Scripture came to my hand, *Cast thy burden upon the Lord, and He shall sustain thee*, Psal. 55. 22.

But I was fain to go and look after something to satisfie my hunger, and going among the Wigwams, I went into one, and there found a Squaw who shewed her self very kind to me, and gave me a piece of Bear. I put it into my pocket, and came home, but could not find an opportunity to broil it, for fear they would get it from me, and there it lay all that day and night in my stinking pocket. In the morning I went to the same Squaw, who had a Kettle of Ground nuts boyling; I asked her to let me boyle my piece of Bear in her Kettle, which she did, and gave me some Ground-nuts to eat with it: and I cannot but think how pleasant it was to me. I have sometime seen Bear baked very handsomly among the English, and some like it, but the thoughts that it was Bear, made me tremble: but now that was savoury to me that one would think was enough to turn the stomach of a bruit Creature.

One bitter cold day, I could find no room to sit down before the fire: I went out, and could not tell what to do, but I went in to another Wigwam, where they were also sitting round the fire, but the Squaw laid a skin for me, and bid me sit down, and gave me some Ground-nuts, and bade me come again: and told me they would buy me, if they were able, and yet these were strangers to me that I never saw before.

The tenth Remove.[1]

That day a small part of the Company removed about three quarters of a mile, intending further the next day.   When they came to the place where they intended to lodge, and had pitched their wigwams, being hungry I went again back to the place we were before at, to get something to eat: being encouraged by the Squaws kindness, who bade me come again; when I was there, there came an Indian to look after me, who when he had found me, kickt me all along: I went home and found Venison roasting that night, but they would not give me one bit of it.   Sometimes I met with favour, and sometimes with nothing but frowns.

The eleventh Remove.[2]

The next day in the morning they took their Travel, intending a dayes journey up the River, I took my load at my back, and quickly we came to wade over the River: and passed over tiresome and wearisome hills.   One hill was so steep that I was fain to creep up upon my knees, and to hold by the twiggs and bushes to keep my self from falling backward.   My head also was so light, that I usually reeled as I went; but I hope all these wearisome steps that I have taken, are but a fore-warning to me of the heavenly rest.   *I know, O Lord, that thy Judgements are right, and that thou in faithfulness hast afflicted me*, Psal. 119. 71.[3]

The twelfth Remove.

It was upon a Sabbath-day-morning, that they prepared for their Travel.   This morning I asked my master whither he would sell me to my Husband; he answered me *Nux*,[4] which did much rejoyce my spirit.   My mistriss, before

[1] The tenth remove seems to have been a change to another location in the Ashuelot valley in New Hampshire.

[2] The eleventh remove, in April, 1676, was as far north as the captive was taken.   The camp was in or near Chesterfield, New Hampshire, where she re·mained until the twelfth remove on Sunday, April 9.

[3] More exactly, Psalm cxix. 75.   [4] Yes.

we went, was gone to the burial of a Papoos, and returning, she found me sitting and reading in my Bible; she snatched it hastily out of my hand, and threw it out of doors; I ran out and catcht it up, and put it into my pocket, and never let her see it afterward. Then they packed up their things to be gone, and gave me my load: I complained it was too heavy, whereupon she gave me a slap in the face, and bade me go; I lifted up my heart to God, hoping the Redemption was not far off: and the rather because their insolency grew worse and worse.

But the thoughts of my going homeward (for so we bent our course) much cheared my Spirit, and made my burden seem light, and almost nothing at all. But (to my amazment and great perplexity) the scale was soon turned: for when we had gone a little way, on a sudden my mistriss gives out, she would go no further, but turn back again, and said, I must go back again with her, and she called her *Sannup*, and would have had him gone back also, but he would not, but said, He would go on, and come to us again in three dayes.[1] My Spirit was upon this, I confess, very impatient, and almost out-ragious. I thought I could as well have dyed as went back: I cannot declare the trouble that I was in about it; but yet back again I must go. As soon as I had an opportunity, I took my Bible to read, and that quieting Scripture came to my hand, Psal. 46. 10. *Be still, and know that I am God.* Which stilled my spirit for the present: But a sore time of tryal, I concluded, I had to go through, My master being gone, who seemed to me the best friend that I had of an In-dian, both in cold and hunger, and quickly so it proved. Down I sat, with my heart as full as it could hold, and yet so hungry that I could not sit neither: but going out to see what I could find, and walking among the Trees, I found six Acorns, and two Ches-nuts, which were some refreshment to me. Towards Night I gathered me some sticks for my own comfort, that I might not ly a-cold: but when we came to ly down they bade me go out, and ly some-where-else, for they had company

---

[1] It was about this time that the news of the death of Canonchet, p. 136, *ante*, reached and discouraged these Indians. Quinnapin seems to have gone forward to see what the outcome would be, taking Philip with him, but the women and children were left in the Connecticut valley for a time.

(they said) come in more than their own: I told them, I could not tell where to go, they bade me go look; I told them, if I went to another Wigwam they would be angry, and send me home again. Then one of the Company drew his sword, and told me he would run me thorough if I did not go presently. Then was I fain to stoop to this rude fellow, and to go out in the night, I knew not whither. Mine eyes have seen that fellow afterwards walking up and down Boston, under the appearance of a Friend-Indian, and severall others of the like Cut. I went to one Wigwam, and they told me they had no room. Then I went to another, and they said the same; at last an old Indian bade me come to him, and his Squaw gave me some Ground-nuts; she gave me also something to lay under my head, and a good fire we had: and through the good providence of God, I had a comfortable lodging that night. In the morning, another Indian bade me come at night, and he would give me six Ground-nuts, which I did. We were at this place and time about two miles from Connecticut River. We went in the morning to gather Ground-nuts, to the River, and went back again that night. I went with a good load at my back (for they when they went, though but a little way, would carry all their trumpery with them) I told them the skin was off my back, but I had no other comforting answer from them than this, That it would be no matter if my head were off too.

The thirteenth Remove.

Instead of going toward the Bay,[1] which was that I desired, I must go with them five or six miles down the River into a mighty Thicket of Brush: where we abode almost a fortnight. Here one asked me to make a shirt for her Papoos, for which she gave me a mess of Broth, which was thickened with meal made of the Bark of a Tree, and to make it the better, she had put into it about a handfull of Pease, and a few roasted Ground-nuts. I had not seen my son a pritty while, and here was an Indian of whom I made inquiry after him, and asked him when he saw him: he answered me, that such a time his master roasted him, and that himself did eat a piece of him, as big as

---

[1] The encampment seems to have been changed for a time to Hinsdale, New Hampshire, near the Connecticut River.

his two fingers, and that he was very good meat: But the Lord upheld my Spirit, under this discouragement; and I considered their horrible addictedness to lying, and that there is not one of them that makes the least conscience of speaking of truth. In this place, on a cold night, as I lay by the fire, I removed a stick that kept the heat from me, a Squaw moved it down again, at which I lookt up, and she threw a handfull of ashes in mine eyes; I thought I should have been quite blinded, and have never seen more: but lying down, the water run out of my eyes, and carried the dirt with it, that by the morning, I recovered my sight again.   Yet upon this, and the like occasions, I hope it is not too much to say with Job, *Have pitty upon me, have pitty upon me, O ye my Friends, for the Hand of the Lord has touched me.*[1] And here I cannot but remember how many times sitting in their Wigwams, and musing on things past, I should suddenly leap up and run out, as if I had been at home, forgetting where I was, and what my condition was: But when I was without, and saw nothing but Wilderness, and Woods, and a company of barbarous heathens, my mind quickly returned to me, which made me think of that, spoken concerning Sampson, who said, *I will go out and shake my self as at other times, but he wist not that the Lord was departed from him.*[2] About this time I began to think that all my hopes of Restoration would come to nothing. I thought of the English Army, and hoped for their coming, and being taken by them, but that failed. I hoped to be carried to Albany, as the Indians had discoursed before, but that failed also. I thought of being sold to my Husband, as my master spake, but in stead of that, my master himself was gone, and I left behind, so that my Spirit was now quite ready to sink. I asked them to let me go out and pick up some sticks, that I might get alone, And poure out my heart unto the Lord. Then also I took my Bible to read, but I found no comfort here neither, which many times I was wont to find: So easie a thing it is with God to dry up the Streames of Scripture-comfort from us. Yet I can say, that in all my sorrows and afflictions, God did not leave me to have my impatience work towards himself, as if his wayes were unrighteous. But I knew that he laid upon me less then I deserved. Afterward, before this dolefull time

[1] Job xix. 21.   [2] Judges xvi. 20.

ended with me, I was turning the leaves of my Bible, and the Lord brought to me some Scriptures, which did a little revive me, as that Isai. 55. 8, *For my thoughts are not your thoughts, neither are your wayes my ways, saith the Lord.* And also that, Psal. 37. 5, *Commit thy way unto the Lord, trust also in him, and he shal bring it to pass.* About this time they came yelping from Hadly, where they had killed three English men, and brought one Captive with them, *viz.* Thomas Read.[1] They all gathered about the poor Man, asking him many Questions. I desired also to go and see him; and when I came, he was crying bitterly, supposing they would quickly kill him. Whereupon I asked one of them, whether they intended to kill him; he answered me, they would not: He being a little cheared with that, I asked him about the wel-fare of my Husband, he told me he saw him such a time in the Bay, and he was well, but very melancholly. By which I certainly understood (though I suspected it before) that whatsoever the Indians told me respecting him was vanity and lies. Some of them told me, he was dead, and they had killed him: some said he was Married again, and that the Governour wished him to Marry; and told him he should have his choice, and that all perswaded I was dead. So like were these barbarous creatures to him who was a lyer from the beginning.

As I was sitting once in the Wigwam here, Phillips Maid came in with the Child in her arms, and asked me to give her a piece of my Apron, to make a flap for it, I told her I would not: then my Mistriss bad me give it, but still I said no: the maid told me if I would not give her a piece, she would tear a piece off it: I told her I would tear her Coat then, with that my Mistriss rises up, and takes up a stick big enough to have killed me, and struck at me with it, but I stept out, and she struck the stick into the Mat of the Wigwam. But while she was pulling of it out, I ran to the Maid and gave her all my Apron, and so that storm went over.

Hearing that my Son was come to this place, I went to see him, and told him his Father was well, but very melancholly: he told me he was as much grieved for his Father as for himself; I wondered at his speech, for I thought I had enough

[1] The prisoner escaped about May 15. The party which had gone to Hadley appears to have been a scouting party only.

upon my spirit in reference to my self, to make me mindless of my Husband and every one else: they being safe among their Friends. He told me also, that a while before, his Master (together with other Indians) where[1] going to the French for Powder; but by the way the Mohawks met with them, and killed four of their Company which made the rest turn back again, for which I desire that my self and he may bless the Lord; for it might have been worse with him, had he been sold to the French, than it proved to be in his remaining with the Indians.

I went to see an English Youth in this place, one John Gilberd[2] of Springfield. I found him lying without dores, upon the ground; I asked him how he did? he told me he was very sick of a flux, with eating so much blood: They had turned him out of the Wigwam, and with him an Indian Papoos, almost dead, (whose Parents had been killed) in a bitter cold day, without fire or clothes: the young man himself had nothing on, but his shirt and wastcoat. This sight was enough to melt a heart of flint. There they lay quivering in the Cold, the youth round like a dog; the Papoos stretcht out, with his eyes and nose and mouth full of dirt, and yet alive, and groaning. I advised John to go and get to some fire: he told me he could not stand, but I perswaded him still, lest he should ly there and die: and with much adoe I got him to a fire, and went my self home. As soon as I was got home, his Masters Daughter came after me, to know what I had done with the English man, I told her I had got him to a fire in such a place. Now had I need to pray Pauls Prayer, 2 Thess. 3. 2. *That we may be delivered from unreasonable and wicked men.* For her satisfaction I went along with her, and brought her to him; but before I got home again, it was noised about, that I was running away and getting the English youth, along with me; that as soon as I came in, they began to rant and domineer: asking me Where I had been, and what I had been doing? and saying they would knock him on the head: I told them, I had been seeing the English Youth, and that I would not run away, they told me I lyed, and taking up a Hatchet, they came to me, and said they would knock me down if I stirred out again; and so confined me to the Wigwam.

---

[1] Were.   [2] John Gilbert had been captured about March 1.

Now may I say with David, 2 Sam. 24. 14. *I am in a great strait.* If I keep in, I must dy with hunger, and if I go out, I must be knockt in head. This distressed condition held that day, and half the next; And then the Lord remembred me, whose mercyes are great. Then came an Indian to me with a pair of stockings that were too big for him, and he would have me ravel them out, and knit them fit for him. I shewed my self willing, and bid him ask my mistriss if I might go along with him a little way; she said yes, I might, but I was not a little refresht with that news, that I had my liberty again. Then I went along with him, and he gave me some roasted Ground-nuts, which did again revive my feeble stomach.

Being got out of her sight, I had time and liberty again to look into my Bible: Which was my Guid by day, and my Pillow by night. Now that comfortable Scripture presented it self to me, Isa. 54. 7. *For a smal moment have I forsaken thee, but with great mercies will I gather thee.* Thus the Lord carried me along from one time to another, and made good to me this precious promise, and many others. Then my Son came to see me, and I asked his master to let him stay a while with me, that I might comb his head, and look over him, for he was almost overcome with lice. He told me, when 1 had done, that he was very hungry, but I had nothing to relieve him; but bid him go into the Wigwams as he went along, and see if he could get any thing among them. Which he did, and it seemes tarried a little too long; for his Master was angry with him, and beat him, and then sold him. Then he came running to tell me he had a new Master, and that he had given him some Groundnuts already. Then I went along with him to his new Master who told me he loved him: and he should not want. So his Master carried him away, and I never saw him afterward, till I saw him at Pascataqua in Portsmouth.

That night they bade me go out of the Wigwam again: my Mistrisses Papoos was sick, and it died that night, and there was one benefit in it, that there was more room. I went to a Wigwam, and they bade me come in, and gave me a skin to ly upon, and a mess of Venson and Ground-nuts, which was a choice Dish among them. On the morrow they buried the Papoos, and afterward, both morning and evening, there came a company to mourn and howle with her: though I confess, I could not much condole with them. Many sorrowfull dayes I had in this place: often getting alone; *like a Crane, or a Swallow, so did I chatter: I did mourn as a Dove, mine eyes ail with looking upward. Oh, Lord, I am oppressed; undertake for me,* Isa. 38. 14. I could tell the Lord as Hezeckiah, ver. 3. *Remember now O Lord, I beseech thee, how I have walked before thee in truth.*[1] Now had I time to examine all my wayes: my Conscience did not accuse me of un-righteousness toward one or other: yet I saw how in my walk with God, I had been a careless creature. As David said, *Against thee, thee only have I sinned:* and I might say with the poor Publican, *God be merciful unto me a sinner.* On the Sabbath-dayes, I could look upon the Sun and think how People were going to the house of God, to have their Souls refresht; and then home, and their bodies also: but I was destitute of both; and might say as the poor Prodigal, *he would fain have filled his belly with the husks that the Swine did eat, and no man gave unto him,* Luke 15. 16. For I must say with him, *Father I have sinned against Heaven, and in thy sight,* ver. 21. I remembred how on the night before and after the Sabbath, when my Family was about me, and Relations and Neighbours with us, we could pray and sing, and then refresh our bodies with the good creatures of God; and then have a comfortable Bed to ly down on: but in stead of all this, I had only a little Swill for the body, and then like a Swine, must ly down on the ground. I cannot express to man the sorrow that lay upon my Spirit, the Lord knows it. Yet that comfortable Scripture would often come to my mind, *For a small moment have I forsaken thee, but with great mercies will I gather thee.*[2]

The fourteenth Remove.[3]

Now must we pack up and be gone from this Thicket, bending our course toward the Bay-towns, I haveing nothing to

---

[1] Isaiah xxxviii. 3.   [2] Isaiah liv. 7.

[3] The fourteenth to nineteenth moves covered the time from April 20 to April 28. The route retraced the path taken earlier. From Hinsdale, New Hampshire, the trail led to the camp on Miller's River in Orange, thence to Niche-waug in Petersham, to Menameset on Barre Plains, to Mount Wachusett in Princeton, where the negotiations for ransom were begun.

eat by the way this day, but a few crumbs of Cake, that an Indian gave my girle the same day we were taken. She gave it me, and I put it in my pocket: there it lay, till it was so mouldy (for want of good baking) that one could not tell what it was made of; it fell all to crumbs, and grew so dry and hard, that it was like little flints; and this refreshed me many times, when I was ready to faint. It was in my thoughts when I put it into my mouth, that if ever I returned, I would tell the World what a blessing the Lord gave to such mean food. As we went along, they killed a Deer, with a young one in her, they gave me a piece of the Fawn, and it was so young and tender, that one might eat the bones as well as the flesh, and yet I thought it very good. When night came on we sate down; it rained, but they quickly got up a Bark Wigwam, where I lay dry that night. I looked out in the morning, and many of them had line in the rain all night, I saw by their Reaking. Thus the Lord dealt mercifully with me many times. and I fared better than many of them. In the morning they took the blood of the Deer, and put it into the Paunch, and so boyled it; I could eat nothing of that, though they ate it sweetly. And yet they were so nice in other things, that when I had fetcht water, and had put the Dish I dipt the water with, into the Kettle of water which I brought, they would say, they would knock me down; for they said, it was a sluttish trick.

The fifteenth Remove.

We went on our Travel. I having got one handfull of Ground-nuts, for my support that day, they gave me my load, and I went on cheerfully (with the thoughts of going homeward) haveing my burden more on my back than my spirit: we came to Baquaug River again that day, near which we abode a few dayes. Sometimes one of them would give me a Pipe, another a little Tobacco, another a little Salt: which I would change for a little Victuals. I cannot but think what a Wolvish appetite persons have in a starving condition: for many times when they gave me that which was hot, I was so greedy, that I should burn my mouth, that it would trouble me hours after, and yet I should quickly do the same again. And after I was thoroughly hungry, I was never again satisfied. For though sometimes it fell out, that I got enough, and did eat till I could eat no more, yet I was as unsatisfied as I was when I began. And now could I see that Scripture verified (there being many Scriptures which we do not take notice of, or understand till we are afflicted) Mic. 6. 14. *Thou shalt eat and not be satisfied.* Now might I see more than ever before, the miseries that sin hath brought upon us: Many times I should be ready to run out against the Heathen, but the Scripture would quiet me again, Amos 3. 6, *Shal there be evil in the City, and the Lord hath not done it?* The Lord help me to make a right improvment of His Word, and that I might learn that great lesson, Mic. 6. 8, 9. *He hath shewed thee (Oh Man) what is good, and what doth the Lord require of thee, but to do justly, and love mercy, and walk humbly with thy God? Hear ye the rod, and who hath appointed it.*

The sixteenth Remove.

We began this Remove with wading over Baquag River: the water was up to the knees, and the stream very swift, and so cold that I thought it would have cut me in sunder. I was so weak and feeble, that I reeled as I went along, and thought there I must end my dayes at last, after my bearing and getting thorough so many difficulties; the Indians stood laughing to see me staggering along: but in my distress the Lord gave me experience of the truth, and goodness of that promise, Isai. 43. 2. *When thou passest thorough the Waters, I will be with thee, and through the Rivers, they shall not overflow thee.* Then I sat down to put on my stockins and shoos, with the teares running down mine eyes, and many sorrowfull thoughts in my heart, but I gat up to go along with them. Quickly there came up to us an Indian, who informed them, that I must go to Wachusit to my master, for there was a Letter come from the Council to the Saggamores, about redeeming the Captives, and that there would be another in fourteen dayes, and that I must be there ready. My heart was so heavy before that I could scarce speak or go in the path; and yet now so light, that I could run. My strength seemed to come again, and recruit my feeble knees, and aking heart: yet it pleased them to go but one mile that night, and there we

stayed two dayes. In that time came a company of Indians
to us, near thirty, all on horseback. My heart skipt within
me. thinking they had been English-men at the first sight of
them, for they were dressed in English Apparel, with Hats,
white Neckcloths, and Sashes about their wasts, and Rib-
bonds upon their shoulders: but when they came near, their
was a vast difference between the lovely faces of Christians,
and the foul looks of those Heathens, which much damped
my spirit again.

The seventeenth Remove.

A comfortable Remove it was to me, because of my hopes.
They gave me a pack, and along we went chearfully; but
quickly my will proved more than my strength; having little
or no refreshing my strength failed me, and my spirit were
almost quite gone. Now may I say with David, Psal. 119. 22,
23, 24. *I am poor and needy, and my heart is wounded within
me. I am gone like the shadow when it declineth: I am tossed up
and down like the locust; my knees are weak through fasting,
and my flesh faileth of fatness.* At night we came to an Indian
Town, and the Indians sate down by a Wigwam discoursing,
but I was almost spent, and could scarce speak. I laid down
my load, and went into the Wigwam, and there sat an Indian
boyling of Horses feet (they being wont to eat the flesh first,
and when the feet were old and dried, and they had nothing
else, they would cut off the feet and use them). I asked him
to give me a little of his Broth, or Water they were boiling in;
he took a dish, and gave me one spoonfull of Samp, and bid
me take as much of the Broth as I would. Then I put some
of the hot water to the Samp, and drank it up, and my spirit
came again. He gave me also a piece of the Ruff or Ridding
of the small Guts, and I broiled it on the coals; and now may
I say with Jonathan, *See, I pray you, how mine eyes have been
enlightened, because I tasted a little of this honey,* 1 Sam. 14. 29.
Now is my Spirit revived again; though means be never so
inconsiderable, yet if the Lord bestow his blessing upon them,
they shall refresh both Soul and Body.

The eighteenth Remove.

We took up our packs and along we went, but a wearisome day I had of it. As we went along I saw an English-man stript naked, and lying dead upon the ground, but knew not who it was. Then we came to another Indian Town, where we stayed all night. In this Town there were four English Children, Captives; and one of them my own Sisters. I went to see how she did, and she was well, considering her Captive-condition. I would have tarried that night with her, but they that owned her would not suffer it. Then I went into another Wigwam, where they were boyling Corn and Beans, which was a lovely sight to see, but I could not get a taste thereof. Then I went to another Wigwam, where there were two of the English Children; the Squaw was boyling Horses feet, then she cut me off a little piece, and gave one of the English Children a piece also. Being very hungry I had quickly eat up mine, but the Child could not bite it, it was so tough and sinewy, but lay sucking, gnawing, chewing and slabbering of it in the mouth and hand, then I took it of the Child, and eat it my self, and savoury it was to my taste. Then I may say as Job, Chap. 6. 7. *The things that my soul refused to touch, are as my sorrowfull meat.* Thus the Lord made that pleasant refreshing, which another time would have been an abomination. Then I went home to my mistresses Wigwam; and they told me I disgraced my master with begging, and if I did so any more, they would knock me in head: I told them, they had as good knock me in head as starve me to death.

The nineteenth Remove.

They said, when we went out, that we must travel to Wachuset this day. But a bitter weary day I had of it, travelling now three dayes together, without resting any day between. At last, after many weary steps, I saw Wachuset hills, but many miles off. Then we came to a great Swamp, through which we travelled, up to the knees in mud and water, which was heavy going to one tyred before. Being almost spent, I thought I should have sunk down at last, and never gat out; but I may say, as in Psal. 94. 18, *When my foot slipped, thy mercy, O Lord, held me up.* Going along, having indeed my life, but little spirit, Philip, who was in the Company, came up and took me by the hand, and said, Two weeks more and you shal be Mistress again. I asked him, if he spake true? he answered, Yes, and quickly you shal come to your master again; who had been gone from us three weeks. After many weary steps we came to Wachuset, where he was: and glad I was to see him. He asked me, When I washt me? I told him not this month, then he fetcht me some water himself, and bid me wash, and gave me the Glass to see how I lookt; and bid his Squaw give me something to eat: so she gave me a mess of Beans and meat, and a little Ground-nut Cake. I was wonderfully revived with this favour shewed me, Psal. 106. 46, *He made them also to be pittied, of all those that carried them Captives.*

My master had three Squaws, living sometimes with one, and sometimes with another one, this old Squaw, at whose Wigwam I was, and with whom my Master had been those three weeks. Another was Wattimore,[1] with whom I had lived and served all this while: A severe and proud Dame she was, bestowing every day in dressing her self neat as much time as any of the Gentry of the land: powdering her hair, and painting her face, going with Neck-laces, with Jewels in her ears, and Bracelets upon her hands: When she had dressed her self, her work was to make Girdles of Wampom and Beads. The third Squaw was a younger one, by whom he had two Papooses. By that time I was refresht by the old Squaw, with whom my master was, Wettimores Maid came to call me home, at which I fell a weeping. Then the old Squaw told me, to encourage me, that if I wanted victuals, I should come to her, and that I should ly there in her Wigwam. Then I went with the maid, and quickly came again and lodged there. The Squaw laid a Mat under me, and a good Rugg over me; the first time I had any such kindness shewed me. I understood that Wettimore thought, that if she should let me go and serve with the old Squaw, she would be in danger to loose, not only my service, but the redemption-pay also. And I was not a little glad to hear this; being by it raised in my hopes,

[1] The name is usually given as Weetamoo.

that in Gods due time there would be an end of this sorrowfull hour. Then came an Indian, and asked me to knit him three pair of Stockins, for which I had a Hat, and a silk Handkerchief. Then another asked me to make her a shift, for which she gave me an Apron.

Then came Tom and Peter,[1] with the second Letter from the Council, about the Captives. Though they were Indians, I gat them by the hand, and burst out into tears; my heart was so full that I could not speak to them; but recovering my self, I asked them how my husband did, and all my friends and acquaintance? they said, They are all very well but melancholy. They brought me two Biskets, and a pound of Tobacco. The Tobacco I quickly gave away; when it was all gone, one asked me to give him a pipe of Tobacco, I told him it was all gone; then began he to rant and threaten. I told him when my Husband came I would give him some: Hang him Rogue (sayes he) I will knock out his brains, if he comes here. And then again, in the same breath they would say, That if there should come an hundred without Guns, they would do them no hurt. So unstable and like mad men they were. So that fearing the worst, I durst not send to my Husband, though there were some thoughts of his coming to Redeem and fetch me, not knowing what might follow. For there was little more trust to them then to the master they served. When the Letter was come, the Saggamores met to consult about the Captives, and called me to them to enquire how much my husband would give to redeem me, when I came I sate down among them, as I was wont to do, as their manner is: Then they bade me stand up, and said, they were the General Court.[2] They bid me speak what I thought he would give. Now knowing that all we had was destroyed by the Indians, I was in a great strait: I thought if I should speak of but a little, it would be slighted, and hinder the matter; if of a great sum, I knew not where it would be pro-

---

[1] Tom Dublet (Nepanet) and Peter Conway (Tatatiquinea) were Christian Indians of Nashobah (Littleton in Lancaster), p. 33, *ante*, who were conducting the negotiations for ransom. Dublet's first visit to the Indians was April 3, when he brought a letter from Governor Leverett of March 31 and bore in return a reply of April 12, to which Mrs. Rowlandson refers on p. 147.

[2] General Court was the official style of the colonial assembly of Massachusetts Bay.

cured: yet at a venture, I said Twenty pounds, yet desired them to take less; but they would not hear of that, but sent that message to Boston, that for Twenty pounds I should be redeemed. It was a Praying-Indian that wrote their Letter for them.[1] There was another Praying Indian, who told me, that he had a brother, that would not eat Horse; his conscience was so tender and scrupulous (though as large as hell, for the destruction of poor Christians). Then he said, he read that Scripture to him, 2 Kings, 6. 25. *There was a famine in Samaria, and behold they besieged it, untill an Asses head was sold for fourscore pieces of silver, and the fourth part of a Kab of Doves dung, for five pieces of silver.* He expounded this place to his brother, and shewed him that it was lawfull to eat that in a Famine which is not at another time. And now, sayes he, he will eat Horse with any Indian of them all. There was another Praying-Indian, who when he had done all the mischief that he could, betrayed his own Father into the English hands, thereby to purchase his own life. Another Praying-Indian was at Sudbury-fight,[2] though, as he deserved, he was afterward hanged for it. There was another Praying Indian, so wicked and cruel, as to wear a string about his neck, strung with Christians fingers. Another Praying-Indian, when they went to Sudbury-fight, went with them, and his Squaw also with him, with her Papoos at her back: Before they went to that fight, they got a company together to *Powaw*; the manner was as followeth. There was one that kneeled upon a Deerskin, with the company round him in a ring who kneeled, and striking upon the ground with their hands, and with sticks, and muttering or humming with their mouths; besides him who kneeled in the ring, there also stood one with a Gun in his hand: Then he on the Deer-skin made a speech, and all manifested assent to it: and so they did many times together. Then they bade him with the Gun go out of the ring, which he

---

[1] Peter Jethro, Indian scribe. The letter, apparently dictated by Philip, is still preserved in the library of the Massachusetts Historical Society. It is printed in Palfrey's *History of New England*, III. 188: "whereupon we ask Mrs. Rolanson how much your husband willing to give for you; she gave an answer 20 pound in goods."

[2] "Sudbury Fight" was on April 18. Captains Samuel Wadsworth of Milton and Samuel Brocklebank of Rowley with some thirty men were killed in an ambush. See p. 92, *ante*.

did, but when he was out, they called him in again; but he seemed to make a stand, then they called the more earnestly, till he returned again: Then they all sang. Then they gave him two Guns, in either hand one: And so he on the Deerskin began again; and at the end of every sentence in his speaking, they all assented, humming or muttering with their mouthes, and striking upon the ground with their hands. Then they bade him with the two Guns go out of the ring again; which he did, a little way. Then they called him in again, but he made a stand; so they called him with greater earnestness; but he stood reeling and wavering as if he knew not whither he should stand or fall, or which way to go. Then they called him with exceeding great vehemency, all of them, one and another: after a little while he turned in, staggering as he went, with his Armes stretched out, in either hand a Gun. As soon as he came in, they all sang and rejoyced exceedingly a while. And then he upon the Deer-skin, made another speech unto which they all assented in a rejoicing manner: and so they ended their business, and forthwith went to Sudbury-fight. To my thinking they went without any scruple, but that they should prosper, and gain the victory. And they went out not so rejoycing, but they came home with as great a Victory. For they said they had killed two Captains, and almost an hundred men. One English-man they brought along with them: and he said, it was too true, for they had made sad work at Sudbury, as indeed it proved. Yet they came home without that rejoycing and triumphing over their victory, which they were wont to shew at other times, but rather like Dogs (as they say) which have lost their ears. Yet I could not perceive that it was for their own loss of men: They said, they had not lost above five or six: and I missed none, except in one Wigwam. When they went, they acted as if the Devil had told them that they should gain the victory: and now they acted, as if the Devil had told them they should have a fall. Whither it were so or no, I cannot tell, but so it proved, for quickly they began to fall, and so held on that Summer, till they came to utter ruine. They came home on a Sabbath day, and the *Powaw* that kneeled upon the Deerskin came home (I may say, without abuse) as black as the Devil. When my master came home, he came to me and bid

me make a shirt for his Papoos, of a holland-laced Pillowbeer.
About that time there came an Indian to me and bid me come
to his Wigwam, at night, and he would give me some Pork
and Ground-nuts. Which I did, and as I was eating, another
Indian said to me, he seems to be your good Friend, but he
killed two Englishmen at Sudbury, and there ly their Cloaths
behind you: I looked behind me, and there I saw bloody
Cloaths, with Bullet-holes in them; yet the Lord suffered not
this wretch to do me any hurt; Yea, instead of that, he many
times refresht me: five or six times did he and his Squaw refresh my feeble carcass. If I went to their Wigwam at any
time, they would alwayes give me something, and yet they
were strangers that I never saw before. Another Squaw gave
me a piece of fresh Pork, and a little Salt with it, and lent me
her Pan to Fry it in; and I cannot but remember what a sweet,
pleasant and delightfull relish that bit had to me, to this day.
So little do we prize common mercies when we have them to
the full.

The twentieth Remove.[1]

It was their usual manner to remove, when they had done
any mischief, lest they should be found out: and so they did
at this time. We went about three or four miles, and there
they built a great Wigwam, big enough to hold an hundred
Indians, which they did in preparation to a great day of
Dancing. They would say now amongst themselves, that the
Governour would be so angry for his loss at Sudbury, that he
would send no more about the Captives, which made me
grieve and tremble. My Sister being not far from the place
where we now were, and hearing that I was here, desired her
master to let her come and see me, and he was willing to it,
and would go with her: but she being ready before him, told
him she would go before, and was come within a Mile or two
of the place; Then he overtook her, and began to rant as if

---

[1] The twentieth remove, April 28–May 2, was to an encampment at about
the southern end of Wachusett Lake, Princeton. On a granite ledge near the
Westminster line which tradition has marked as the Redemption Rock, the late
Senator George F. Hoar had the date May 2, 1676, inscribed as the date of the
agreement made between the Indians and John Hoar for the ransom of Mrs.
Rowlandson. See pp. 157, 158, *post*.

he had been mad; and made her go back again in the Rain; so that I never saw her till I saw her in Charlestown. But the Lord requited many of their ill doings, for this Indian her Master, was hanged afterward at Boston.[1] The Indians now began to come from all quarters, against their merry dancing day. Among some of them came one Goodwife Kettle:[2] I told her my heart was so heavy that it was ready to break: so is mine too said she, but yet said, I hope we shall hear some good news shortly. I could hear how earnestly my Sister desired to see me, and I as earnestly desired to see her: and yet neither of us could get an opportunity. My Daughter was also now about a mile off, and I had not seen her in nine or ten weeks, as I had not seen my Sister since our first taking. I earnestly desired them to let me go and see them: yea, I intreated, begged, and perswaded them, but to let me see my Daughter; and yet so hard hearted were they, that they would not suffer it. They made use of their tyrannical power whilst they had it: but through the Lords wonderfull mercy, their time was now but short.

On a Sabbath day, the Sun being about an hour high in the afternoon, came Mr. John Hoar[3] (the Council permitting him, and his own foreward spirit inclining him) together with the two forementioned Indians, Tom and Peter, with their third Letter from the Council. When they came near, I was abroad: though I saw them not, they presently called me in, and bade me sit down and not stir. Then they catched up their Guns, and away they ran, as if an Enemy had been at hand; and the Guns went off apace. I manifested some great trouble, and they asked me what was the matter? I told them, I thought they had killed the English-man (for they had in the mean time informed me that an English-man was come) they said, No; They shot over his Horse and under, and before his Horse; and they pusht him this way and that way, at their pleasure: shewing what they could do: Then they let them

---

[1] Mrs. Divoll had Sagamore Sam for her master; he was hanged in Boston, September 26, 1676.

[2] Arrangements looking toward her ransom are mentioned in the letter described in note 1, on p. 152.

[3] John Hoar of Concord, to whose services Mrs. Rowlandson owed more than to the colonial government. He was an ancestor of the late Senator Hoar.

come to their Wigwams. I begged of them to let me see the
English-man, but they would not. But there was I fain to
sit their pleasure. When they had talked their fill with him,
they suffered me to go to him. We asked each other of our
welfare, and how my Husband did, and all my Friends? He
told me they were all well, and would be glad to see me.
Amongst other things which my Husband sent me, there came
a pound of Tobacco: which I sold for nine shillings in Money:
for many of the Indians for want of Tobacco, smoaked Hemlock,
and Ground-Ivy. It was a great mistake in any, who thought
I sent for Tobacco: for through the favour of God, that desire
was overcome. I now asked them, whither I should go home
with Mr. Hoar? They answered No, one and another of
them: and it being night, we lay down with that answer; in
the morning, Mr Hoar invited the Saggamores to Dinner; but
when we went to get it ready, we found that they had stollen
the greatest part of the Provision Mr. Hoar had brought, out
of his Bags, in the night. And we may see the wonderfull
power of God, in that one passage, in that when there was such
a great number of the Indians together, and so greedy of a little
good food; and no English there, but Mr. Hoar and my self:
that there they did not knock us in the head, and take what
we had: there being not only some Provision, but also Trading-
cloth, a part of the twenty pounds agreed upon: But instead
of doing us any mischief, they seemed to be ashamed of the
fact, and said, it were some Matchit Indian[1] that did it.
Oh, that we could believe that there is no thing too hard for
God! God shewed his Power over the Heathen in this, as
he did over the hungry Lyons when Daniel was cast into the
Den. Mr. Hoar called them betime to Dinner, but they ate
very little, they being so busie in dressing themselves, and
getting ready for their Dance: which was carried on by eight
of them, four Men and four Squaws: My master and mistress
being two. He was dressed in his Holland shirt, with great
Laces sewed at the tail of it, he had his silver Buttons, his
white Stockins, his Garters were hung round with Shillings,
and he had Girdles of Wampom upon his head and shoulders.
She had a Kersey Coat, and covered with Girdles of Wampom
from the Loins upward: her armes from her elbows to her hands

---

[1] *I. e.*, bad Indian.

were covered with Bracelets; there were handfulls of Necklaces about her neck, and severall sorts of Jewels in her ears. She had fine red Stokins, and white Shoos, her hair powdered and face painted Red, that was alwayes before Black. And all the Dancers were after the same manner. There were two other singing and knocking on a Kettle for their musick. They keept hopping up and down one after another, with a Kettle of water in the midst, standing warm upon some Embers, to drink of when they were dry. They held on till it was almost night, throwing out Wampom to the standers by. At night I asked them again, if I should go home? They all as one said No, except my Husband would come for me. When we were lain down, my Master went out of the Wigwam, and by and by sent in an Indian called James the Printer,[1] who told Mr. Hoar, that my Master would let me go home to morrow, if he would let him have one pint of Liquors. Then Mr. Hoar called his own Indians, Tom and Peter, and bid them go and see whither he would promise it before them three: and if he would, he should have it; which he did, and he had it. Then Philip smeling the business cal'd me to him, and asked me what I would give him, to tell me some good news, and speak a good word for me. I told him, I could not tell what to give him, I would any thing I had, and asked him what he would have? He said, two Coats and twenty shillings in Mony, and half a bushel of seed Corn, and some Tobacco. I thanked him for his love: but I knew the good news as well as the crafty Fox. My Master after he had had his drink, quickly came ranting into the Wigwam again, and called for Mr. Hoar, drinking to him, and saying, He was a good man: and then again he would say, Hang him Rogue: Being almost drunk, he would drink to him, and yet presently say he should be hanged. Then he called for me. I trembled to hear him, yet I was fain to go to him, and he drank to me, shewing no incivility. He was the first Indian I saw drunk all the while that I was amongst them.[2] At last his Squaw

[1] James the Printer was a Praying Indian, who had assisted at Cambridge in the printing of Eliot's Indian Bible. Later, July 1, he and 140 followers surrendered on the faith of a proclamation which offered pardon to those who did so.

[2] A striking testimony, but whether to the discipline among the Indians or to the remoteness of their successive "removes" Mrs. Rowlandson gives no hint.

ran out, and he after her, round the Wigwam, with his mony jingling at his knees: But she escaped him: But having an old Squaw he ran to her: and so through the Lords mercy, we were no more troubled that night. Yet I had not a comfortable nights rest: for I think I can say, I did not sleep for three nights together. The night before the Letter came from the Council, I could not rest, I was so full of feares and troubles, God many times leaving us most in the dark, when deliverance is nearest: yea, at this time I could not rest night nor day. The next night I was overjoyed, Mr. Hoar being come, and that with such good tidings. The third night I was even swallowed up with the thoughts of things, *viz.* that ever I should go home again; and that I must go, leaving my Children behind me in the Wilderness; so that sleep was now almost departed from mine eyes.

On Tuesday morning they called their General Court (as they call it) to consult and determine, whether I should go home or no: And they all as one man did seemingly consent to it, that I should go home; except Philip, who would not come among them.

But before I go any further, I would take leave to mention a few remarkable passages of providence, which I took special notice of in my afflicted time.

1. Of the fair opportunity lost in the long March, a little after the Fort-fight, when our English Army was so numerous, and in pursuit of the Enemy, and so near as to take several and destroy them: and the Enemy in such distress for food, that our men might track them by their rooting in the earth for Ground-nuts, whilest they were flying for their lives. I say, that then our Army should want Provision, and be forced to leave their pursuit and return homeward: and the very next week the Enemy came upon our Town, like Bears bereft of their whelps, or so many ravenous Wolves, rending us and our Lambs to death. But what shall I say? God seemed to leave his People to themselves, and order all things for his own holy ends. *Shal there be evil in the City and the Lord hath not done it? They are not grieved for the affliction of Joseph, therefore shal they go Captive, with the first that go Captive.* It is the Lords doing, and it should be marvelous in our eyes.

2. I cannot but remember how the Indians derided the

slowness, and dulness of the English Army, in its setting out.
For after the desolations at Lancaster and Medfield, as I went
along with them, they asked me when I thought the English
Army would come after them? I told them I could not tell:
It may be they will come in May, said they. Thus did they
scoffe at us, as if the English would be a quarter of a year getting ready.

3. Which also I have hinted before, when the English
Army with new supplies were sent forth to pursue after the
enemy, and they understanding it, fled before them till they
came to Baquaug River, where they forthwith went over safely:
that that River should be impassable to the English. I can
but admire to see the wonderfull providence of God in preserving the heathen for farther affliction to our poor Countrey.
They could go in great numbers over, but the English must
stop: God had an over-ruling hand in all those things.

4. It was thought, if their Corn were cut down, they would
starve and dy with hunger: and all their Corn that could be
found, was destroyed, and they driven from that little they
had in store, into the Woods in the midst of Winter; and yet
how to admiration did the Lord preserve them for his holy
ends, and the destruction of many still amongst the English!
strangely did the Lord provide for them; that I did not see
(all the time I was among them) one Man, Woman, or Child,
die with hunger.

Though many times they would eat that, that a Hog or a
Dog would hardly touch; yet by that God strengthned them
to be a scourge to his People.

The chief and commonest food was Ground-nuts: They
eat also Nuts and Acorns, Harty-choaks, Lilly roots, Ground-
beans, and several other weeds and roots, that I know not.

They would pick up old bones, and cut them to pieces at
the joynts, and if they were full of wormes and magots, they
would scald them over the fire to make the vermine come
out, and then boile them, and drink up the Liquor, and then
beat the great ends of them in a Morter, and so eat them.
They would eat Horses guts, and ears, and all sorts of wild
Birds which they could catch: also Bear, Vennison, Beaver,
Tortois, Frogs, Squirrels, Dogs, Skunks, Rattle-snakes; yea,
the very Bark of Trees; besides all sorts of creatures, and pro-

vision which they plundered from the English. I can but stand in admiration to see the wonderful power of God, in providing for such a vast number of our Enemies in the Wilderness, where there was nothing to be seen, but from hand to mouth. Many times in a morning, the generality of them would eat up all they had, and yet have some forther supply against they wanted. It is said, Psal. 81. 13, 14. *Oh, that my People had hearkned to me, and Israel had walked in my wayes, I should soon have subdued their Enemies, and turned my hand against their Adversaries.* But now our perverse and evil carriages in the sight of the Lord, have so offended him, that instead of turning his hand against them, the Lord feeds and nourishes them up to be a scourge to the whole Land.

5. Another thing that I would observe is, the strange providence of God, in turning things about when the Indians was at the highest, and the English at the lowest. I was with the Enemy eleven weeks and five dayes, and not one Week passed without the fury of the Enemy, and some desolation by fire and sword upon one place or other. They mourned (with their black faces) for their own lossess, yet triumphed and rejoyced in their inhumane, and many times devilish cruelty to the English. They would boast much of their Victories; saying, that in two hours time they had destroyed such a Captain, and his Company at such a place; and such a Captain and his Company in such a place; and such a Captain and his Company in such a place: and boast how many Towns they had destroyed, and then scoffe, and say, They had done them a good turn, to send them to Heaven so soon. Again, they would say, This Summer that they would knock all the Rogues in the head, or drive them into the Sea, or make them flie the Countrey: thinking surely, Agag-like, *The bitterness of Death is past.*[1] Now the Heathen begins to think all is their own, and the poor Christians hopes to fail (as to man) and now their eyes are more to God, and their hearts sigh heaven-ward: and to say in good earnest, *Help Lord, or we perish:* When the Lord had brought his people to this, that they saw no help in any thing but himself: then he takes the quarrel into his own hand: and though they had made a pit, in their own imaginations, as deep as hell for the Christians

[1] I Samuel xv. 32.

that Summer, yet the Lord hurll'd them selves into it.   And the Lord had not so many wayes before to preserve them, but now he hath as many to destroy them.

But to return again to my going home, where we may see a remarkable change of Providence: At first they were all against it, except my Husband would come for me; but afterwards they assented to it, and seemed much to rejoyce in it; some askt me to send them some Bread, others some Tobacco, others shaking me by the hand, offering me a Hood and Scarfe to ride in; not one moving hand or tongue against it.   Thus hath the Lord answered my poor desire, and the many earnest requests of others put up unto God for me.   In my travels an Indian came to me, and told me, if I were willing, he and his Squaw would run away, and go home along with me: I told him No: I was not willing to run away, but desired to wait Gods time, that I might go home quietly, and without fear.   And now God hath granted me my desire.   O the wonderfull power of God that I have seen, and the experience that I have had: I have been in the midst of those roaring Lyons, and Salvage Bears, that feared neither God, nor Man, nor the Devil, by night and day, alone and in company: sleeping all sorts together, and yet not one of them ever offered me the least abuse of unchastity to me, in word or action.   Though some are ready to say, I speak it for my own credit; But I speak it in the presence of God, and to his Glory.   Gods Power is as great now, and as sufficient to save, as when he preserved Daniel in the Lions Den;   or the three Children in the fiery Furnace.   I may well say as his Psal. 107. 12, *Oh give thanks unto the Lord for he is good, for his mercy endureth for ever*.   Let the Redeemed of the Lord say so, whom he hath redeemed from the hand of the Enemy, especially that I should come away in the midst of so many hundreds of Enemies quietly and peacably, and not a Dog moving his tongue.   So I took my leave of them, and in coming along my heart melted into tears, more then all the while I was with them, and I was almost swallowed up with the thoughts that ever I should go home again.   About the Sun going down, Mr. Hoar, and my self, and the two Indians came to Lancaster, and a solemn sight it was to me.   There had I lived many comfortable years amongst my Relations and Neighbours, and now not one Christian to be seen, nor one house left standing. We went on to a Farm house[1] that was yet standing, where we lay all night: and a comfortable lodging we had, though nothing but straw to ly on. The Lord preserved us in safety that night, and raised us up again in the morning, and carried us along, that before noon, we came to Concord. Now was I full of joy, and yet not without sorrow: joy to see such a lovely sight, so many Christians together, and some of them my Neighbours: There I met with my Brother, and my Brother in Law,[2] who asked me, if I knew where his Wife was? Poor heart! he had helped to bury her, and knew it not; she being shot down by the house was partly burnt: so that those who were at Boston at the desolation of the Town, and came back afterward, and buried the dead, did not know her. Yet I was not without sorrow, to think how many were looking and longing, and my own Children amongst the rest, to enjoy that deliverance that I had now received, and I did not know whither ever I should see them again. Being recruited with food and raiment we went to Boston that day, where I met with my dear Husband, but the thoughts of our dear Children, one being dead, and the other we could not tell where, abated our comfort each to other. I was not before so much hem'd in with the merciless and cruel Heathen, but now as much with pittiful, tender-hearted and compassionate Christians. In that poor, and destressed, and beggerly condition I was received in, I was kindly entertained in severall Houses: so much love I received from several (some of whom I knew, and others I knew not) that I am not capable to declare it. But the Lord knows them all by name: The Lord reward them seven fold into their bosoms of his spirituals, for their temporals. The twenty pounds the price of my redemption was raised by some Boston Gentlemen, and Mrs. Usher,[3] whose bounty and religious charity, I would not forget to make mention of. Then Mr. Thomas Shepard[4] of Charlstown received us

---

[1] This farmhouse was on the road to Marlborough, as "not one house was left standing" in Lancaster.

[2] Josiah White and Henry Kerley.

[3] Wife of Hezekiah Usher, bookseller, a selectman of Boston.

[4] Rev. Thomas Shepard of Charlestown was a son of the more famous Rev. Thomas Shepard of Cambridge.

into his House, where we continued eleven weeks; and a Father and Mother they were to us. And many more tender-hearted Friends we met with in that place. We were now in the midst of love, yet not without much and frequent heaviness of heart for our poor Children, and other Relations, who were still in affliction. The week following, after my coming in, the Governour and Council sent forth to the Indians again; and that not without success; for they brought in my Sister, and Good-wife Kettle: Their not knowing where our Children were, was a sore tryal to us still, and yet we were not without secret hopes that we should see them again. That which was dead lay heavier upon my spirit, than those which were alive and amongst the Heathen; thinking how it suffered with its wounds, and I was no way able to relieve it; and how it was buried by the Heathen in the Wilderness from among all Christians. We were hurried up and down in our thoughts, some-time we should hear a report that they were gone this way, and sometimes that; and that they were come in, in this place or that: We kept enquiring and listning to hear concerning them, but no certain news as yet. About this time the Council had ordered a day of publick Thanks-giving:[1] though I thought I had still cause of mourning, and being unsettled in our minds, we thought we would ride toward the Eastward, to see if we could hear any thing concerning our Children. And as we were riding along (God is the wise disposer of all things) between Ipswich and Rowly we met with Mr. William Hubbard,[2] who told us that our Son Joseph was come in to Major Waldrens,[3] and another with him, which was my Sisters Son. I asked him how he knew it? He said, the Major himself told him so. So along we went till we came to Newbury; and their Minister being absent, they desired my Husband to Preach the Thanks giving for them; but he was not willing to stay there that night, but would go over to Salisbury,

---

[1] This was the Thanksgiving of June 29, 1676. The broadside appointing it, the earliest American thanksgiving broadside known, is extant in the library of the Massachusetts Historical Society, and is reproduced in Rev. W. D. Love's *The Fast and Thanksgiving Days of New England*, p. 200.

[2] Minister of Ipswich and historian of the war; see p. 22, *supra.*

[3] Major Richard Waldron or Waldren of Dover, New Hampshire, a man of much prominence in his region.

to hear further, and come again in the morning; which he did, and Preached there that day. At night, when he had done, one came and told him that his Daughter was come in at Providence: Here was mercy on both hands: Now hath God fulfiled that precious Scripture which was such a comfort to me in my distressed condition. When my heart was ready to sink into the Earth (my Children being gone I could not tell whither) and my knees trembled under me, And I was walking through the valley of the shadow of Death: Then the Lord brought, and now has fulfilled that reviving word unto me: *Thus saith the Lord, Refrain thy voice from weeping, and thine eyes from tears, for thy Work shall be rewarded, saith the Lord, and they shall come again from the Land of the Enemy.*[1] Now we were between them, the one on the East, and the other on the West: Our Son being nearest, we went to him first, to Portsmouth, where we met with him, and with the Major also: who told us he had done what he could, but could not redeem him under seven pounds; which the good People thereabouts were pleased to pay. The Lord reward the Major, and all the rest, though unknown to me, for their labour of Love. My Sisters Son was redeemed for four pounds, which the Council gave order for the payment of. Having now received one of our Children, we hastened toward the other; going back through Newbury, my Husband preached there on the Sabbath-day: for which they rewarded him many fold.

On Munday we came to Charlstown, where we heard that the Governour of Road-Island[2] had sent over for our Daughter, to take care of her, being now within his Jurisdiction: which should not pass without our acknowledgments. But she being nearer Rehoboth than Road-Island, Mr. Newman[3] went over, and took care of her, and brought her to his own House. And the goodness of God was admirable to us in our low estate, in that he raised up passionate[4] Friends on every side to us, when we had nothing to recompance any for their love. The Indians were now gone that way, that it was apprehended dangerous to go to her: But the Carts which carried Provision to the English Army, being guarded, brought

---

[1] Jeremiah xxxi. 16.
[2] William Coddington was governor of Rhode Island at this time.
[3] Rev. Noah Newman of Rehoboth.   [4] Compassionate.

her with them to Dorchester, where we received her safe:
blessed be the Lord for it, For great is his Power, and he can
do whatsoever seemeth him good.   Her coming in was after
this manner: She was travelling one day with the Indians,
with her basket at her back; the company of Indians were
got before her, and gone out of sight, all except one Squaw;
she followed the Squaw till night, and then both of them lay
down, having nothing over them but the heavens, and under
them but the earth.   Thus she travelled three dayes together,
not knowing whither she was going: having nothing to eat or
drink but water, and green Hirtle-berries.   At last they came
into Providence, where she was kindly entertained by several
of that Town.   The Indians often said, that I should never
have her under twenty pounds: But now the Lord hath
brought her in upon free-cost, and given her to me the second
time.   The Lord make us a blessing indeed, each to others.
Now have I seen that Scripture also fulfilled, Deut. 30:4, 7.
*If any of thine be driven out to the outmost parts of heaven,
from thence will the Lord thy God gather thee, and from thence
will he fetch thee.   And the Lord thy God will put all these curses
upon thine enemies, and on them which hate thee, which persecuted thee.*   Thus hath the Lord brought me and mine out of
that horrible pit, and hath set us in the midst of tender-hearted
and compassionate Christians.   It is the desire of my soul,
that we may walk worthy of the mercies received, and which
we are receiving.

Our Family being now gathered together (those of us that
were living) the South Church in Boston hired an House for
us: Then we removed from Mr. Shepards, those cordial
Friends, and went to Boston, where we continued about three
quarters of a year: Still the Lord went along with us, and provided graciously for us.   I thought it somewhat strange to
set up House-keeping with bare walls; but as Solomon says,
Mony answers all things;[1] and that we had through the be-
nevolence of Christian-friends, some in this Town, and some in
that, and others: And some from England, that in a little
time we might look, and see the House furnished with love.
The Lord hath been exceeding good to us in our low estate,
in that when we had neither house nor home, nor other neces-

[1] Ecclesiastes x. 19.

saries; the Lord so moved the hearts of these and those towards us, that we wanted neither food, nor raiment for our selves or ours, Prov. 18. 24. *There is a Friend which sticketh closer than a Brother.* And how many such Friends have we found, and now living amongst? And truly such a Friend have we found him to be unto us, in whose house we lived, *viz.* Mr. James Whitcomb,[1] a Friend unto us near hand, and afar off.

I can remember the time, when I used to sleep quietly without workings in my thoughts, whole nights together, but now it is other wayes with me. When all are fast about me, and no eye open, but his who ever waketh, my thoughts are upon things past, upon the awfull dispensation of the Lord towards us; upon his wonderfull power and might, in carrying of us through so many difficulties, in returning us in safety, and suffering none to hurt us. I remember in the night season, how the other day I was in the midst of thousands of enemies, and nothing but death before me: It is then hard work to perswade my self, that ever I should be satisfied with bread again. But now we are fed with the finest of the Wheat, and, as I may say, With honey out of the rock: In stead of the Husk, we have the fatted Calf: The thoughts of these things in the particulars of them, and of the love and goodness of God towards us, make it true of me, what David said of himself, Psal. 6. 5.[2] *I watered my Couch with my tears.* Oh! the wonderfull power of God that mine eyes have seen, affording matter enough for my thoughts to run in, that when others are sleeping mine eyes are weeping.

I have seen the extrem vanity of this World: One hour I have been in health, and wealth, wanting nothing: But the next hour in sickness and wounds, and death, having nothing but sorrow and affliction.

Before I knew what affliction meant, I was ready sometimes to wish for it. When I lived in prosperity, having the comforts of the World about me, my relations by me, my Heart chearfull, and taking little care for any thing; and yet seeing many, whom I preferred before my self, under many tryals and afflictions, in sickness, weakness, poverty, losses, crosses, and

[1] James Whitecomb of Boston lived about where the Tremont Building was erected.

[2] More exactly, Psalm vi. 6.

cares of the World, I should be sometimes jealous least I should have my portion in this life, and that Scripture would come to my mind, Heb. 12. 6. *For whom the Lord loveth he chasteneth, and scourgeth every Son whom he receiveth.* But now I see the Lord had his time to scourge and chasten me. The portion of some is to have their afflictions by drops, now one drop and then another; but the dregs of the Cup, the Wine of astonishment, like a sweeping rain that leaveth no food, did the Lord prepare to be my portion. Affliction I wanted, and affliction I had, full measure (I thought) pressed down and running over; yet I see, when God calls a Person to any thing, and through never so many difficulties, yet he is fully able to carry them through and make them see, and say they have been gainers thereby. And I hope I can say in some measure, As David did, *It is good for me that I have been afflicted.* The Lord hath shewed me the vanity of these outward things. That they are the Vanity of vanities, and vexation of spirit; that they are but a shadow, a blast, a bubble, and things of no continuance. That we must rely on God himself, and our whole dependance must be upon him. If trouble from smaller matters begin to arise in me, I have something at hand to check my self with, and say, why am I troubled? It was but the other day that if I had had the world, I would have given it for my freedom, or to have been a Servant to a Christian. I have learned to look beyond present and smaller troubles, and to be quieted under them, as Moses said, Exod. 14. 13. *Stand still and see the salvation of the Lord.*

Finis.

DECENNIUM LUCTUOSUM, BY
COTTON MATHER, 1699

INTRODUCTION

FOR an understanding of any conflict between the French and English in America the difference between the purposes of the two peoples in colonization must be kept constantly before us. The English, whether Puritan or Cavalier, came to America to make new homes. They identified themselves with the country in which they settled, and sought to reproduce the conditions existing in the land from which they had come. The French and in a less degree the Dutch were not seeking homes. Their purpose was to obtain new territories and new trade for their mother countries or new wealth for themselves. This done they could return to France or to Holland and live with an increased political and social prestige. The Englishman became an American. The Frenchman less often became a Canadian. The navigation laws would have been a matter of course to a French colony. They irritated English colonists intensely.

These reasons explain the cause and the result of the conflict between the French and English in America. For purposes of trade the French boundaries must be continually expanding and their relations with the Indians friendly. The more gradual development of the English self-governing and self-supporting communities demanded a secure frontier and an assimilation or destruction of all hostile peoples within those boundaries, but the English would not incorporate the Indians among themselves. The first successes were with the French under leaders like Champlain, Talon, and Frontenac. The final victory lay with the gradual advance of the English township. The *coureur de bois* was no match for the permanent settler.

Behind this inevitable conflict in America was the immediate conflict in Europe. Since the rule of Cromwell England had not been politically independent of France. The interference of Louis XIV. in British affairs had become more and more galling to Englishmen, but the probable extinction of the male line of the Stuarts with the death of James II. had prevented an open alliance between the Whigs within and the Dutch without the kingdom. The birth of a son to the English king removed the hope of a Protestant successor who would oppose France, and the rivalry between the two peoples, each seeking a controlling influence in Europe and America, broke out into open war. The colonists had no option but war even had they desired to remain at peace. From the viewpoint of the New England Puritan much can be found in the conditions prevailing both in England and in America at this time to justify the title of *Decennium Luctuosum* (Sorrowful Decade) which Cotton Mather chose for his history of the period. In England the memory of the harsh control exercised by the Puritans of 1648 and by Cromwell remained so vivid that neither the carelessness of the early reign of Charles II. nor the unscrupulousness of Danby during the later years of that reign had aroused any effective protest. In America the weakness of Massachusetts and New England resulting from the efforts put forth during King Philip's war determined the home government to improve this opportunity to coerce the independent colonists. Edward Randolph came to Boston to learn how this coercion might be effected, and from 1676 to the close of the century he was a thorn in the flesh of Massachusetts. Largely because of his influence and that of his friend William Blathwayt the Bay Colony was kept in a broil with New Hampshire, was obliged to buy out the claims of the Gorges heirs to the province of Maine, lost the charter under which she had chosen her own governors, and was reduced to what she considered the low estate of a royal province. The administrations of Joseph Dudley and of Sir Edmund Andros are among the bitterest periods of Massachusetts history.

The revolution of 1689 and the reign of William and Mary did not restore the balance in New England. It brought a change from the Andros government, but neither the religious nor the political authority of the Puritan returned to its former high position. The promises which had been read into the "Declaration" of William when he invaded England were regarded by the colonists as unfulfilled. The charge of ill faith to his Massachusetts supporters was urged continuously, and seemed justified when Rhode Island and Connecticut, but not Massachusetts, were allowed to resume their old frames of government. Pride in the European victories of the British king did not remove nor make adequate compensation for the failure of Increase Mather, the colonial agent at London, to secure a restoration of the old charter lost in 1684, and the war at home, continued from the Andros régime, and waged against the combined French and Indian adversaries, was a grievous burden to the exhausted Americans. The beginning of Mather's ten years was certainly a period of woe to the Puritan at Boston, nor had the atmosphere cleared at the end of that decade. The king had lost many of his prerogatives in England by virtue of the revolution against the Stuarts. The English government and its gubernatorial representative in Massachusetts had apparently gained new prerogatives in America as a result of the same uprising. A centralized government with Frontenac at its head had been a success in Canada, but Massachusetts wished no Frontenac at Boston.

With the invasion of the military powers belonging to Connecticut and Rhode Island under their restored charters the Massachusetts Puritans had no sympathy. Had it been a governor of their own choice who took command of the troops from the more southern colonies they might have acquiesced, but when royal appointees like Fletcher, of New York, and Sir William Phips, in obedience to English directions, thus interfered, it was another evidence of decreasing colonial importance. Little wonder that Mather should be discouraged, for he could not see the end which this policy must bring.

From the Puritan viewpoint the religious outlook was little brighter. The removal of Increase Mather from the presidency of Harvard College in 1701 has been said to mark the end of Biblical rule in New England. Not that religion or the Bible had no further influence, but New England history was no longer recorded as an illustration of the fulfilment of Biblical prophecy. Such were the conditions when the following narrative was written. The general history of the war of 1688–1698 can best be followed in Parkman's *Count Frontenac and New France under Louis XIV.* or in Shea's edition of Charlevoix.

Cotton Mather was the most learned writer in colonial America. His *Magnalia* or *Ecclesiastical History of New England* (into which the *Decennium Luctuosum* was incorporated) is the most noteworthy history written by any American previous to the revolution of 1776. For the preparation of this ambitious work no contemporary author could have had better advantage than he. Cotton Mather's father and grandfather had not only lived during the period covered by this history, but they had lived at the centre of New England's political and religious activity, leading figures in the Puritan theocracy, and had been men of sufficient ability to realize the importance of the changes through which the colonies were passing. Of even greater importance for the years between the loss by Massachusetts of her old charter in 1684 and the grant of the new in 1691 was the experience of Increase Mather as special agent of the colony in England. These years gave him and his son a knowledge of men and conditions abroad supple-

menting the father's earlier experience of men and events in
New England. Both Richard and Increase Mather were pro-
lific writers for their time and their store of knowledge was
thereby continued. The nine publications credited to the
former and the more than one hundred and thirty distinct
contributions of the latter show the literary influence and in-
heritance which came to the yet more industrious grandson.
Thus the experience and writings of his immediate ancestors,
among whom John Cotton must also be reckoned, united with
the testimony of their fellows and the wide correspondence
of Mather himself in furnishing a rich field upon which our
author could draw for his material. It was a field somewhat
comparable to the archives in Europe and America which
Parkman covered two centuries later in his history of the
French side of the conflict.

Cotton Mather was born February 12, 1662/3, and was
graduated from Harvard College in 1678. He spent his youth
among the incidents related in the preceding pages of this
volume and of which his father made careful record in his
Brief History. From 1684 to 1728 he was minister of the
Second (Old North) Church in Boston. Eager to do good, but
also eager for prominence and distinction, he published more
than four hundred books and pamphlets, marked by piety and
learning, but also by pedantry, vanity, and great defects of
judgment. Several of them were historical in intention. The
Decennium Luctuosum was first published at Boston in 1699.
This edition has now become excessively rare. The text here
printed is that of the nearly unique copy in the Boston Public
Library. A sermon, *Observable Things : The History of Ten
Years Rolled away under the great Calamities of a War with Indian Salvages, Repeated and Improved in a Sermon at Boston-
Lecture, 27 d. 7 m.* [*i. e.*, September 27] 1698, is appended in
the original volume, but is no necessary part of the narrative.

A few years later, Mather incorporated the *Decennium*

Luctuosum, as an appendix or seventh chapter to book VII., in
his chief historical work, the famous *Magnalia Christi Ameri-
cana.* That strange mosaic, so valuable for New England history but so disorderly and inaccurate, was in good part made
up out of pieces already printed—and insufficiently revised.
Its first edition was published in London in 1702. There are
modern editions of 1820 and 1853. The spirit in which the
"bulky thing," as the author calls the entire work, was written
may be fairly judged from the following quotations. The twelfth
of January, 1698, writes Mather in his private records, "I set
apart . . . for the exercise of a secret fast before the Lord,"
in order to obtain "the direction of Heaven about my Church
History." So soon as the author had seen the completed volume in print a second day was set apart "for solemn thanksgiving unto God for his watchful and gracious Providence
over that work and for the harvest of so many prayers and
cares and tears and resignations as I had employed upon it."

The secret of the weakness as well as of the strength of
Cotton Mather as an historian is found in these statements.
His *Magnalia* is more a series of sermons to prove the manner
in which God's peculiar care over New England had been made
manifest than a careful statement of the exact facts as they
occurred. The result is a strange and imperfect thing, showing great knowledge and industry but giving almost as much
irritation as pleasure to the reader. Among other advantages
generally conceded to Mather was that of an excellent memory,
but the critic is tempted to remark that it would have been
better if our author had not trusted his memory so absolutely
when writing his history. Much the same might be said of
his frequent use of Latin quotations and the numerous digres-
sions for illustrative purposes. Both practices show a wealth
of knowledge on the part of the author, but they assume an
equal familiarity with Latin on the part of the reader and an
equal desire to turn aside from the narrative in hand, an as-

sumption which often confuses if it does not vex the student.
Despite these criticisms of details, the *Decennium Luctuosum*
as a whole covers the last years of conflict in the seventeenth
century better than any other contemporary history, perhaps
as well as all others combined. Errors of fact and of fancy
are to be found, but the narrative is interesting, and with the
above cautions may usually be trusted.

Cotton Mather, the more distinguished son of a notable
father, was not only the most complete type of the old-fashioned
divine in New England, as Professor Barrett Wendell remarks
in his biography, but also New England's best specimen of
the late-seventeenth-century historian. His life and his historical writings show what in New England history during the
last quarter of that century most appealed to the ablest men
of the time. For this reason if for no other, the *Decennium
Luctuosum* has its proper place in this series of narratives.
The author's description of his work will form a fitting close
to this introduction.

"In the Month of *August*, I sett myself to Consider on
Some further and Special Services for the Name of my Lord
Jesus Christ. And I foresaw a very Comprehensive One to
be done, first, in Collecting and Improving the *observable Dispensations* of God, which have occurred, in the Long *War*,
which wee have had with our Indian Savages, and uttering
my Observations, in a Sermon or Two, at our Countrey-
Lecture: And, then, in composing as agreeable an History of
our *Indian War* as I can and Incorporating into it as charming
and useful entertainments for the Countrey, as I may think
upon: so, Resigning myself up to the Conduct of the Spirit
of Grace, I sett about the Service thus before mee; hoping
within a few weeks time, in the midst of my other undertak-
ings, to dispatch it, for the glory of my Heavenly Lord.

"The work, being accomplished, I putt upon it, the Title
of *Decennium Luctuosum*. It is filled with a great Variety of

Things contrived as well as I can together, for the Glory of my Lord Jesus Christ, and the welfare of the people throughout the Land.

"O my God, I exceedingly give Thanks to thy Name, for the Help thou hast given mee, in Dispatching this work."

DECENNIUM LUCTUOSUM, BY
COTTON MATHER, 1699

Decennium Luctuosum: An History of Remarkable Occurrences in the Long War, which New-England hath had with the Indian Salvages, from the year 1688, to the year 1698, faithfully Composed and Improved.
Infandum, Jubes Renovare Dolorem.
Boston in New England. Printed by B. Green, and J. Allen, for Samuel Phillips, at the Brick Shop near the Old-Meeting-House, 1699.[1]

To the People of New England.

Sirs,

You are Welcome unto the History of a Tedious war, and unto a Period of that War so far in prospect, as to render its History Seasonable.

Every Reasonable man will readily allow, that it is a duty to God, and a Service to the World, for to preserve the Memory of such matters, as have been the more Memorable Occurrences in the War, that has for Ten Years together been multiplying Changes and Sorrows upon us. And the Author, in whose Historical Writings the most Inquisitive Envy has never to this hour detected so much as one Voluntary and Material Mistake, or one farthing paid unto the Readers in the Coin of Candia,[2] has now chosen to preserve the Memory of these matters while they are Fresh and New, and one hath not Fifty years, which is the Channel of the River of Oblivion, to pass over unto them. This Expedition is used in the publication of our *Decennium Luctuosum*, in hope that if any mistake worth Noting do appear in these Writings, it may

---

[1] Title-page of the original.   [2] Counterfeit coin.

Like, and perhaps With, a Second Edition, be Corrected and Amended.

He Expects no Thanks for his Essayes to do Good, in this way or any other, unto any part of his Country, to whom he would gladly devote all his Talents, if he were a Thousand Times better Talented than he is; and though the most ungrateful Treats Imaginable (which are too well known by the name of Country-pay) should be given him, he would still be of that Opinion, *Recte fecisse Merces est*, If a man may Do Good, it is enough.

All the Favour he desires of you is, That you would not Enquire after him; or ask, who he is? but that as he is at best but an Obscure Person, he may continue in yet more Obscurity: which will be a greater pleasure to him than to be placed among the Great men of Achaia.[1]

For indeed, He hath often thought on a passage written by Holy Mr. Row[2] to his Excellent Son, *I pray that God would make use of my self and you in such a way, as that God only may be seen and we not be taken notice of at all; that He may have the Glory, and we may not be seen.*

Could he have invited his Excellency unto such a glorious Table as that in a certain Cabinet at Florence, which is furnished with Birds and flowers, all consisting of Neatly polished Jewels inlaid into it; a work Fifteen years in making, and worth an Hundred Thousand crowns: or could he have written a Book worthy to be laid up in the Cabinet of Darius: the Author might have been under a Temptation to have had his Name Engraved upon his Work. But a little Boiled Indian Corn in a Tray, is as much as our Best History of an Indian War, composed perhaps in fewer Dayes than there were Years in the War, may presume to be compar'd unto. And since our History will not afford such a Diversion unto His Excellency, under the Indispositions of His Health, as those of Livy and Curtius did unto the Princes that Recovered their lost Health by Reading them; nor can any passage here be so

---

[1] Such professions of aversion to notoriety are frequent with Mather. The emptiness of the present elaborate expression of this fine sentiment is manifest from the fact that the sermon *Observable Things*, which every one in Boston knew to be by Cotton Mather, since it had been publicly delivered September 27, 1698, is included as a part of the volume. See the Introduction, p. 175 above.

[2] John Row (1525?-1580), the Scottish reformer.

happy, as that which cured Laurentius Medices [1] of a Malady
by having it read unto him: it will require no more than a
Nameless Writer to Assure that Great Person on this Occasion,
That all the good People of New-England make their Fervent
Vows unto the Almighty, For His Excellencies Prosperity,
and the Welfare of his Excellent Lady, and of his Noble and
Hopeful Offspring.

And the naming of the Author, is as little Necessary to
Qualify him, that he may pay publick Acknowledgments unto
the Honourable the Lieutenant Governour; not only for His
Cares about the Publick, while it was Tempestuated with the
Indian War, which now makes an History; but chiefly for his
more than ordinary Tenderness of that Society, which has
been the very *Decus ac Tutamen* [2] of New-England. The
Nameless Writer of this History may Report, that with a
Greater Expence than that of the First-Founder, this Honourable Person proves that he Loves our Nation, by Building us
another Edifice for the Supply of all our Synagogues, and
Stoughton-Hall outshines Harvard-Colledge: and he Speaks
Kinder Language, as well as Better Latin, than that eminent
States-man in Flanders, whose Answer to a Petition for the
priviledges of an University there to be restored, was, *non
curamus vostros privilegios*. [3] This Report may be given without being obliged for to confess any other Name than this,
which he readily Confesses; One that was once a Member of
Harvard-Colledge.

I pray, Sirs, Ask no further; Let this Writing be, like that
on the Wall to Belshazzar, where the Hand only was to be
seen, and not who'se it was. The History is compiled with
Incontestable Veracity; and since there is no Ingenuity in it,
but less than what many Pens in the Land might Command,
he knows not why his Writing Anonymously may not Shelter
him from the Inconveniencies of having any Notice, one way
or other, taken of him. Though among his other small Furniture, he hath not left himself unfurnished with skill in the

---

[1] Lorenzo de' Medici. The governor here alluded to was Lord Bellomont,
the lieutenant-governor William Stoughton, who was in actual charge of the government until Bellomont's arrival.

[2] "Glory and protection."

[3] He meant to say, "We do not care for your privileges," but *curamus* is
not the proper word.

Spanish Language, yet he never could bring himself to the Belief of the Spanish Proverb, *Quien no parece, perece; i. e.* He that appears not, perishes; He that Shows not himself to the world is undone. At Milain there is an Academy of Sensible Persons, called The Nascosti, or, Hidden men; At Venice there is one of such persons called, The Incogniti;[1] and at Parma there is one of them, called, The Innominati.[2] If there were nothing else Disagreeable in them, the Author of this History would be glad of an Admission into such an Academy.

The History is indeed of no very Fine Thread; and the Readers, who every where Fish for nothing but Carps, and who Love, like Augustus, to Tax all the World may find Fault enough with it. Nevertheless, while the Fault of an Untruth can't be found in it, the Author pretends that the famous History of the Trojan War it self comes behind our little History of the Indian War; For the best Antiquaries have now confuted Homer; the Walls of Troy were, it seems, all made of Poets Paper; and the Siege of the Town, with the Tragedies of the Wooden Horse, were all but a piece of Poetry.

And if a War between Us and an Handful of Indians do appear no more than a *Batrachomyomachie*[3] to the World abroad, yet unto us at home it hath been considerable enough to make an History. Nor is the Author afraid of promising, that of all the Thirty Articles which make up this History, there shall not be One without something in it that may by our selves be justly thought Considerable.

Should any Petit Monsieur complain, (as the Captain that found not himself in the Tapestry Hangings, which exhibited the story of the Spanish Invasion in 1588) that he don't find himself mentioned in this History, the Author has this Apology. He has done as well and as much as he could, that whatever was worthy of a mention, might have it; and if this Collection of Matters be not compleat, yet he supposes it may be more compleat than any one else hath made; and now he hath done, he hath not pull'd up the Ladder after him; others may go on as they please with a compleater Composure.

If the Author had taken Delight, in this History, and at all Times, to Celebrate the Merits of such as have Deserved well

---

[1] The unknown.   [2] The nameless.
[3] " Battle of Frogs and Mice," a poem attributed to Homer.

of his Country, (which he has here done, it may be, for some that never could afford him a good word!) Especially, if he do Erect Statues for Dead Worthies, when there is no Room Left for Flattery, (for who will bestow paint upon a Dead Face!) And if he do all this with all possible concern, to avoid casting Aspersions upon others: Why should any betray such Ill Nature as to be angry at it? My Good Country, forgive him this Injury!

Huic Uni forsan poteram Succumbere culpæ.[1]

But whatever this History be, it aims at the Doing of Good, as well as the Telling of Truth; and if its Aim shall be attained, That will be a sufficient Reward for all the Trouble of Writing it. When he Desires any more, he'll give you his Name; in the mean Time, as a far greater man once was called, Ludovicus Nihili, which you may make Lewis of Nothingham; so the Author will count himself not a little favoured, if he may pass for one of no more Account than a No-body; which would certainly make a very Blameless person of him.

However, that the History may not altogether want a Subscription, the Author, finding it a Custome among the Christian Writers of the Orient, when they have written a Treatise, to Subscribe it after this manner: *Scriptum per Servum vilem pauperem, omnibus Justitiis privatum, peccatorem magis quam omnis Caro*; Or, *Scripsit hoc pauper N. N.* Or, *Est Scriptura servi pauperis, et qui Benevolentia Dei indiget, et miserationibus*;[2] he will accordingly Subscribe himself, The Chief of Sinners. Nevertheless, he will humbly Lay claim to the Words used by the Nameless Author of a Treatise Entituled, *The Faithful Steward*; "Tho' I am worse than they speak of me, who cast Disgrace upon me, and I can Espy Ten Faults in my self, where they can discern One; yet I can, thro' Grace, Appeal to Thee, O Lord, with some Comfort, that I am Displeased with my self for my Sins, and would fain please Thee in all Things, at all Times, in all places, and in every Condition."

[1] "Perhaps I may have incurred this one fault."
[2] "Written by a poor mean slave lacking all righteousness, and a greater sinner than all other flesh," or, "Written by poor N. N.," or, "Written by a poor slave who needs the pity and loving kindness of God."

DECENNIUM LUCTUOSUM: OR, THE REMARK-ABLES OF A LONG WAR WITH INDIAN SALVAGES

Introduction.

TWENTY THREE Years have Rolled away since the Nations of Indians within the Confines of New England, generally began a fierce War upon the English Inhabitants of that Country. The Flame of War then Raged thro' a great part of the Country, whereby many whole Towns were Laid in Ashes, and many Lives were Sacrificed. But in little more than one years Time, the United Colonies of Plymouth, Massachusetts, and Connecticut, with their United Endeavours, bravely Conquered the Salvages. The Evident Hand of Heaven appearing on the Side of a people whose Hope and Help was alone in the Almighty Lord of Hosts, Extinguished whole Nations of the Salvages at such a rate, that there can hardly any of them now be found under any Distinction upon the face of the Earth. Onely the Fate of our Northern and Eastern Regions in that War was very different from that of the rest. The Desolations of the War had overwhelmed all the Settlements to the North-East of Wells.[1] And when the Time arrived, that all hands were weary of the War, a sort of a Peace was patched up, which Left a Body of Indians, not only with Horrible Murders Unrevenged, but also in the possession of no little part of the Countrey, with circumstances which the English might think not very Honourable. Upon this Peace the English returned unto their Plantations; their Number increased; they Stock'd their Farms, and Sow'd their Fields; they found the Air as Healthful, as the Earth was Fruitful; their Lumber and their Fishery became a considerable Merchandize; continual Accessions were made unto

---

[1] In the western part of the coast of Maine.

them, until Ten or a Dozen Towns in the Province of Main, and the County of Cornwall,[1] were suddenly Started up into something of Observation.

But in the Year 1688, the Indians which dwelt after the Indian manner among them, Commenced another War upon these Plantations which hath broke them up, and strangely held us in play for Ten Years together. In these Ten Years there hath been a variety of Remarkable Occurrences; and because I have supposed that a Relation of those Occurrences may be Acceptable and Profitable to some of my Country men, I shall now with all Faithfulness Endeavour it. With all Faithfulness, I say; because tho' there should happen any Circumstantial Mistake in our Story, (for 'tis a rare thing for any Two men concern'd in the same Action, to give the Story of it without some Circumstantial Difference) yet even this also I shall be willing to Retract and Correct, if there be found any just occasion: But for any one Material Error in the whole Composure, I challenge the most Sagacious Malice upon Earth to detect it, while matters are yet so fresh as to allow the Detection of it. I disdain to make the Apology once made by the Roman Historian, *Nemo Historicus non aliquid mentitus, et habiturus sum mendaciorum Comites, quos Historiæ et eloquentiæ miramur Authores.*[2] No, I will write with an Irreproachable and Incontestable Veracity; and I will write not one Thing but what I am furnished with so good Authority for, that any Reasonable man, who will please to Examine it, shall say, I do well to insert it as I do: And I will hope that my reader hath not been Studying of Godefridus de Valle's book, *De arte nihil Credendi*; About The Art of Believing Nothing.[3] Wherefore having at the very Beginning thus given such a Knock upon thy Head, O Malice, that thou canst never with Reason Hiss at our History, we will proceed unto the several Articles of it.

[1] The region from the Kennebec to the St. Croix (eastern Maine), included in the patent of Charles II. to the Duke of York, his brother, had been erected by the latter into the county of Cornwall.

[2] "There is no historian without some falsehood and I shall have for companions in mendacity writers whom all admire as models of historic truth and eloquence."

[3] Geoffroi Vallée, sieur de la Planchette, sceptical writer, executed at Paris in 1574.

Article I.

The Occasion and Beginning of the War.

If Diodorus Siculus had never given it as a great Rule of History, *Historiæ primum Studium, primariaq' consideratio esse videtur, insoliti gravisq' Casus principio causas investigare,*[1] Yet my Reader would have expected that I should Begin the History of our War, with an History of the Occurrences and Occasions which did Begin the War. Now, Reader, I am at the very first fallen upon a Difficult Point; and I am in danger of pulling a War upon my self, by Endeavouring of thy Satisfaction. In Truth, I had rather be called a Coward, than undertake my self to Determine the Truth in this matter; but having Armed my self with some good Authority for it, I will Transcribe Two or Three Reports of the matter, now in my Hands, and Leave it unto thy own Determination.

One Account I have now lying by me, Written by a Gentleman of Dover,[2] in these Terms.

The Eastern Indians, and especially those of Saco and Ammonoscoggin, pretend many Reasons for the late Quarrel against the English, which began this long and bloody War.

1. Because the English refused to pay that yearly Tribute of Corn, agreed upon in the Articles of Peace formerly concluded with them by the English Commissioners.

2. Because they were Invaded in their Fishery, at Saco River, by certain Gentlemen, who stop'd the Fish from coming up the River with their Nets and Sains. This they were greatly Affronted at, saying, They thought (though the English had got away their Lands as they had, yet) the Fishery of the Rivers had been a priviledge Reserved Entire unto themselves.

3. Because they were Abused by the English, in Suffering, if not Turning, their Cattel over to a certain Island to destroy their Corn.

4. But the Fourth and Main provocation was, The Granting or Pattenting of their Lands to some English; at which they were greatly

---

[1] "The first object and primary consideration of history seems to be the investigation of the original causes of great and unusual happenings."

[2] Rev. John Pike.

Enraged, threatning the Surveyor to knock him on the Head if he came to lay out any Lands there.

5. To these may be added the Common Abuses in Trading, *viz.* Drunkenness, Cheating, etc. which such as Trade much with them are seldom Innocent of.

Doubtless these Indian Allegations may be answered with many English Vindications. But I shall at present Intermeddle no further than to offer another Account, which also I have in my Hands, written by a Gentleman of Casco.[1] It runs in such terms as these.

Many were the Outrages and Insultings of the Indians upon the English, while Sir E. A.[2] was Governour. At North-Yarmouth, and other places at the Eastward, the Indians killed sundry Cattel, came into Houses, and threatned to knock the people on the Head; and at several Times gave out Reports that they would make a War upon the English, and that they were animated to do so by the French. The Indians behaving themselves so insultingly, gave just occasion of great suspicion. In order for the finding out the Truth, and to Endeavour the preventing of a War, Capt. Blackman,[3] Justice of Peace, with some of the Neighbourhood of Saco River, Seized several Indians that had been bloody murderous Rogues in the first Indian War, being the chief Ring-Leaders, and most capable to do mischief. The said Capt. Blackman Seized to the Number of between Sixteen and Twenty, in order for their Examination, and to bring in the rest to a Treaty. The said Blackman soon sent the said Indians with a Good Guard to Falmouth[4] in Casco-bay, there to be Secured, until orders could come from Boston concerning them. And in the mean Time the said Indians were well provided with Provisions and Suitable Necessaries. The rest of the Indians Robb'd the English, and took some English Prisoners: Whereupon Post was sent to Boston. Sir Edmond Andross being at New-York, the Gentlemen of Boston sent to Falmouth some Souldiers for the Defence of the Country, and also the Worshipful Mr. Stoughton,[5] with others, to Treat with the Indians in order for the Settling of a Peace, and getting in of our English Captives. As soon as the said Gentlemen arrived to the East-ward, they sent away one of the Indian Prisoners to the rest of the Indians, to Summon them to bring

[1] Rev. Shubael Dummer, of York, Maine.
[2] Sir Edmund Andros. North Yarmouth is in Maine.
[3] Benjamin Blackman.   [4] Near and in Portland, Maine.
[5] William Stoughton, lieutenant-governor of Massachusetts.

in the English they had taken; Also that their Sachims should come
in to treat with the English, in order that a Just Satisfaction should
be made on both sides.   The Gentlemen waited the Return of the
Indian Messenger; and when he Returned he brought Answer, That
they would meet our English at a place called Macquoit,[1] and there
they would bring in the English Captives, and Treat with the English.
And although the place appointed by the Indians for the Meeting
was some Leagues distant from Falmouth, yet our English Gentlemen
did condescend to it, in hope of getting in our Captives, and putting
a stop to further Trouble.   They Dispatch'd away to the place, and
carried the Indian Prisoners with them, and staid at the place appointed, expecting the coming of the Indians that had promised a
Meeting.   But they, like false perfidious Rogues, did not appear.
Without doubt they had been counselled what to do by the French
and their Abettors, as the Indians did declare afterwards; and that
they were near the place, and saw our English that were to Treat
with them, but would not shew themselves; but did Endeavour to
take an Opportunity to Destroy our English that were to Treat [with]
them.   Such was their Treachery!   Our Gentlemen staid days to
wait their coming; but seeing they did not appear at the place appointed, they Returned to Falmouth, and brought the Indian Prisoners, expecting that the other Indians would have sent down some
Reason why they did not appear at the place appointed, and to make
some excuse for themselves.   But instead of any compliance, they
fell upon North Yarmouth, and there kill'd several of our English.
Whereupon the Eastern parts were ordered to get into Garrisons, and
to be upon their Guard until further Orders from Sir Edmond Andros;
and that the Indian Prisoners should be sent to Boston, which was
done with great care, and not one of them hurt; and care taken daily
for provision.   But Sir E. A. Returning from New-York, set them all
at Liberty; not so much as taking care to Redeem those of our English for them, that were in their hands.   I had kept one at Falmouth
a Prisoner, to be a Guide into the Woods for our English, to find out
the Haunts of our Heathen Enemies.   But Sir E. A. sent an Express
to me, that upon my utmost peril I should set the said Indian at
Liberty, and take care that all the Arms that were taken from him,
and all the rest of those Capt. Blackman had seized, should be delivered up to them, without any Orders to Receive the like of ours
from them.

It will be readily Acknowledged, that here was enough done
to render the Indians Inexcusable for not coming in upon the

[1] In Freeport, Maine.

Proclamation, which Sir Edmond Andros, then Governour of New-England, immediately Emitted thereupon, requiring them to Surrender the Murderers now among them. A Spaniard, that was a Souldier, would say, That if we have a good Cause, the smell of Gunpowder in the Field is as sweet as the Incense at the Altar. Let the Reader judge after these things, what scent there was in the Gunpowder spent for Nine or Ten years together in our War with the Indian Salvages.

Now that while we are upon this Head, we may at once dispatch it; I will unto these two Accounts add certain passages of one more, which was published in September, 1689.

Such were the Obscure Measures taken at that Time of Day, that the Rise of this War hath been as dark as that of the River Nilus; only the Generality of Thinking People through the Country can Remember When and Where every one did foretel A War. If any Wild English (for there are such as well as of another nation) did then Begin to Provoke and Affront the Indians, yet those Indians had a fairer way to come by Right than that of Bloodshed, nothing worthy of, or calling for, any Such Revenge was done unto them. The most Injured of them all, (if there were any Such) were afterwards dismissed by the English with Favours, that were then Admirable even to Our selves; and These too, instead of Surrendring the Persons, did increase the Numbers of the Murderers. But upon the Revolution of the Government (April, 1689.) the State of the War became wholly New: and we are more arrived unto Righteousness as the Light, and Justice as the Noon day. A great Sachem of the East we then immediately Applied our selves unto, and with no small Expences to our selves, we Engaged Him to Employ his Interest for a Good Understanding between us, and the party of Indians then in Hostility against us. This was the Likely, the Only way of coming at those Wandring Salvages: But That very Sachem now treacherously of an Embassador became a Traitor, and annexed himself with his People to the Heard of our Enemies, which have since been Ravaging, Pillaging and Murdering, at a rate which we ought to count Intolerable. The Penacook Indians,[1] of whom we were Jealous, we likewise Treated with; and while we were by our Kindnesses and Courtesies Endeavouring to render them utterly Inexcusable, if ever they

---

[1] The Pennacook Indians were a part of the Abenakis, a term covering practically all the Indians from the Kennebec to the St. John Rivers. The Pennacooks occupied a region on the Merrimac River, the present region of Concord and Manchester, New Hampshire.

sought our Harm; Even Then, did Those also by some Evil Instigation, (the Devils, no doubt!) quickly Surprize a Plantation where they
had been Civilly treated a Day or Two before, and Commit at once
more Plunder and Murder than can be heard with patience.[1]

Reader, Having so placed these Three Accounts as to defend my Teeth, I think I may safely proceed with our Story.
But because Tacitus teaches us to distinguish between the meer
Occasions and the real Causes of a War, it may be some will
go a little Higher up in their Enquiries: They will Enquire
whether no body seized a parcel of Wines that were Landed
at a French Plantation to the East ward?   Whether an Order
were not obtained from the King of England, at the Instance
of the French Embassador, to Restore these Wines?   Whether
upon the Vexation of this Order, we none of us ran a New Line
for the Bounds of the Province?   Whether we did not contrive
our New Line so as to take in the Country of Monsieur St.
Casteen?   Whether Monsieur St. Casteen, flying from our
Encroachments, we did not seize upon his Arms and Goods,
and bring them away to Pemmaquid?   And Who were the We
which did these things?   And whether the Indians, who were
Extremely under the Influence of St. Casteen, that had Married a Sagamore's Daughter among them, did not from this
very Moment begin to be obstreperous?   And whether all the
Sober English in the Country did not from this very Moment
foretel a War?   But for any Answer to all these Enquiries I
will be my self a Tacitus.[2]

ARTICLE II.

The first Acts of Hostility between the Indians and the English.

When one Capt. Sargeant[3] had Seized some of the principal Indians about Saco by order of Justice Blackman, pres-

[1] From Mather's own sermon, *Souldiers Counselled and Comforted* (Boston, 1689), pp. 29–31.

[2] *I. e.,* "I will be silent." Jean Vincent de l'Abadie, baron de St. Castin, was
a Frenchman, who had established himself among the Indians, on the east side
of the Penobscot near its mouth, at the place now called Castine, Maine.   Remains of his fort can still be seen there.   Andros dispossessed him in the spring
of 1688.

[3] Peter Sargent.

ently the Indians fell to Seizing as many of the English, as
they could catch. Capt. Rowden, with many more, in one
place, and Capt. Gendal,[1] with sundry more, in another place,
particularly fell into the Hands of these desperate Man-
catchers. Rowden, with many of his Folks, never got out of
their Cruel Hands; but Gendal, with his, got a Release, one
can scarce tell, How, upon the Return of those which had been
detain'd in Boston. Hitherto there was no Spilling of Blood!
But some Time in September following, this Capt. Gendal
went up, with Soldiers and others, to a place above Casco,
called North Yarmouth, having Orders to build Stockados on
both sides the River, for Defence of the place, in case of any
Sudden Invasion. While they were at work, an English Captive came to 'em with Information, that Seventy or Eighty of
the Enemy were just coming upon 'em; and he advised 'em,
To yield quietly, that they might Save their Lives. The Soldiers that went thither from the Southward being terrifyed at
this Report, Ran with an Hasty Terror to get over the River;
but with more Hast than good speed; for they ran directly
into the Hands of the Indians. The Indians dragging along
these their Prisoners with 'em, came up towards the Casconians;
who, having but a very Little Time to Consult, yet in this
Time Resolved; First, That they would not be Siezed by the
Salvages: Next, That they would free their Friends out of the
Hands of the Salvages, if it were possible; Thirdly, That if it
were possible they would use all other Force upon the Salvages,
without coming to down right Fight. Accordingly They laid
hold on their Neighbours, whom the Salvages had Siezed, and
this with so much Dexterity that they cleared them all, Except
one or Two; whereof the whole Number was about a Dozen.
But in the Scuffle one Sturdy and Surly Indian held his prey
so fast, that one Benedict Pulcifer gave the Mastiff a Blow
with the Edge of his Broad Ax upon the Shoulder, upon which
they fell to't with a Vengeance, and Fired their Guns on both
sides, till some on both sides were Slain. These were, as one
may call them, the Scower-pit of a long War to follow. At
last, the English Victoriously chased away the Salvages, and
Returned safely unto the other side of the River. And Thus
was the Vein of New-England first opened, that afterwards

[1] Walter Gendell.

Bled for Ten years together![1] The Skirmish being over, Captain Gendal in the Evening passed over the River in a Canoo, with none but a Servant; but Landing where the Enemy lay hid in the Bushes, they were both Slain immediately. And the same Evening, one Ryal,[2] with another man, fell unawares into the Hands of the Enemy; Ryal was afterwards Ransomed by Monsieur St. Casteen, but the other man, was barbarously Butchered. Soon after this, the Enemy went Eastward unto a place call'd Merry-Meeting, (from the Concourse of divers Rivers there)[3] where several English had a Sad-Meeting with them; for they were killed several of them even in Cold Blood, after the Indians had Seized upon their Houses and their Persons. And about this Time, the Town call'd Sheepscote was entered by these Rapacious Wolves, who burnt all the Houses of the Town, save Two or Three. The People saved themselves by getting into the Fort, all but one Man, who going out of the Fort, for to Treat with 'em, was Treacherously Assassinated. Thus the place, which was counted, The Garden of the East, was infested by Serpents; and a Sword Expell'd the poor Inhabitants. Little more Spoil was done by the Salvages before Winter, Except only, that a place called Kennebunk, near Winter-harbour, they cut off Two Families, to wit, Barrows, and Bussies; but Winter coming on, the Serpents retired into their Holes. When Summer comes, Reader, look for Tornadoes enough to overset a greater Vessel, than little New-England.

ARTICLE III.

The First Expedition of the English against the Indians.

When the Keeper of the Wild Beasts, at Florence, has entertain'd the Spectators with their Encounters on the Stage,

---

[1] Other writers date this attack on North Yarmouth in July, 1688, and as Mather refers to the attack upon Sheepscot a little later as occurring on September 5 the date given here is probably too late.

[2] John Royall or Royal.

[3] Merrymeeting Bay is in the Kennebec River, where the Androscoggin flows into it, just above Bath. The Sheepscot Falls settlement was at the head of tidewater on the Sheepscot River, a few miles above Wiscasset. Winter Harbor was Saco.

he has this Device to make 'em Retire into the several Dens of their Seraglio. He has a fearful Machin of Wood, made like a Great Green Dragon, which a man within it rouls upon Wheels, and holding out a Couple of Lighted Torches at the Eyes of it, frights the fiercest Beast of them all into the Cell that belongs unto him.   Sir Edmond Andros, the Governour of New-England, that he might Express his Resolutions, to force the Wild Beasts of the East into order, in the Winter now coming on, turned upon them as Effectual a Machin as the Green Dragon of Florence; that is to say, An Army of near a Thousand men.[1]   With this Army he marched himself in Person into the Caucasæan Regions, where he built a Fort at Pemmaquid, and another Fort at Pechypscot Falls, besides the Fort at Sheepscote.   He, and his Army underwent no little Hardship, thus in the Depth of Winter to Expose themselves unto the Circumstances of a Campaign, in all the Bleak Winds and Thick Snows of that Northern Country. But it was Hop'd That Good Forts being thus Garrison'd with Stout Hearts in several Convenient places, the Indians might be kept from their usual Retreats, both for Planting and for Fishing, and lye open also to perpetual Incursions from the English, in the fittest seasons thereof: and it was Thought by the most sensible, this method would in a little while compel the Enemy to Submit unto any Terms: albeit others considering the Vast Woods of the Wilderness, and the French on the back of these Woods, fancied that this was but a project to Hedge in the Cuckow.   However, partly the Army, and partly the Winter, frighted the salvages into their Inaccessible Dens: and yet not one of the Indians was killed; but Sickness and Service kill'd it may be more of our English, than there were Indians then in Hostility against them.   The News of matters approaching towards a Revolution in England, caused the Governor to Return unto Boston in the Spring,[2] and upon his Return, there fell out several odd Events, with Rumours, whereof I have now nothing to say, but, that I love my eyes

---

[1] Andros set out in November, 1688.   Other estimates place the number of the army at 700.   His fort at Pemaquid was a mere stockade, which Phips in 1692 replaced by an extensive stone fort, still largely remaining.   Pechypscot (Pejebscot) is now Brunswick, Maine.

[2] He returned to Boston toward the end of March.

too well, to mention them.[1] Some of the Soldiers took Advantage from the Absence of the Governor to desert their Stations in the Army; and tho' this Action was by Good men generally condemned, as an Evil Action, yet their Friends began to gather together here and there in Little Bodies to protect them from the Governor, concerning whom, abundance of odd Stories then buzz'd about the Country, made 'em to imagine, that he had carried 'em out only to Sacrifice 'em. Some of the principal Gentlemen in Boston, consulting what was to be done, in this Extraordinary Juncture, They Agreed, that altho' New-England had as much to Justifie a Revolution as old, yet they would, if it were possible, extinguish all Essays in the people, towards an Insurrection; in daily hopes of Orders from England for our Safety: but that if the Country people, by any unrestrainable Violences pushed the business on so far, as to make a Revolution unavoidable, Then to prevent the Shedding of Blood by an ungoverned Mobile, some of the Gentlemen present, should appear at the Head of it, with a Declaration [2] accordingly prepared. He that Reads the Narrative of Grievances under the Male Administrations of the Government then Tyranizing, Written and Signed by the Chief Gentlemen of the Governour's Council, will not wonder at it, that a Revolution was now rendered indeed unavoidable. It was a Government whereof Ned Randolph, a Bird of their own Feather, confess'd as we find in one of his published Letters, That they were as Arbitrary as the Great Turk. And for such a Government a better Similitude cannot perhaps be thought on, than that of Mons. Souligne; 'Tis like the Condition of persons possessed with Evil Spirits, which will go an Hundred Leagues in less time than others can Ten; but at the Journeys End find themselves to be so Bruised that they never can Recover it. The Revolution (and ye Tories, a Just one) was accordingly Made on the Eighteenth of April, which their Majesties, then happily Seated on the British Throne, kindly Accepted and Approved. The Governor and

---

[1] There was a rumor that in case of an uprising in favor of William and Mary, Andros had been instructed to turn New England over to the French.

[2] This "declaration," issued in April, 1689, is generally considered to have been prepared by Cotton Mather himself and probably some time before this date. In the revolution which followed, Andros was deposed.

Magistrates of the Massachusets-Colony, which were in power Three years and Half before, (a period often observed!) did some Time after this Resume their places, and apply themselves to such Acts of Government, as Emergencies made necessary for them, Fortified with a Letter from the King to Authorize and Empower them in their Administrations. Thus they waited for further Directions from the Authority of England, and such a Settlement as would most Conduce (which were the words of the King's Letter, bearing Date Aug. 12, 1689.) to the Security and Satisfaction of the Subjects in that Colony.

ARTICLE IV.

A Flame Spreading, upon the best Endeavours to Quench it.

It was hop'd the War would now come to an Immediate End; but the Great God who Creates that Evil, had further Intentions to Chastise a Sinful People, by those who are not a People. The Government sent Capt. Greenleaf,[1] to treat with the Indians at Penacook,[2] who answered him with fair pretences and Promises of Amity. They procured an Interview, with some of the more Eastern Sagamores, who not only promised Friendship themselves, but also undertook to make our Enemies become our Friends. They sent unto the Soldiers, yet remaining at Pammaquid for to keep their Post, Engaging to them that they should not want their Pay. But all this care, was defeated by Methods of Mischiefs too deep for our present penetration. The Salvages began to Renew their Hostilities at Saco Falls, in the Beginning of April, on a Lord's day morning, some while before the Revolution. The Penacook Indians were all this while peaceably Conversant at Quochecho; and so long as that Conversation continued, the Inhabitants were very Secure of any Danger, not only from those Cut-throats, but also from their Brethren. Happy had it been for those Honest People, if their Fear had made so much Haste as my Pen has done, to call 'em Cut-throats!

---

[1] Probably Enoch Greenleaf.
[2] Pennacook was at Rumford or Concord, New Hampshire.

For the Penacookian joining with the Saconian Indians, hovered about Quochecho,[1] where one Mesandowit, a Sagamore, being that Night kindly Entertained by Major Richard Waldein, horribly betray'd his kind Host, with the Neighbours, into the hands of Murderers. Above an Hundred, some say Five Hundred of the Indians, about break of Day having Surprized the Secure and Silent English, they particularly rushed into the Garrison of the Generous Major, which was by Simon Mesandowit (for bestowing a Heathen Name upon him, we now call him so,) opened for them, and having first barbarously Murthered the Old Gentleman, who was Equivalent unto Two and Twenty, then they Murdered Two and Twenty more, and Captived Nine and Twenty of the People; burn't four or five of the best Houses, took much Plunder, and so drew off; but kill'd Mr. John Broughton in their drawing off: while Mr. John Emmerson, a worthy Preacher at Berwick, by declining to lodge at the hospitable Major's that Night, when strongly Invited, received a remarkable Deliverance. Hereupon Forces were dispatch'd for the Relief of what Remained in Quochecho; Capt. Noyes also with more Forces, visited Penacook, where though the Men escaped him, he destroy'd the Corn of our New Enemies: but the Sculking Enemies at the same Time Slew several Persons at an out-farm on the North-side of Merrimack-River. A party of men were soon after sent out of Piscataqua, under the Command of Capt. Wincal, who went up to Winnopisseag ponds,[2] (upon Advice of one John Church, who ran from them, that the Indians were there) where they kill'd One or Two of the Monsters they Hunted for, and cut down their Corn. Four young men of Saco, desirous to join with them, went into the woods to Seek their Horses, and Found their Deaths by an Ambush of Indians. Twenty-four Armed men, going forth from Saco falls, to bury the Slain, had a brisk Encounter with the Indians, whom they pursued into a Vast Swamp, until a Greater Number of Indians pouring in upon them, obliged 'em, with the loss of about Five or Six more, to retire from any further Action.

[1] Dover, New Hampshire. Waldein is a misprint for Waldern (Waldron). Major Richard Waldron had for years been the principal man of the Cocheco district, and had been chief justice of New Hampshire and acting president.

[2] John Wincol or Winkle of Portsmouth; Lake Winnepiseogee.

But before the Dogs-dayes were out, there was more Bleeding still, that prov'd fatal to us. On Aug. 2 One Starky, going early in the Morning from the Fort at Pemmaquid unto New Harbour, fell into the Hands of the Indians, who to obtain his own Liberty informed Them, That the Fort had at that Instant but Few men in it: and that one Mr. Giles, with Fourteen men, was gone up to his Farm, and the rest Scattered abroad about their Occasions. The Indians hereupon divided their Army; Part going up to the Falls, kill'd Mr. Giles,[1] and others; Part, upon the Advantage of the Tide, Snapt the rest, before they could Recover the Fort. From a Rock near the Fort, which inconveniently overlook'd it, the Assailants now overlook'd it, as over Lincoln, and grievously galled the Defendants. Capt. Weems had but few with him, that were able to Fight; and his own face was in the Fight, by an Accident, horribly Scorched with Gun Powder. Wherefore, the day following, they Surrendered the Fort, upon Capitulations for Life and Liberty; which yet the Indians broke, by Butchering and Captiving many of them. Capt. Skynner and Capt. Farnham, repairing to the Fort, from an Island about half a Mile distant from it, were both Slain as they Landed on the Rocks; and Mr. Patishal,[2] as he lay with his Sloop in the Barbican, was also taken and Slain. This, together with more Spoil done by the Indians on the English, at Sheepscote, and Kennebeck, and other places East-ward, caused the inhabitants to draw off unto Falmouth as fast as they could: and, Well if they could have made Good their Standing there!

Mantissa.

The Foregoing Article of our Tragedies hath Related the Taking of Quochecho! The Condition of Two persons, under and after the Fate of Quochecho, may have in it, an Entertain-

---

[1] Thomas Gyles, chief justice of the county of Cornwall under the government of the Duke of York. His son John, carried away captive at this time, and afterward for many years Indian interpreter to the Massachusetts government, was author of one of the most famous narratives of Indian captivity, *Memoirs of the Odd Adventures*, etc. (Boston, 1736).

[2] Richard Pattishall, a sea-captain of Boston, who figures in the *Journal of Jasper Danckaerts*, in this series.

ment Acceptable for some sort of Readers. It shall be in this place Reported, from the Communications of Mr. John Pike, the worthy Minister of Dover, to whom I have been beholden, for Communicating to me many other passages also, which occur in this our History.

I. Mrs. Elizabeth Heard, a Widow of a Good Estate, a Mother of many Children, and a Daughter of Mr. Hull, a Reverend Minister formerly Living at Piscataqua, now lived at Quochecho. Happening to be at Portsmouth, on the Day before Quochecho was cut off, She Returned thither in the Night, with one Daughter and Three Sons, all masters of Families. When they came near Quochecho, they were astonished, with a prodigious Noise of Indians, Howling, Shooting, Shouting, and Roaring, according to their manner in making an Assault. Their Distress for their Families carried them still further up the River, till they Secretly and Silently passed by some Numbers of the Raging Salvages. They Landed about an Hundred Rods from Major Waldern's Garrison; and running up the Hill, they saw many Lights in the Windows of the Garrison, which they concluded the English within had set up, for the Direction of those who might seek Refuge there. Coming to the Gate, they desired entrance; which not being readily granted, they called Earnestly, and bounced, and knocked, and cried out of their unkindness within, that they would not open to them in this Extremity. No Answer being yet made, they began to doubt, whether all was well; and one of the young men then climbing up the wall, saw a horrible Tawny in the Entry, with a Gun in his Hand. A grievous Consternation Seiz'd now upon them; and Mrs. Heard sitting down without the Gate, through Despair and Faintness, unable to Stir any further, charg'd her Children to Shift for themselves, for She must unavoidably There End her Days. They finding it impossible to carry her with them, with heavy hearts forsook her; but then coming better to herself, she fled and hid among the Barberry-bushes in the Garden: and then hastning from thence, because the Day-Light advanced, She sheltered herself (though seen by Two of the Indians) in a Thicket of other Bushes, about Thirty Rods from the House. Here she had not been long, before an Indian came towards her, with a Pistol in his Hand: the Fellow came up to her, and Stared her in the Face, but said nothing to her, nor she to him. He went a little way back, and came again, and Stared upon her as before, but said nothing; whereupon she asked him, what he would have? He still said nothing, but went away to the House Co-hooping, and Returned unto her no more. Being thus unaccountably preserved, She made several Essays to pass the River; but found herself unable to do it; and finding all places on that side the River fill'd with Blood, and Fire, and hideous Outcries, thereupon she Return'd to her old bush, and there poured out her ardent Prayers to God for help in this Distress. She continued in the Bush, until the Garrison was Burnt, and the Enemy was gone; and then she Stole along by the River side, until she came to a Boom, where she passed over. Many sad Effects of Cruelty she Saw left by the Indians in her way; until arriving at Captain Gerish's Garrison, she there found a Refuge from the Storm; and here she soon had the Satisfaction to understand, that her own Garrison, though one of the first that was assaulted, had been bravely Defended and maintained against the Adversary. This Gentlewoman's Garrison was the most Extream Frontier of the Province, and more Obnoxious than any other, and more uncapable of Relief; nevertheless, by her presence and courage, it held out all the War, even for Ten Years together; and the Persons in it have Enjoy'd very Eminent preservations. The Garrison had been deserted, if She had accepted Offers that were made her by her Friends, of Living in more safety at Portsmouth; which would have been a Damage to the Town and Land: but by her Encouragement this Post was thus kept: and She is yet Living in much Esteem among her Neighbours.[1]

II. Mrs. Sarah Gerish, Daughter to Captain John Gerish of Quochecho, a very Beautiful and Ingenious Damsel, about Seven years of Age, lodg'd at the Garrison of her affectionate Grandfather, Major Waldern, when the Indians brought an horrible Destruction upon it. She was always very Fearful of the Indians; but what Fear may we think now Surprised her, when they fiercely bid her go into such a Chamber and call the People out? Finding only a little Child in the Cham-

---

[1] Her daughter was recovered from captivity when, in September, 1690, Major Benjamin Church captured the Indian fort at Lewiston Falls.

ber, she got into the Bed unto the Child, and hid herself in the Cloaths as well as she could. The Fell-Salvages quickly pull'd her out, and made her Dress for a March, but led her away with no more than one Stockin upon her, a terrible March through the Thick Woods, and a thousand other Miseries, till they came to the Norway-Plains. From thence they made her go to the end of Winnopisseag Lake, and from thence to the Eastward, through horrid Swamps, where sometimes they must Scramble over huge Trees fallen by Storm or Age for a vast way together, and sometimes they must Climb up long, steep, tiresome, and almost Inaccessible Mountains. Her First Master was one Sebundowit, a Dull sort of a Fellow, and not such a Devil as many of 'em were; but he Sold her, to a Fellow that was a more harsh, and mad, sort of a Dragon, and he carried her away to Canada.

A long and a sad Journey she had of it, thro' the midst of an hideous Desart, in the midst of a dreadful Winter: And who can enumerate the Frights, that she endured, before the End of her Journey? Once her Master commanded her to loosen some of her upper-Garments, and stand against a Tree while he charged his Gun; whereas the poor Child Shrieked out, He's going to kill me! God knows what he was going to do; but the Villain having charged his Gun, he call'd her from the Tree, and forbore doing her any Damage. Another time, her Master ordered her to run along the Shore with some Indian Girls, while he paddled up the River in his canoo. As they were upon a precipice, a Tawny Wench violently push'd her Headlong into the River: but it so fell out, that in that very place, the Bushes hung over the Water; so that getting Hold of them she Recovered herself. The Indians ask'd her How she became so wet? but she durst not say, how, through Dread of the young Indians, who were always very Abusive to her, when they had her alone. Moreover, once being spent with Travelling all Day, and lying down Spent and Wet at Night, she fell into so profound a Sleep, that in the Morning she waked not. The Barbarous Indians left her Asleep, and covered with Snow; but at length waking, what Agonies may you imagine she was in, to find herself left a prey for Bears and Wolves, and without any Sustenance, in an howling Wilderness many Scores of Leagues from any Plantation? She Ran crying after them; and Providence having ordered a Snow to fall, by means whereof, she Track'd them until she overtook them. Now the young Indians began to Terrifie her, with daily Intimations, that she was quickly to be Roasted unto Death; and one Evening much Fuel was prepared, between Two Logs, which they told her, was for her. A mighty fire being made, her Master call'd her to him, and told her, that she should presently be Burnt alive. At first, she stood Amazed; afterwards she burst into Tears; and then she hung about the Tygre, and begg'd of him, with an inexpressible Anguish, that he would Save her from the Fire. Hereupon the Monster so Relented, as to tell her, That if she would be a Good Girl she should not be Burnt.

At last, they arrived at Canada, and she was carried unto the Lord Intendant's House, where many Persons of quality took much notice of her. It was a Week after this that she remained in the Indian Hands, before the price of her Ransom could be agreed on. But then the Lady Intendant sent her to the Nunnery, where she was comfortably provided for; and it was the Design, as was said, for to have brought her up in the Romish Religion, and then have Married her unto the Son of the Lord Intendant.[1] She was kindly used there, until Sir William Phips, lying before Quebeck, did, upon Exchange of Prisoners, obtain her Liberty. After Sixteen Months Captivity, she was Restored unto her Friends; who had the Consolation of having this their Desireable Daughter again with them, Returned from the Dead; But coming to be Sixteen years old, in the Month of July 1697, Death by a Malignant Feavor, more Irrecoverably took her from them.

Article V.

New Forces Rais'd, and New Actions done.

On Aug. 28, 1689, Major Swayn, with Seven or Eight Companies, raised by the Massachuset-Colony, marched Eastward;

---

[1] It was Madame de Champigny, wife of the intendant of Quebec, who placed Sarah in the Hôtel Dieu. Phips's expedition against Quebec in August, 1690, the history of which can be followed in Parkman's *Frontenac*, had little other result than this exchange of prisoners.

and soon after, Major Church,[1] with a party of English and
Christian-Indians, raised in Plymouth-Colony, follow'd them.
While these were on their March, the Indians, that lay Sculk-
ing after the Indian-fashion in the Thick Woods, took notice
how many men belong'd unto Lieut. Huckin's Garrison:[2]
And seeing 'em all go out unto their daily work, nimbly ran
so between them and the Garrison, as to kill 'em all (about
Eighteen) but one, who being accidentally gone over the
River, escaped them. They then Attacqued the Garrison, in
which there now were only Two Boys, (and one of them Lame)
with some Women and Children; but these Two Boys very
Manfully held 'em in play a Considerable while, and wounded
several of them, and kept 'em off, till the assailants had found
a way to set the House on a Light Fire over their Heads.
They then urging 'em to Surrender, for the sake of the Goods,
the Boys (Brave Boys, truly!) would not, until they had
Solemnly promised 'em their Lives: But the perfidious
Wretches broke their promise, for they persently kill'd Three
or Four of the Children: However one of these Minutius's's,
the Day after, very happily got out of their Clutches. It was
by a particular Accident, that these Indians were delivered
from falling into the Hands of Captain Garner, who pursued
'em Vigourously. But while the Forces now gone into the
East, were settling of Garrisons in convenient places, a huge
Body of Indians fell upon Casco,[3] where one of their first
Exploits was their killing of Capt. Bracket. Nevertheless,
Captain Hall, (a valiant Souldier in the Former War, and a
valiant Commander in This) with his Vigorous Lieutenant
Dawes, just then arriving with his Company, the English
hotly Engaged them for several Hours; and after a deal of
true English Valour discovered in this Engagement, and the
loss of Ten or a Dozen men, the Indians Ran for it, with What
loss on their part, we do not know: That with some we Do.
Presently after this, Major Swayn passing through Extream

---

[1] Major Jeremiah Swain and Major Benjamin Church. The latter's account
of his expedition may be found in his *Entertaining Passages*, pp. 55-65.

[2] In present Durham, New Hampshire.

[3] Near Falmouth and the present Portland. Captain Anthony Brackett
of Back Cove; Captain Nathaniel Hall of Yarmouth; Lieutenant Sylvanus Davis
of Falmouth. Blue Point was in Scarborough.

Difficulties to get at it, gave some Relief to a Garrison at Blue point, which was beset by the Indians, who still Fled into their Inaccessible Swamps, when our Bullets began to be Hail'd upon them. It was judg'd, That here one or Two Opportunities of bringing the War unto an End were strangely mist, and lost: But where the mismanagement lay I cannot Remember; nor what were the *Faux Pas* of the Actors. Our Honest Major will clear himself, who Returning then to his Head Quarters at Berwick, sent abroad Scouts, to Learn, if it were possible, where they might have the best Game at the *Chasse a La Bete noire*,[1] then to be followed. Capt. Wiswel[2] having with him a party of Indian Auxiliaries, they were sent out, under the Conduct of Lieut. Flag: But coming to Winnopisseag, these Indians had a Consult in their own Language, and Sending back their Lieutenant, with two Indians, Nineteen of them Staid in that Country Eleven Days, not having any English with them: At which the Major was justly and greatly offended. It was then Suspected, and afterwards (by escap'd Captives) Asserted, that these Wretches found the Enemy, and Lodg'd with 'em Two Nights, and told 'em what they knew of the English Numbers and Motions. The Enemy then Retired into the howling Desarts where there was no Coming at them: And no endeavours being able to reach them, the Army in the Month of November following was Dismissed: Only some Soldiers were left in Garrison at Wells, at York, at Berwick, and at Quechecho, for the Assistance of the poor Inhabitants against any more Invasions. There has been little Doubt that our Northern Indians are Originally Scythians; and it is become less a Doubt, since it appears from later Discoveries, That the pretended Straits of Anian[3] are a Sham; for Asia and America, it seems, are there Contiguous. Now of these our Scythians in America, we have still found what Julius Cæsar does report concerning Them of Asia:

Difficilius Invenire quam Interficere:
It is harder to Find them than to Foil them.

[1] This "Hunt of the Black Beast" appears to be the name of a game much in vogue at the time of writing.

[2] Noah Wiswell.

[3] Bering Strait. Mather's confidence that it did not exist was doubtless derived from his reading of Hennepin.

A Digression,

Relating some Wonderful Judgments of God.

Before we pass to another year, Stand still, Reader, and Behold some Wonderful Events proper here to be Introduced. The Relation thereof shall be given, as I have Received it.

Portsmouth, Feb.27, 1698/9.

Monsieur Vincelotte of Quebeck, arrived here, the 25th of the last Month,[1] and since Embarked for France by way of Bilboa, as Agent to Represent the Affairs of Canada.

He says, That about Nine or Ten years since, the Earl of Frontenac, Governor of that place (who died last November), did personally Attempt to Subdue the Maqua's, etc., having no less than Fifteen Hundred Soldiers in his Army.

After a few Days March, they (being much Wearied and very Thirsty) came unto a certain small Well, of which they drank very plentifully.   But in a few Hours after, sundry complained of much Illness, and according to their various Constitutions fell Sick (as it seem'd) of different Distempers;   which occasioned so great Disorder and Confusion in the Army, that no less than Four well men, for a while, were Engaged in taking care of every one that was Sick. About Three Days after, the Maqua scout, narrowly observing the Motions of the French, rallied together, as many as possible, to give a Check unto their Undertaking;   which they soon accomplished, with very considerable Advantage.   But the French appearing so Numerous, forced them to Retreat, and in pursuit of them, took and ransackt a Small Town.

The Sickness by this Time increased unto so great an Height, as to occasion a Council of War, which ordered their speedy Return; and in a short Time, no less than Eight Hundred persons Dyed out of the Army.

Now about Three Years ago, a certain Soldier, who belong'd at that Time to the Army, went into France.   In a short Time after his Arrival, he Robb'd one of the Churches of a considerable value of Plate;   but being soon discovered, he was Sentenced to be Burnt: He then sent unto sundry Father-Confessors, unto whom he acknowledged his many Sins;   particularly the Fact for which he was Con-

---

[1] The Sieur de Vincelotte, Canadian, had on Frontenac's death been sent to France by the intendant Champigny, in a fruitless endeavor to secure the governorship for the latter. Maquas signifies the Iroquois, or Five Nations.

demned. But he therewithal said, that he had something else of
more considerable moment to Impart, which did much afflict his
Conscience; Namely, an Action of his, about Seven Years before
committed, when Listed under the Conduct of the Earl of Frontenac,
in an enterprize against the Sennakers[1] and Maqua's; (for said he) I
was the only person at that Time Instrumental to the Death of near
Eight Hundred Souls. Having Received some Affront, from some
of the Officers, I was prompted to seek some speedy Revenge, which
my own corrupt Nature with the Instigation of Satan, did instantly
Acomplish; for being plentifully stored with some Rank poison upon
another account, I threw it all into a Well, of which the Thirsty Army
drank freely, and in the Event it proved so fatal unto them.

For the further Confirmation of this Report, Monsieur Vincelotte at the same Time told me, That he was himself Wounded in
the Engagement, and should continue Lame to his Dying Day.

Reverend Sir, Your most Humble Servant,

S. Penhallow.[2]

Article VI.

*New Assaults from the Indians, with some Remarkables of Cap-
tives taken in those Assaults.*

The Sun and the War be again Returning! The year 1690
must begin, very Inauspiciously. In February, the French,
with Indians, made a Descent from Canada, upon a Dutch
Town called Schenectada, Twenty Miles above Albany, under
the Government of New-York, and in that Surprising Incur-
sion, they killed about Sixty Persons, whereof one was their
Minister,[3] and carried about Half as many into Captivity;
but the People there, assisted by the Maqua's, pursued them,
and Recovered some of their Captives from them. Upon the
Advice of this Mischief in the West, order was dispatch'd
unto Major Frost[4] in the East, that the Towns there should

---

[1] Senecas.

[2] Samuel Penhallow (1665–1726), a rich merchant of Portsmouth, and chief
justice of New Hampshire, whose *Narrative of the Indian Wars of New England
from* 1703 *to* 1726 is a chief source for the period named.

[3] Domine Petrus Tesschenmaker; see the *Journal of Jasper Danckaerts*, in this
series. Frontenac, governor of Canada, sent out three expeditions of French and
Indians this winter, one against Albany, which destroyed Schenectady, one against
the frontier settlements of New Hampshire, and one against those of Maine.

[4] Charles Frost.

stand upon their Guard. The Major did his Duty; but they
did not Theirs: They Dream't that while the Deep Snow of
the Winter continued, they were Safe Enough; but this prov'd
as vain as a Dream of a Dry Summer. On March 18th, the
French, with Indians, being Half one, half t'other, Half In-
dianized French, and Half Frenchified Indians, commanded
by Monsieur Artel and Hope-hood [1] fell Suddenly upon
Salmon Falls, destroying the best part of the Town, with Fire
and Sword. Near Thirty Persons were Slain, and more than
Fifty were led into what the Reader will by 'nd by call, The
worst Captivity in the World. It would be a Long Story to
tell, what a particular Share in this Calamity, fell to the Family
of One Clement Short: This Honest Man, with his Pious
Wife, and Three Children, were killed: and Six or Seven of
their Children, were made Prisoners: the most of which arrived
safe to Canada, through a thousand Hardships; and the most
of these were with more than a Thousand Mercies afterwards
Redeemed from Canada, unto their English Friends again.
But my Readers will be so Reasonable, as to excuse me, if I
do not mention the Fate of every Family, that hath Suffered a
Share in the Calamity of this Grievous War; for 'tis impossible that I should Know All that hath happened; and it would
be improper for me to Write All that I know: And very
little is the Advantage of having a Name Standing upon Record
only among unhappy Sufferers. About Seven Score English
went out after 'em, and came up with 'em: nevertheless,
through the Disadvantages of their Feet by the Snow, they
could make no Hand on it. Four or five of ours were kill'd,
and as many of the Enemy; but the Night put an End unto the
Action. Ours took one Prisoner, a French man, who Confessed, that they came from Canada, where both French and
Indians were in Pay at Ten Livers [2] Per Month, and he particularly Declared the State of Canada. This Prisoner met
with such kind usage from us, that he became a Freeman of
Christ, and Embraced and Professed the Protestant Religion.
But of the Prisoners, which the Enemy took from us, there
were Two which immediately met with a very Different Fate.

[1] Hopehood is often called Wohawa; Artel is properly François Hertel, a
French officer.
[2] Livres.

Three Indians hotly pursued one Thomas Toogood, and One of them overtaking him, while the rest perceiving it, staid behind the Hill, he yielded himself a Prisoner. While the Salvage was getting Strings to bind him, he held his Gun under his Arm; which Toogood Observing, Suddenly pluck't it from his Friend Stark Naught, Threatening and Protesting, that he would Shoot him down, if he made any Noise, and so Away he ran with it, unto Quochecho.

If my Reader be inclined now to Smile, when he thinks, how Simply poor Isgrim look'd, returning to his Mates behind the Hill, without either Gun or Prey, or any thing but Strings, to Remember him of his own Deserts, the Smiles will all be presently turn'd into Tears. The Indians had now made a Prisoner of one Robert Rogers, and being on their Journey they came to an Hill, where this man, being through his Corpulency, (for which he was usually Nicknamed, Robin Pork) and an Insupportable and Intolerable Burden laid upon his Back, not so able to Travel as the rest, he Absconded. The Wretches missing him, immediately went in pursuit of him; and it was not long before they found his Burden cast in the way, and the Track of his going out of the way, which they follow'd, until they found him hidden in a Hollow Tree. They Took him out, they Stript him, they beat him, and prickt him, and push'd him forward with their Swords, until they were got back to the Hill; and it being almost Night, they fastned him to a Tree with his Hands behind him, and made themselves a Supper, Singing, Dancing, Roaring, and Uttering many Signs of Joy, but with Joy little enough to the poor Creature, who foresaw, what all this Tended unto. They then cut a parcel of Wood, and bringing it into a plain place, they cut off the Top of a small Red Oak Tree, Leaving the Trunk for a Stake, whereto they bound their Sacrifice. They first made a Great Fire near this Tree of Death, and bringing him unto it, they bid him take his Leave of his Friends; which he did in a doleful manner; no Pen, though made of an Harpies Quill, were able to describe the Dolour of it! They then allow'd him a little Time, to make his Prayers unto Heaven, which he did with an Extream Fervency and Agony: whereupon they bound him to the Stake, and brought the rest of the Prisoners, with their Arms tied each to other, so setting them round the Fire.

This being done, they went behind the Fire, and thrust it forwards upon the man, with much Laughther and Shouting; and when the Fire had burnt some while upon him, even till he was near Stifled, they pull'd it again from him. They Danc'd about him, and at every Turn, they did with their knives cut collops of his Flesh, from his Naked Limbs, and throw them with his Blood into his Face. When he was Dead, they set his Body down upon the Glowing Coals, and left him tyed with his Back to the Stake; where the English Army soon after found him. He was left for Us, to put out the Fire with our Tears!

Reader, Who should be the Father of these Myrmidons?

ARTICLE VII.

The Condition of the Captives, that from time to time fell into the Hands of the Indians ; with some very Remarkable Accidents.

We have had some Occasion, and shall have More, to mention Captives falling into the Hands of the Indians. We will here, without any thing worthy to be call'd A Digression, a little Stand Still, and with mournful Hearts look upon the Condition of the Captives in those cruel Hands. Their Condition truly might be Express'd in the Terms of the ancient Lamentations, (thus by some Translated) Lam. 4:3. *The Daughter of my People is in the Hands of the Cruel, that are like the Ostrich in the Wilderness.* Truly, the Dark places of New-England, where the Indians had their Unapproachable Kennels, were Habitations of Cruelty; and no words can Sufficiently describe the Cruelty undergone by our Captives in those Habitations. The Cold, and Heat, and Hunger, and Weariness, and Mockings, and Scourgings, and Insolencies Endured by the Captives, would enough deserve the Name of Cruelty; but there was this also added unto the rest, that they must ever now and then have their Friends made a Sacrafice of Devils before their Eyes, but be afraid of dropping a Tear from those Eyes, lest it should, upon that provocation, be next their own Turn, to be so Barbarously Sacrificed. Indeed, some few of the Captives, did very happily Escape from their Barbarous Oppressors, by a Flight wisely managed;

and many more of them, were Bought by the French, who treated them with a Civility ever to be acknowledged, until care was taken to fetch 'em home.   Nevertheless many Scores of 'em Dyed among the Indians; and what usage they had, may be gathered from the following Relations, which I have obtained from Credible Witnesses.

Relation I.

James Key, Son to John Key of Quochecho, was a Child of about Five years of Age, taken Captive by the Indians at Salmon Falls; and that Hellish Fellow, Hope-Hood, once a Servant of a Christian Master in Boston, was become the Master of this Little Christian.   This Child, Lamenting with Tears the want of Parents, his Master Threatned him with Death, if he did not Refrain his Tears; but these Threatnings could not Extinguish the Natural Affections of a Child.   Wherefore, upon his Next Lamentations, this Monster Stript him Stark Naked, and lash'd both his Hands round a Tree, and Scourg'd him, so that from the Crown of his Head unto the Sole of his Foot, he was all over Bloody and Swollen; and when he was Tired with laying on his Blows, on the Forlorn Infant, he would lay him on the Ground, with Taunts remembering him of his Parents.   In this misery, the poor Creature lay horribly Roaring for divers Days together, while his Master, gratified with the Musick, lay contriving of New Torments, wherewith to Martyr him.   It was not long, before the Child had a Sore Eye, which his Master said, proceeded from his Weeping on the Forbidden Accounts: Whereupon, laying Hold on the Head of the Child with his Left Hand, with the Thumb of his Right he forced the Ball of his Eye quite out, therewithal telling him, That when he heard him Cry again he would Serve t'other so too, and leave him never an Eye to Weep withal.   About Nine or Ten Days after, this Wretch had Occasion to Remove, with his Family, about Thirty Miles further; and when they had gone about Six Miles of the Thirty, the Child being Tir'd and Faint, sat him down to rest, at which this Horrid Fellow, being provoked, he Buried the Blade of his Hatchet, in the Brains of the Child, and then chopt the Breathless Body to pieces before the rest of the Company,

and threw it into the River.   But for the sake of these and
other such Truculent Things, done by Hope-Hood, I am Resolved, that in the course of our Story, I will watch to see what
becomes of that hideous Loup-Garou,[1] if he come to his
End, as I am apt to think he will, before the Story.

Relation II.

Mehetabel Goodwin, being a Captive among the Indians,
had with her a Child about Five Months old; which thro'
Hunger and Hardship, she being unable to nourish it, often
made most grievous Ejaculations.   Her Indian Master told
her, that if the Child were not quiet, he would soon dispose of
it; which caused her to use all possible means, that his Ne-
topship[2] might not be offended; and sometimes carry it from
the Fire, out of his Hearing, where she sat up to the wast in
Snow and Frost for several Hours until it was Lull'd asleep.
She thus for several dayes preserved the Life of her Babe,
until he saw cause to Travel, with his own Cubs, farther afield;
and then, lest he should be Retarded in his Travel, he violently
Snatcht the Babe out of its Mother's Arms, and before her Face
knockt out its Brains, and stript it of the Few Rags it had
hitherto Enjoy'd, and order'd her the Task, to go wash the
Bloody Cloaths.   Returning from this Melancholy Task, She
found the Infant hanging by the Neck in a Forked Bough of a
Tree.   She desired leave to lay it in the Earth; but he said, it
was better as it was, for now the Wild Beasts would not come
at it, (I am sure, they had been at it!) and she might have
the Comfort of seeing it again, if ever they came that way.
The Journey now before them, was like to be very long, even
as far as Canada, where his purpose was to make Merchandise
of his Captive, and glad was the Captive of such happy Tidings.   But the Desperate length of the way, and want of Food,
and grief of Mind, wherewith she now encountred, caused her
within a few Days to faint under her Difficulties.   When at
length she sat down for some Repose, with many Prayers,
and Tears unto God, for the Salvation of her Soul, she found
her self unable to Rise, until she espied her Furious Executioner

[1] Were-wolf.
[2] *Netop*, in the language of the Massachusetts Indians, meant "friend."

coming towards her, with Fire in his Eyes, the Devil in his
Heart, and his Hatchet in his Hand, ready to bestow a Mercy-
Stroak of Death upon her. But then this miserable Creature
got on her Knees, and with Weeping, and Wailing, and all
Expressions of Agony and Entreaty, prevailed on him, to
spare her Life a little, and she did not question but God would
enable her to Walk a little faster. The merciless Tyrant was
prevailed withal, to spare her this Time; nevertheless her
former Weakness quickly Returning upon her, he was just
going to Murder her; but a Couple of Indians, just at that
Instant, coming in, suddenly call'd upon him to Hold his
Hand; whereat such an Horror Surprized his Guilty Soul, that
he ran away. But hearing them call his Name, he Returned,
and then permitted these his Friends, to Ransom his prisoner
from him. After this, being Seated by a River side, they
heard several Guns go off, on the other side; which they concluded, was from a party of Albany Indians, who were Enemies
unto these; whereupon this Bold Blade would needs go in a
Canoo to discover what they were. They Fired upon him,
and shot through him, and several of his Friends, before the
Discovery could be made unto Satisfaction. But some dayes
after this, divers of his Friends gathered a party to Revenge
his Death, on their Supposed Enemies; with whom they joyned
Battel, and fought several Hours, until their Supposed Enemies
did Really put 'em to the Rout. Among the Captives, which
they left in their Flight, one was this poor Goodwin, who was
Overjoyed in seeing her self thus at Liberty; but the Joy did
not last long, for these Indians were of the Same Sort with the
other, and had been by their own Friends, thus through a strange
Mistake set upon. However, this crew proved more Favourable to her than the former, and went away Silently with their
Booty, being loth to have any Noise made of their foul Mistake.
And yet, a few Dayes after, such another Mistake happened;
for, meeting with another party of Indians, which they imag-
ined in the English Interests, they furiously engaged each other,
And many were killed and wounded on either side; but they
proved a party of the French Indians, who took this poor
Goodwin, and presented her to the French Captain, by whom
she was carried unto Canada, where she continued Five years,
and then was brought safe Back into New-England.

Relation III.

Mary Plaisted, the Wife of Mr. James Plaisted, was made
a Captive by the Indians about Three Weeks after her Delivery of a Male Child.[1] They then Took her, with her
Infant, off her Bed, and forced her to Travel in this her Weakness the best part of a Day, without any Respect or Pitty.
At Night the Cold Ground in the Open Air was her Lodging;
and for many a Day she had no Nourishment, but a little
Water with a little Bears-flesh: which rendred her so feeble,
that she, with her Infant, were not far from totally Starved.
Upon her Cries to God, there was at length some Supply sent
in, by her Masters taking a Moose, the Broth whereof Recovered her.   But she must now Travel, many Days, thro' Woods,
and Swamps, and Rocks, and over Mountains, and Frost and
Snow, until she could stir no farther.   Sitting down to Rest,
she was not able to Rise, until her Diabolical Master help'd
her up; which when he did, he took her Child from her, and
carried it unto a River, where stripping it of the few Rags it
had, he took it by the Heels, and against a Tree dash'd out its
Brains, and then flang it into the river.   So he Returned unto
the miserable Mother, telling her, she was now eased of her
Burden, and must walk faster than she did before!

Relation IV.

Mary Ferguson, taken Captive by the Indians at Salmon
Falls, declares, that another Maid of about Fifteen or Sixteen
years of Age, taken at the same Time, had a Great Burden
Imposed on her.   Being over-born with her Burden, she burst
out into Tears, telling her Indian Master, That she could go
no further.   Whereupon he immediately took off her Burden,
and leading her aside into the Bushes, he cut off her Head,
and Scalping it, he ran about Laughing and Bragging what

[1] She must have been well known to Mather, her sister being the wife of his
friend Rev. Shubael Dummer.   She embraced the Catholic faith at Montreal in
1693, but was redeemed in 1695.   A daughter, captured at the same time, became
a nun, and head of the mission school for girls at Sault au Recollet; another was
married in Canada and remained there.

an Act he had now done; and showing the Scalp unto the rest, he told them, They should all be Served so if they were not patient.

In fine, when the Children of the English Captives Cried at any Time, so that they were not presently quieted, the manner of the Indians was, to dash out their Brains against a Tree.

And very often, when the Indians were on, or near the Water, they took the Small Children, and held 'em under Water, till they had near Drowned them, and then gave 'em unto their Distressed Mothers to quiet 'em.

And the Indians in their Frolicks would Whip and Beat the Small Children, until they set 'em into grievous outcries, and then throw 'em to their Amazed Mothers, for them to quiet 'em again as well as they could.

This was Indian Captivity!

Reader, a Modern Traveller assures us, that at the Villa Ludovisia, not far from Rome, there is to be seen the Body of a Petrified Man; and that he himself saw, by a piece of the man's Leg, Broken for Satisfaction, both the Bone and the Stone Crusted over it. All that I will say, is, That if thou canst Read these passages without Relenting Bowels, thou thyself art as really Petrified as the man at Villa Ludovisia.

Nescio tu quibus es, Lector, Lecturus Ocellis;
Hoc Scio quod Siccis scribere non potui.[1]

Article VIII.

A Little Account of the Greatest Action that ever New-England Attempted.

I have Read or Heard, That when the Insufferable Abuses which the English Nation suffered from the Abbeys were in the Parliament complained of, the Total Dissolution of those Abbeys was much forwarded, by a Speech of a Gentleman in the House of Commons, to this purpose; that his own House had been much annoy'd by Rooks building in a Tree, near unto

---

[1] "I know not, reader, whether you will be moved to tears by this narrative; I know I could not write it without weeping."

it, and that he had used many ineffectual ways to disturb, and disroost these mischievous Rooks, until at Last he found out an infallible way to be delivered from the Rooks, and that was to cut down the Tree that Lodged 'em. The Distresses into which New-England was now fallen, made this very comparison to be thought of. The Indian Rooks grievously infested the Country; and while the Country was only on the Defensive Part, their Men were Thinned, their Towns were Broken, and their Treasures consumed, without any Hope of seeing an End of these Troublesome Tragedies. The French Colonies to the Northward were the Tree in which those Rooks had their Nests; and the French having in person first fallen upon the English of New-England, it was thought that the New-Englanders might very justly take this Occasion to Reduce those French Colonies under the English Government, and so at once take away from all the Rooks for ever, all that gave 'em any Advantage to Infest us. Accordingly, a Naval Force, with about Seven Hundred men, under the Conduct of Sir William Phips, was dispatched away to L'Accady and Nova Scotia. This Fleet setting Sail from New-England, April 28, 1690, in a Fortnight Arrived at Port-Royal, and Sir William having the Fort Surrenderd unto him, took Possession of that Province, for the Crown of England. But this was only a step towards a far greater Action! There was no Speech about the Methods of Safety made, which did not conclude with a, *Delenda est Carthago*. It was become the concurring Resolution of all New-England, with New-York, that a vigorous Attack should be made upon Canada at once, both by Sea and Land.[1] A fleet of Thirty-Two Sail, under the Command of Sr. William Phips, was Equipp'd at Boston, and began their Voyage, Aug. 9, and the whole Matter was put into Form, with so much Contrivance and Caution and Courage, that nothing but an Evident Hand of Heaven was likely to have given such a Defeat unto it, as has been indeed generally and Remarkably given unto all the Colonies of America, when they have Invaded one onother. If this Expedition did miscarry, and if Canada proved unto New-England, what it prov'd unto the Spaniards, when at their Deserting it, they call'd it, *Il Capo de Nada*; or, The Cape of Nothing, (whence

[1] See p. 201, note.

the Name Canada)[1] there is no New-Englander, but what
will maintain, that it was with a less Disgraceful miscarriage,
than what baffled every one of those, that were made in this
War, against the French Islands, by more powerful Fleets of
those, who were forward Enough to Reproach New-England.
I am sure, he that Reads the Account of what was done at
Martineco, in the *Relation of the Voyage of M. de Gennes*,
lately published,[2] must be very easy in his Reflections upon
what was done at Canada.　And I will add, That if the New-
England-men return'd *re infecta*[3] from Canada, yet they did
not leave Two Hundred men behind them to the mercy of the
French, as they who most Reproached New-England, soon
after did at Guadalupa.

The fuller narrative of these memorable Things the Reader
may find written in *The Life of Sir William Phipps*, lately
published;[4] of which I must here give this Attestation, That
as my Acquaintance with the Author, gives me Assurance of
his being as Willing to Retract a Mistake, as unwilling to Commit one, and of his Care in whatever he writes, to be able to
make the profession of Oecolampadius, *Nolui aliquid Scribere,
quod improbaturum putem Christum*:[5] so I have Compared
this Narrative with the Journals of the Expedition; and I
find the most Contested passages of the Story, (nor did I ever
hear of any more than one or two little circumstantial passages
contested, as carrying a sound a little too Rhetorical; but, I
say, I find them) to be the very Express Words thereof, contained in those Journals; and more than so, that very credible
Persons, concerned therein, have readily offered their Deposi-

---

[1] A derivation wholly without warrant.　By "French islands," below, the
French West Indies are meant.

[2] *Relation d'un Voyage fait en* 1695, 1696, 1697, *aux Côtes d'Afrique, Détroit
de Magellan, Brésil, Cayenne, et Iles Antilles, par une Escadre commandée par M.
de Gennes* (Paris and Amsterdam, 1699), by Froger.

[3] "With unaccomplished purpose."

[4] *Pietas in Patriam*, the life of Sir William Phips here referred to, was written
by Mather himself and published in London in 1697.　It is reprinted in the *Magnalia*, as an appendix to book II.　It is highly eulogistic in character, as might
be expected when we remember that the Mathers endorsed Phips for the post
of governor.

[5] "I have been unwilling to write anything which I think Christ would not
approve."

tions upon Oath, to the Truth of what is Written. So I take
my leave of that History, and of Sir William Phipps, the
Memorable Subject of that History, whom I leave under this

EPITAPH.

Bonus non est, qui non ad Invidium usque Bonus est.[1]

(*A Digression.*)

Reader, since we can give no better an Account of the Last
English Expedition to Canada, why may we not for a Minute
or Two Refresh our selves with a Story of an Old one.

In the very year, when the Massachuset-Colony began, the
English Attempted the Conquest of Canada; and though the
First Attempt miscarried, the Second prospered. The Story of
it makes a Chapter in Father Hennepin's Account of the Vast
Country lately discovered, betwixt Canada and Mexico;[2]
and this is the Sum of it.

While a Colony was forming it self at Canada, an English
Fleet was Equipp'd, in the year, 1628, under the Command
of Admiral Kirk, with a Design to take Possession of that
Country. In their Voyage, having taken a French Ship, at
the Isle Percee, they Sailed up the River, as far as Tadousac,
where they found a Bark in which they set ashore some Soldiers, to Seize on Cape Tourment. And here a Couple of
Salvages discovering them, ran away to advise the people of
Quebeck, that the English were approaching. When the Fleet
arrived, the Admiral Summoned the Town to Surrender by
a Letter to Monsieur Champelin,[3] the governour: but the
Governour notwithstanding his being so Surprized with the
Invasion, made such a Resolute Answer, that the English,
(though as the Historian says, they are a People that will
sooner Die than quit what they once undertake) did conclude
the fort Quebeck, was in a much better condition for Defence
than it really was; and therefore desisting from any further

---

[1] "He is not good who is not good enough to be hated."

[2] Louis Hennepin, *Nouvelle Description d'un très grand Pays Situé dans
l'Amérique entre le Nouveau Mexique et la Mer glaciale* (Utrecht, 1697). But it
contains no such chapter.

[3] Champlain. The English commander was David Kirke.

Attempt at this Time, they returned into England with Resolution further to pursue their Design at a more favourable Opportunity.

Accordingly, on July 19, 1629, in the Morning, the English Fleet appear'd again, over against in the Great Bay of Quebeck, at the point of the Isle of Orleans; which Fleet Consisted of Three men of War and Six other Vessels. Admiral Kirk sending a Summons form'd in very Civil Expressions, for the Surrender of the Place, the miserable State of the Country, which had been by the English Interceptions, hindred of Supplies from France, for Two years together, oblig'd the Sieur Champelin to make a softer Answer than he did before. He sent Father Joseph Le Caron aboard the Admiral to treat about the Surrender, and none of his Demands for Fifteen Dayes, and then for five dayes, Time to consider on't, could obtain any longer Time, than till the Evening, to prepare their Articles. Upon the Delivery of this Message, a Council was held, wherein some urged, that the English had no more than Two Hundred men of Regular Troops aboard, and some others which had not much of the Air of Soldiers; and that the Courage of the Inhabitants was much to be relied upon, and therefore it was best for to run the risk of a Siege: but Monsieur Champelin, apprehending the Bravery of the English, remonstrated unto the Council, that it was better to make a Surrender on Good Terms, than be all cut in pieces by an unreasonable Endeavour to Defend themselves. Upon this, the Articles regulating all matters, were got ready, and Father Joseph had his Commission, to carry them aboard the English Admiral, where the Signing of them was deferred until To Morrow. On July 20, the Articles of Capitulation were Signed, on both sides, and the English being Landed, were put in possession of Canada by the Governour of it. The French Inhabitants, who were then in the Country, had twenty Crowns apiece given them, the rest of their Effects remained unto the Conquerors, but those who were willing to stay, were favoured by the English with great Advantages. The Fleet set Sail again for England, Sept. 14, and arrived at Plymouth, Oct. 18, in that year.[1]

[1] Canada was given back to France by the treaty of St. Germain-en-Laye, March 29. 1632.

Article IX.

Casco Lost.

When the Indians at last perceived that the New-Englanders were upon a Likely Design to Swallow up the French Territories, the Prospect of it began to have the same Operation upon them, that the Success of the Design would have made Perpetual; that is, to Dis-spirit them, for giving the New-Englanders any further Molestations. Nevertheless, Before and Until they were thoroughly Advised of what was a doing, and likely to be done, they did molest the Country with some Tragical Efforts of their Fury. Captain James Converse was Marching through the vast Wilderness to Albany, with some Forces, which the Massachusets Colony were willing to send by Land (besides what they did send by Sea unto Quebeck,) for the Assistance of the Army, in the West, that was to go from thence over the Lake, and there fall upon Mount Real;[1] but unhappy Tidings out of the East required the Diversion of those Forces thither. About the Beginning of May, the French and Indians, between Four and Five Hundred,[2] were seen at Casco, in a great Fleet of canoos passing over the Bay; but not Seeing or Hearing any more of them, for Two or Three Weeks together, the Casconians flattered themselves with Hopes, That they were gone another way. But about May 16. those Hopes were over; for one Gresson,[3] a Scotchman, then going out Early, fell into the mouths of these Hungry Salvages. It proved no kindness to Casco, tho' it proved a great one to himself, that a Commander so qualified as Captain Willard, was called off, Two or Three Days before.[4] But the Officers of the place, now concluding, that the whole Army of the Enemy were watching for an Advantage to Sur-

[1] Montreal.

[2] Some other writers place the number of French and Indians at above 500. Casco is Falmouth (Portland). The commander of the French forces was M. Robineau de Portneuf.

[3] Robert Gresson or Greason.

[4] Major Simon Willard was succeeded by Captain Sylvanus Davis, later taken prisoner and held at Quebec until exchanged at the time of the expedition of Phips in November, 1690.

prize The town, Resolved that they would keep a Strict
watch, for Two or Three days, to make some further Discovery,
before they salley'd forth. Notwithstanding this, one Lieut.
Clark,[1] with near Thirty of their Stoutest young men, would
venture out, as far as the Top of an Hill in the Entrance of
the Wood, half a mile distant from the Town. The out-let
from the Town to the Wood was thro' a Lane, that had a
Fence on each side, which had a certain Block-house at one
End of it; and the English were Suspicious, when they came
to Enter the Lane, that the Indians were lying behind the Fence
because the Cattel stood staring that way, and would not
pass into the Wood as they use to do. This mettlesome Company then ran up to the Fence with an, Huzza! thinking thereby
to discourage the Enemy, if they should be lurking there;
but the Enemy were so well prepared for them, that they answered them with an horrible Vengeance, which kill'd the
Lieutenant, with Thirteen more upon the Spot, and the rest
escaped with much ado unto one of the Garrisons. The Enemy
then coming into Town, beset all the Garrisons at once, Except
the Fort; which were manfully Defended so long as their
Ammunition lasted; but That being spent, without a prospect
of a Recruit, they quitted all the Four Garrisons, and by the
Advantage of the Night, got into the Fort. Upon this, the
Enemy Setting the Town on Fire, bent their whole Force
against the Fort, which had hard by it a deep Gully, that con-
tributed not a little unto the Ruin of it: For the Besiegers
getting into that Gully, lay below the Danger of our Guns.
Here the Enemy began their Mine, which was carried so near
the Walls, that the English, who by Fighting Five Days and
Four Nights, had the greatest part of their men killed and
wounded, (Captain Lawrence mortally, among the rest,)
began a parley with them. Articles were Agreed, That they
should have liberty to March unto the Next English Town,
and have a Guard for their Safety in their March; and the
French Commander, lifting up His Hand, Swore by the Everlasting God, for the performance of these Articles. But the
Agreement was kept, as those that are made with Hugonots
use to be: The English being first Admonished, by the French,

[1] Thaddeus Clark. The capture and entire destruction of Casco (Falmouth) was one of the great disasters of the war.

that they were all rebels, for proclaiming the Prince of Orange
their King, were Captived, and many of them cruelly Murdered
by the Indians: Only some of them (and particularly, Major
Davis,) were Carried unto Canada, where the Gentry very
civilly Treated them.   The Garrisons at Papoodack, Spurwink,
Black Point, and Blue Point,[1] were so disanimated at these
Disasters, that, without Orders they drew off immediately, to
Saco, Twenty miles within Casco, and from Saco in a few Days
also they drew off to Wells, Twenty miles within the said
Saco; and about Half Wells drew off as far as Lieutenant
Storers.   But the Arrival of Orders and Soldiers from the Government, stopt them from Retiring any further; and Hope-
Hood, with a party that staid for further mischief, meeting
with some Resistance here, turn'd about, and having first had
a skirmish with Captain Sherborn, they appear'd the next
Lords day at Newichawannick, or, Berwick, where they Burnt
some Houses, and Slew a man.   Three Days after, they came
upon a Small Hamlet, on the South side of Piscataqua River,
called Fox Point, and besides the Burning of several Houses,
they Took Half a Dozen, and kill'd more than a Dozen, of the
too Securely Ungarrisoned People; which it was as easy to
do, as to have Spoiled an ordinary Hen-Roost.   But Captain
Floyd[2] and Captain Greenleaf coming upon those Indians,
made some Slaughter among them, Recovered some Captives
with much Plunder, and bestow'd a Good wound upon
Hope-Hood, who left his gun (which was next his life) in this
Action.[3]

All that shall further belong to this Paragraph of our Story,
is, That when the Indians were got into the Woods, they made
one Goody Stockford their messenger to her Neighbours,
whose Charity she so well Sollicited, that she got a Shalop full
of it unto Casco, where the Indians permitted us to Redeem
several of the Prisoners.

[1] Purpooduck and Spurwick were in Cape Elizabeth, Black Point and
Blue Point in Scarborough.

[2] James Floyd.

[3] Marginal note: "Villain! Thou shalt not escape so: There must quickly
be another stroke upon thee!"

Article X.

Harm Watch'd and Catch'd by the Indians, and several Rare Instances of Mortal wounds upon the English, not proving Mortal.

That memorable Tygre, Hope-Hood, (called also Wohawa,) finding the Coast hereabouts too hot for him, went away with his Crew, a great way to the West-ward, with a Design to Bewitch another Crew at Aquadocta into his Assistance. Here a party of French Indians, by a strange Mistake, supposing Hope-Hood and his Wretches to have been the Indians, who had lately done some Spoil upon them at Canada, furiously fell upon them, and in their Blind Fury slew him, and a considerable part of his Company. So we have now done with him! In the mean Time, some other Indians came upon an Helpless place, called Spruce Creek, and kill'd an old man, and carried a Woman into Captivity; but tho' Captain Converse pursued 'em Three Days, they were too Nimble for him. On July 4, Eight or Nine persons working in a Field, at a place call'd Lampereel River,[1] the Scythe of Death unhappily mow'd them down, in that Field of Blood: The Indians by Surprize kill'd 'em all, and carried a Lad Captive. About this Time a Council of War was called at Portsmouth, by which 'twas thought adviseable to send out Captain Wiswel, with a considerable Scout, for to Scour the Woods as far as Casco; and it being Resolved, That one of the other Captains with about Fourscore Stout men should accompany Captain Wiswel in this Action, they All with such a Generous Emulation offered it, that it was necessary to determine it by a Lot, which fell upon Captain Floyd. On July 4, assisted with Lieut. Andrews, and a Detachment of Twenty-two men from Wells, they took their March from Quochecho into the Woods. But the Day following, the Enemy set upon Captain Hilton's Garrison in Exeter, which Lieutenant Bancroft, then posted at Exeter, with the loss of a few of his men Relieved. At this Time there happened a Remarkable Thing. I know not whether the Story told by Plato[2] be true, That one Herus Armenius

---

[1] Now Newmarket, New Hampshire.   [2] *Republic*, X. 614.

(whom Clemens will have to be Zoroaster) being Slain in War, lay Ten Days among the Dead, and then being brought away, and on the Twelfth Day laid on the funeral pile, he came to Life again.   But it is true, that one Simon Stone being here wounded with Shot, in Nine several places, lay for Dead (as it was Time!) among the Dead.   The Indians coming to Strip him, attempted with Two several Blows of an Hatchet at his Neck, to cut off his Head, which Blows added, you may be sure, more Enormous wounds unto those Port-holes of Death, at which the Life of the poor man, was already running out, as fast as it could.   Being charged hard by Lieut. Bancroft, they left the man, without Scalping him; and the English now coming to Bury the Dead, one of the Soldiers perceived this poor man to fetch a gasp: whereupon an Irish Fellow then present, advised 'em to give him another Dab with an Hatchet, and so Bury him with the rest.   The English detesting this Barbarous Advice, lifted up the wounded man, and poured a little Fair Water into his Mouth, at which he Coughed; then they poured a little Strong Water after it, at which he opened his Eyes. The Irish Fellow was ordered now to hale a Canoo ashore, to carry the wounded men up the River unto a Chirurgeon; and as Teague was foolishly pulling the Canoo ashore, with the Cock of his Gun, while he held the Muzzle in his Hand, his Gun went off, and broke his Arm, whereof he remains a Cripple to this Day: But Simon Stone was thoroughly cured, and is at this Day a very lusty man; and as he was Born with Two Thumbs on one Hand, his Neighbours have thought him to have at least as many Hearts as Thumbs!

Reader, Let us Leave it now unto the Sons of Æsculapius, to Dispute out the Problem, What Wounds are to be Judged Mortal?   The Sovereign Arbiter of Life and Death, seems to have determined it,   That no Wounds are Mortal, but such as He shall in his Holy Providence Actually make so.   On the one side, let it be Remembered, That a Scratch of a Comb has proved Mortal; That the Incomparable Anatomist Spigelius, at the Wedding of his Daughter, gathering up the Reliques of a Broken Glass, a Fragment of it scratched one of his Fingers; and all his Exquisite Skill in Anatomy, could not prevent its producing an Empyema, that Killed him: That Colonel Rossiter, cracking a Plumb-stone with his Teeth, broke his Tooth, and Lost his Life; That the Lord Fairfax, cutting a Corn in his Foot, Cut asunder the Thread of his Life; That Mr. Fowler, a Vintner, playing with his Child, received a little scratch of a Pin, which turn'd unto a Gangrene, that Cost him his Life. And, Reader, Let the Remembrance of such Things, cause thee to Live, preparing for Death continually. But then, on the other side, That nothing may be Despaired of, Remember Simon Stone. And, besides him, I call to Remembrance, That the Indians making an Assault upon Deerfield, in this Present War, they struck an Hatchet some inches into the Scull of a Boy there, even so deep, that the Boy felt the Force of a Wrench used by 'em to get it out. There he lay a long while Weltring in his Blood; they found him, they Dress'd him, considerable Quantities of his Brain came out from time to time, when they opened the Wound; yet the Lad Recovered, and is now a Living Monument of the Power and Goodness of God. And in our Former War, there was one Jabez Musgrove, who tho' he were Shot by the Indians, with a Bullet, that went in at his Ear, and went out at his Eye on the other side of his head; and a Brace of Bullets, that went into his Right Side, a little above his Hip, and passing thro' his Body within the Back-Bone, went out at his Left Side; yet he Recovered, and Lived many years after it.

ARTICLE XI.

A Worthy Captain Dying in the Bed of Honour.

On July 6. Lord's-Day, Captain Floyd, and Captain Wiswel, sent out their Scouts before their Breakfast, who immediately returned, with Tidings of Breakfast enough provided for those, who had their Stomach sharp set for Fighting: Tidings of a considerable Track of the Enemy, going to the Westward. Our Forces vigorously followed the Track, till they came up with the Enemy, at a place call'd Wheelwright's Pond; where they engaged 'em in a Bloody Action for several Hours. The manner of the Fight here was as it is at all times, with Indians; namely, what your Artists at Fighting do call, *A la disbandad :* [1] And here, the Worthy Captain Wiswel, a man

---

[1] Spanish, meaning, "separately, not in company formation."

worthy to have been Shot (if he must have been Shot), with no Gun inferior to that at Florence, the Barrel whereof is all pure Gold, behaving himself with much Bravery, Sold his Life as dear as he could; and his Lieutenant Flag, and Sergeant Walker, who were Valient in their Lives, in their Death were not divided. Fifteen of ours were Slain, and more Wounded; but how many of the Enemy 'twas not exactly known, because of a singular care used by them in all their Battels to carry off their Dead, tho' they were forced now to Leave a good Number of them on the Spot. Captain Floyd maintained the Fight, after the Death of Captain Wiswel, several Hours, until so many of his Tired and Wounded men Drew off, that it was Time for him to Draw off also; for which he was blamed perhaps, by some that would not have continued at it so long as he. Hereupon Captain Converse repaired with about a score Hands to look after the Wounded men, and finding seven yet Alive, he brought 'em to the Hospital by Sun-rise the next morning. He then Returned with more Hands, to Bury the Dead, which was done immediately; and Plunder left by the Enemy at their going off, was then also taken by them. But the same Week, these Rovers made their Descent as far as Amesbury, where Captain Foot being Ensnared by them, they Tortured him to Death; which Disaster of the Captain, was an Alarum to the Town, and an Effectual Word of Command, causing 'em to fly out of their Beds into their Garrisons; otherwise they had all undoubtedly before next morning Slept their last; their Beds would have been their Graves. However, the enemy Kill'd Three Persons, Burnt Three Houses, Butchered many Cattel; and so, that Scene of the Tragedy being over, away they went.

In fine, From the First Mischief done, at Lampereel River, to the Last at Amesbury, all belong'd unto one Indian Expedition, in which, though no English Places were taken, yet Forty English People were cut off.

Article XII.

An Indian Fort or Two taken, and some other Actions.

Reader, I remember the prolixity of Guicciardine, the Historian,[1] gave such Offence, that Boccalini brings in an Offender at Verbosity, Ordered for his punishment by the Judges at Parnassus, to Read that punctual Historian; but the poor Fellow begg'd rather to be Fley'd alive, than to be Tortured with Reading an Historian, who in relating the War between the Florentines and Pisans made longer Narrations about the Taking of a Pigeon-House, than there needed of the most Fortified Castle in the World.　For this cause, let me be excused, Reader, if I make Short Work, in our Story, and Leave the Honest Actors themselves to Run over Circumstances more at large, with their Friends by the Fireside.

The Enemy appearing a Little Numerous and Vexatious, the Government sent more Forces to break up the Enemies Quarters; and Auxiliaries both of English and Indians, under the Command of Major Church, assisted the Enterprize.[2] About Three Hundred Men, were dispatched away upon this Design, in the Beginning of September, who Landed by Night in Casco Bay, at a place called Macquoit, and by Night Marched up to Pechypscot-fort;[3] where, from the Information of some Escaped Captives, they had an Expectation to meet with the Enemy; but found that the Wretches were gone farther afield.　They then marched away for Amonoscoggin Fort,[4] which was about Forty Miles up the River; and Wading through many Difficulties, whereof one was a Branch of the River it self, they met with Four or Five Salvages, going to their Fort, with two English Prisoners.　They sav'd the Prisoners, but could not catch the Salvages; however, on the Lord's-Day they got up to the Fort undiscovered, where to their sorrowful Disappointment, they found no more than one and Twenty of the Enemy, whereof they Took and Slew

[1] Francesco Guicciardini (1483–1540), the historian of Florence; Trajano Boccalini (1556–1613), satirist.

[2] See Church, *Entertaining Passages*, pp. 66–76.

[3] Freeport; Brunswick.　　　　　　　　　　　　　　　[4] At Lewiston.

Twenty. They found some Considerable Store of Plunder, and Rescued Five English Captives, and laid the Fort in Ashes; but one Disaster they much Complained of; That the Captain of the Fort, whose Name was Agamcus, alias, Great Tom, slipt away from the Hands of his too Careless keepers. But if this piece of Carelessness did any Harm, there was another which did some Good: for Great Tom having terribly Scared a party of his Country-men, with the Tidings of what had happened, and an English Lad in their Hands also telling some Truth unto them, they betook themselves to such a Flight, in their Fright, as gave one Mr. Anthony Bracket,[1] then a Prisoner with 'em, an Opportunity to Fly Four-score miles another way. Our Forces returning to Macquoit, one of our Vessels was there Carelessly ran aground, and compelled thereby to stay for the next Tide; and Mr. Bracket had been miserably aground, if it had not so fell out; for he thereby got thither before she was afloat, otherwise He might have perished, who was afterwards much Improved in Service against the Murderers of his Father. Arriving at Winter harbour, a party of men were sent up the River, who coming upon a parcel of the Mankeen Wolves then hunted for, killed some of them, and Seized most of their Arms, and Stores, and Recovered from them an English man, who told them, that the Enemy were intending to Rendezvouz on Pechypscot Plain, in order to an attempt upon the Town of Wells. Upon this, they Reimbark'd for Macquoit, and repaired as fast as they could unto Pechypscot Plain, and being Divided into Three parties, they there waited for the Approach of the Enemy. But being tyred with one of the three Italian miseries, Waiting for those who did not come, they only possessed themselves of more Plunder there hid by the Enemy, and returned unto Casco-harbour. The Enemy it seems dogg'd their Motions; and in the Night they made a mischievous Assault upon such of the English Army, as were too Remiss in providing for their own Safety in their going ashore; Killing Five of our Plymouth Friends, who had Lodg'd themselves in an House, without Commanders or Centinels. The English, as soon as the Light of the Day (which was the Lord's-day, Sept. 21,) gave 'em

---

[1] Son of the Anthony Brackett previously mentioned, p. 202, *supra.* Agamagus was a Penobscot chief, also called Moxus.

leave, quickly Ran upon the Enemy, and Eased the world of
some of them, and made the rest Scamper from that part of
the world, and got many of their Canoos, and not a little of
their Ammunition, and their best Furniture for the Winter.
The Army was after this Dismiss'd, only an Hundred men
were left, with Captain Converse, and Lieutenant Plaisted,[1]
who spent their Time, as profitably as they could, in Scouting
about the Frontiers, to prevent Surprizals, from an Enemy
which rarely did Annoy, but when they could Surprize.

Article XIII.

A Flag of Truce.

New-England was now quite out of Breath! A tedious,
lingring, expensive Defence, against an Ever-Approaching
and Unapproachable Adversary, had made it so. But nothing
had made it more so, than the Expedition to Canada, which
had Exhausted its best Spirits, and seem'd its *Ultimus Cona-
tus.*[2] While the Country was now in too Great Amazements
to proceed any farther in the War, the Indians themselves
Entreat them to proceed no farther. The Indians came in to
Wells, with a Flag of Truce: and there Ensued some Overtures,
with the English Commissioners, Major Hutchinson,[3] and
Captain Townsend, sent from Boston to join with some others
at Wells. At length a meeting was Appointed and obtained
at Sagadehock,[4] Nov. 23, Where the Redemption of Ten
English Captives was accomplished; one of whom was Mrs.
Hull, whom the Indians were very loth to part withal, because
being able to Write well, they made her serve them in the
Quality of a Secretary: another was named Nathanael White,
whom the Barbarous Canibals had already ty'd unto a Stake,
and cut off one of his Ears, and made him Eat it Raw, and intended for to have Roasted the rest of him alive: the poor
man, being astonished at his own Deliverance! At last, they

---

[1] James Converse of Woburn; Ichabod Plaisted of Kittery.
[2] "Last effort."
[3] Elisha Hutchinson, grandson of Anne Hutchinson.
[4] Sagadahoc, at the mouth of the Kennebec River, where Popham had
built his fort of St. George in 1607.

Signed Articles, dated, Nov. 29, 1691, wherein they Engaged, that no Indians in those parts of the World should do any Injury to the Persons or Estates of the English in any of the English Colonies, until the first of May, next Ensuing: and that on the said First of May, they would bring into Storer's Garrison at Wells all the English Captives in their Hands, and there Make, and Sign, and Seal Articles of Peace with the English; and in the mean time give seasonable Advice of any Plots, which they might know the French to have against them.   To this Instrument were set the Paws of Edgeremet,[1] and Five more of their Sagamores, and noblemen.

But as it was not upon the Firm Land, but in their Canoos upon the Water, that they Signed and Sealed this Instrument; so, Reader, we will be Jealous, that it will prove but a Fluctuating, and unstable sort of a Business; and that the Indians will Do a Ly, as they use to do.   However, we will Dismiss all our Soldiers to their several Homes, Leaving only Captain Converse to keep Wells in some Order, until the First of May do show, whether any more than a meer Flag of Truce be yet shown unto us.

ARTICLE XIV.

Remarkable Encounters.

At the Day appointed, there came to the place Mr. Danforth, Mr. Moodey, Mr. Vaughan, Mr. Brattle, and several other Gentlemen, guarded with a Troop, to see how the Frenchified Indians would keep their Faith with the Hereticks of New-England.   The Indians being poor Musicians for keeping of Time, came not according to their Articles, and when Captain Converse had the courage to go fetch in some of them, they would have made a Lying excuse, That they did not know the Time.   They brought in Two Captives, and promised That in Twenty Days more, they would bring in to Captain Converse all the rest; but finding that in Two and Twenty days they came not, with much concern upon his Mind, he got himself Supplied, as fast as he could, with Five and Thirty men, from the County of Essex.   His men were not come half an Hour

---

[1] Edgeremet or Egeremet was an Indian leader near Machias.

to Storer's House, on June 9, 1691, nor had they got their Indian Weed fairly lighted into their Mouths, before Fierce Moxus, with Two Hundred Indians, made an Attacque upon the Garrison.   This Recruit of Men, thus at the very Nick of Time, Saved the place; for Moxus meeting with a brave Repulse, drew off; and gave Modockawando cause to say, (as a Captive aftewards related it) My Brother Moxus has miss'd it now, but I will go my self the next year, and have the Dog Converse out of his Hole.   About this Time, the Enemy Slew Two men at Berwick, Two more at Exeter, and the biggest part of Nine, loading a Vessel at Cape Nidduck.   But about the latter End of July, we sent out a small Army under the Command of Captain March, Captain King, Captain Sherburn, and Captain Walten, (Converse lying Sick all Summer, had this to make him yet more Sick that he could have no part in these Actions,) who landing at Macquoit, Marched up to Pechypscot, but not finding any signs of the Enemy, Marched down again.   While the Commanders were waiting ashore, till the Soldiers were got aboard, such Great Numbers of Indians poured in upon them, that tho' the Commanders wanted not for Courage or Conduct, yet they found themselves obliged, with much ado, (and not without the Death of Worthy Captain Sherburn) to retire into the Vessels which then lay aground. Here they kept pelting at one another all night; but unto little other purpose than this, which was indeed Remarkable: that the Enemy was at this Time Going to Take the Isle of Shoales, and no doubt had they gone, they would have Taken it, but having Exhausted all their Ammunition on this Occasion, they desisted from what they designed.   For the Rest of the Year, the Compassion of Heaven towards Distressed New-England, kept the Indians under a strange Inactivity; only, on Sept. 28, Seven persons were Murthered and Captived at Berwick; and the Day following, Thrice Seven of Sandy-Beach; on Octob. 23, One Goodridge and his Wife, were murthered at Newberry,[1] and his Children Captived: and the Day following, the like Fate befel a Family at Haverhil.   And this year, a very Good Strong Fort at Cape Nidduck, owned by a Widdow, was unhappily Deserted; after which, the Enemy came, and burnt the Houses in it.

---

[1] In the *Magnalia* this is corrected to Rowley.

ARTICLE XV.

The Martyrdome of Mr. Shubael Dummer, with the Fate of York.

But the Winter must not pass over, without a Storm of Blood! The Popish Indians, after long Silence and Repose in their Inaccessible Kennels, which made our Frontier Towns a little Remit their Tired Vigilance, did, Jan. 25, 1691,[1] Set upon the Town of York, where the Inhabitants were in their unguarded Houses, here and there scattered, Quiet and Secure. Upon the Firing of a Gun by the Indians, which was their Signal, the Inhabitants looked out, but unto their Amazement, found their Houses to be Invested with horrid Salvages, who immediately kill'd many of those unprovided Inhabitants, and more they took Prisoners. This Body of Indians, Consisting of divers Hundreds, then sent in their Summons, to some of the Garrison'd Houses; and those Garrisons, whereof some had no more than Two or Three Men in them, yet being so well Manned, as to Reply, That they would Spend their Blood unto the last Drop, e'er they would Surrender, these Cowardly miscreants had not mettle enough to meddle with 'em. So they Retired into their Howling Thickets, having first Murdered about Fifty, and Captivated near an Hundred of that unhappy People.[2] In this Calamity great was the Share that fell to the Family of Mr. Shubael Dummer, the Pastor of the Little Flock thus prey'd upon; Those Blood-Hounds, being set on by some Romish Missionaries, had long been wishing, that they might Embrue their Hands in the Blood of some New-English Minister; and in this Action, they had their Diabolical Satisfaction. Our Dummer, the Minister of York,[3] was One of whom, for his Exemplary Holiness, Humbleness, Modesty, Industry and Fidelity, the world was not worthy. He was a Gentleman Well-Descended, Well-Tempered, Well-Educated;

[1] *I. e.*, 1692.

[2] Rev. John Pike in his diary gives the loss as 48 killed and 73 captured. The captives were taken to Sagadahoc and many were redeemed later; see p. 232, *post*.

[3] Shubael Dummer was born in 1632, was graduated from Harvard in 1656, had been minister at York for many years, and was one of Mather's most valued correspondents.

and now short of Sixty years of Age. He might have taken for
his Coat of Arms the same that the Holy Martyr Hooper
Prophetically did, A Lamb in a Flaming Bush, with Rays from
Heaven shining on it. He had been Sollicited with many
Temptations to Leave his Place, when the Clouds grew Thick
and Black in the Indian Hostilities, and were like to break
upon it; but he chose rather, with a paternal Affection, to
stay amongst those who had been, so many of them, Converted
and Edified by his Ministry, and he spent very much of his
own Patrimony to Subsist among them, when their Distresses
made them unable to support him as otherwise they would have
done. In a word, He was one that might, by way of Eminency,
be called, A Good Man. This Good Man was just going to
Take Horse, at his own Door, upon a Journey in the Service
of God, when the Tygres, that were making their Depredations
upon the Sheep of York, seiz'd upon this their Shepherd; and
they shot him so, that they left him Dead among the Tribe
of Abel on the Ground. Thus was he, as Ambrose in his Ele-
gant Oration, *De obitu Fratris*,[1] expresses it, *Non nobis ereptus,
sed periculis*.[2] His Wife they carried into Captivity, where
through Sorrows and Hardships among those Dragons of the
Desert, she also quickly Died; and his Church, as many of
them as were in that Captivity, Endured This, among other
Anguishes, that on the next Lord's Day, one of those Tawnies
chose to Exhibit himself unto them, (A Devil as an Angel of
Light!) in the Cloaths, whereof they had Strip the Dead Body
of this their Father. Many were the Tears that were dropt
throughout New-England, on this Occasion; and These among
the rest; for Tho' we do not, as Tradition tells us, the Ante-
diluvians did use to do, By the Blood of Abel, yet we cannot
but mournfully Sing of the Blood of such an Abel.

Epitaph.

Dummer The Shepherd Sacrific'd,
By Wolves, because the Sheep he priz'd,
The Orphans Father, Churches Light,

---

[1] "On the Death of a Brother." The allusion is to a funeral discourse delivered by St. Ambrose (d. 397), commonly called *De Excessu Fratris sui Satyri*.
[2] "Not snatched from us but from dangers."

The Love of Heav'n, of Hell the Spight.
The Countries Gapman, and the Face
That Shone, but knew it not, with Grace.
Hunted by Devils, but Reliev'd
By Angels, and on High Receiv'd.
The Martyr'd Pelican, who Bled
Rather than leave his Charge Unfed.
A proper Bird of Paradise,
Shot, and Flown thither in a Trice.

Lord, Hear the Cry of Righteous Dummer's wounds,
Ascending still against the Salvage Hounds,
That Worry thy dear Flocks; and let the Cry
Add Force to Theirs, that at thine Altar ly.

To Compleat the Epitaph of this Good man, there now
needs no more, than the famous old Chaucer's Motto.

Mors mihi ærumnarum Requies.[1]

Article XVI.

The Memorable Action at Wells.

A Vessel, the Name whereof I know not, (Reader, Let it be
the *Charity*) being immediately dispatched unto Sagadehock,
by the charitable Compassions of the more Southward Neighbours, with Effects to accomplish it, happily Effected the Redemption of many that were taken Captives at York.   But the
rest of the People in that Broken Town talking of Drawing off,
the Government sent Captain Converse and Captain Greenleaf,
with such Encouragements unto them, to keep their Station,
as prevailed with 'em still to Stand their Ground.   In February Major Hutchinson was made Commander in Chief, and
Forces under the Command of Captain Converse, Captain
Floyd, and Captain Thaxter, were by him so prudently posted,
on the Frontiers, that by maintaining a continual Communication, it became a Difficult Thing for the Enemy to make any

[1] "Death is the end of my misfortunes."

more Approaches.   Lieutenant Wilson particularly hearing of
a man Shot at, in Quochecho-Woods, went out with a Scout of
about Eighteen men, who came upon the Indians that had shot
at the man; and killed and wounded all but one of the whole
Company.   But now, Reader, the Longest Day [of] the Year is
to come on, and if I mistake not, the Bravest Act in the War,
fell out upon it.[1]—Modockawando is now come, according
to his Promise a Twelve-Month ago.   Captain Converse was
lodg'd in Storer's Garrison at Wells, with but Fifteen men;
and there came into Wells Two Sloops, with a Shallop, which
had aboard Supplies of Ammunition for the Soldiers, and Contribution for the Needy.   The Cattel this Day came Frighted
and Bleeding out of the Woods, which was a more certain
Omen of Indians a coming, than all the Prodigies that Livy
reports of the Sacrificed Oxen.   Converse immediately issued
out his Commands unto all Quarters, but especially to the
Sloops just then arrived.   The Sloops were Commanded by
Samuel Storer, and James Gouge, and Gouges being two miles
up the River, he wisely brought her down undiscovered, unto
Storers, by the advantage of a Mist then prevailing.   A careful Night they had on't!   The next Morning, before Day-
Light, one John Diamond, a Stranger that came in the Shallop
on a Visit, came to Captain Converse's Garrison, where the
Watch invited him in; but he chose rather to go aboard the
Sloops, which were little more than a Gun-Shot off; and, alas,
the Enemy issuing out from their Lurking-places, immediately
Seiz'd him, and haled him away by the Hair of the Head, (in
spight of all the Attempts used by the Garrison, to Recover
him) for an horrible Story to be told by and by concerning him.
The General of the Enemies Army was Monsieur Burniff;[2]
and one Monsieur Labrocree[3] was a principal Commander;
(the Enemy said, he was Lieutenant General:) there were also
Divers other Frenchmen of Quality, Accompanied with Modockawando, and Moxus, and Egeremet, and Warumbo, and
several more Indian Sagamores; The Army made up in all,
about Five Hundred Men, or Fierce Things in the Shape of
Men, all to Encounter Fifteen Men in one little Garrison,

[1] The attack and repulse at Wells occurred on June 10 and 11, 1692, old
style; June 20 and 21, new style.

[2] Burniff is a corruption of Portneuf.   [3] La Broquerie.

and about Fifteen more Men, (worthily called Such!) in a Couple
of open Sloops. Diamond Having informed 'em How 'twas in
all points, (only that for Fifteen, by a mistake he said Thirty,)
they fell to Dividing the Persons and Plunder, and Agreeing,
that such an English Captain should be Slave to such a one, and
such a Gentleman in the Town should serve such a one, and his
Wife be a Maid of Honour to such or such a Squaw proposed, and
Mr. Wheelright[1] (instead of being a Worthy Counsellor of the
Province, which he Now is!) was to be the Servant of such a
Netop; and the Sloops, with their Stores, to be so and so
parted among them. There wanted but One Thing to Con-
summate the whole matter, even the Chief Thing of all, which
I suppose they had not thought of; That was, For Heaven to
Deliver all this prize into their Hands: But, *Aliter Statutum
est in Cœlo!* [2] A man Habited like a Gentleman made a
Speech to them in English, Exhorting 'em to Courage, and
Assuring 'em, that if they would Courageously fall upon the
English, all was their own. The Speech being Ended, they fell
to the Work, and with an horrid Shout and Shot, made their
Assault, upon the Feeble Garrison; but the English answered
with a brisk Volley, and sent such a Leaden Shower among
them, that they retired from the Garrison to spend the Storm
of their Fury upon the Sloops.

You must know, That Wells Harbour is rather a Creek
than a River, for 'tis very Narrow, and at low water, in many
places Dry; nevertheless, where the Vessels ride, it is Deep
enough, and so far off the Bank, that there is from thence no
Leaping aboard. But our Sloops were sorely incommoded by
a Turn of the Creek, where the Enemy could ly out of danger
so near 'em as to throw Mud aboard with their Hands. The
Enemy was also priviledged with a Great Heap of Plank,
lying on the Bank, and with an Hay Stock, which they Strengthened with Posts and Rayles; and from all these places, they
poured in their Vengeance upon the poor Sloops, while they so
placed Smaller parties of their Salvages, as to make it impossible for any of the Garrisons to afford 'em any relief. Lying
thus, within a Dozen yards of the Sloops, they did with their
Fire Arrows, divers times desperately set the Sloops on Fire:
but the brave Defendants, with a Swab at the End of a Rope

---

[1] Samuel Wheelwright.   [2] "It was ordered otherwise in Heaven."

tyed unto a Pole, and so dipt into the Water, happily put the Fire out. In brief, the Sloops gave the Enemy so brave a Repulse, that at Night they Retreated: when they Renewed their Assault, finding that their Fortitude would not assure the Success of the Assault unto them, they had recourse unto their Policy. First, an Indian comes on with a Slab for a Shield, before him; when a Shot from one of the Sloops pierced the Slab, which fell down instead of a Tombstone with the Dead Indian under it; on which, as little a Fellow as he was, I know not whether some will not reckon it proper to inscribe the Epitaph, which the Italians use to bestow upon their Dead Popes: When the Dog is Dead, all his Malice is Dead with him. Their next Stratagem was This: They brought out of the Woods a kind of a Cart, which they Trimm'd and Rigg'd, and Fitted up into a Thing, that might be called, A Chariot: whereupon they built a platform, shot-proof in the Front, and placed many men upon that platform. Such an Engine they understood how to Shape, without having Read (I suppose) the Description of the *Pluteus* in Vegetius![1] This Chariot they push'd on, towards the Sloops, till they were got, it may be, within Fifteen yards of them; when, lo, one of their Wheels, to their Admiration, Sunk into the Ground. A Frenchman Stepping to heave the Wheel, with an Helpful Shoulder, Storer Shot him down; Another Stepping to the Wheel, Storer with a well-placed Shot, sent him after his Mate: so the Rest thought it was best to let it stand as it was. The Enemy kept galling the Sloops, from their Several Batteries, and calling 'em to Surrender, with many fine promises to make them Happy, which ours answered with a just Laughter, that had now and then a mortiferous Bullet at the End of it. The Tide Rising, the Chariot overset, so that the men behind it lay open to the Sloops, which immediately Dispenced an horrible Slaughter among them; and they that could get away, got as fast, and as far off, as they could. In the Night the Enemy had much Discourse with the Sloops; they Enquired, Who were their Commanders? and the English gave an Answer, which in some other Cases and Places would have been too true, That they had a great many Commanders: but the

---

[1] Vegetius was the chief Roman writer on the military art; the *pluteus* was a shed or penthouse to protect soldiers while attacking a fortification.

Indians Replied, You ly, you have none but Converse, and
we will have him too before Morning! They also knowing,
that the Magazine was in the Garrison, lay under an Hill-
Side, Pelting at That by Times; but Captain Converse, once
in the Night, sent out Three or Four of his men into a Field
of Wheat, for a Shot, if they could get one. There seeing a
Black Heap lying together, Ours all at once let Fly upon them,
a Shot that Slew several of them that were thus Caught in the
Corn, and made the rest glad, that they found themselves Able
to Run for it. Captain Converse was this while in much Distress, about a Scout of Six men, which he had sent forth
to Newichawannick,[1] the Morning before the Arrival of the
Enemy, ordering them to Return the Day following. The
Scout Return'd, into the very Mouth of the Enemy, that lay
before the Garrison; but the Corporal, having his Wits about
him, call'd out aloud, (as if he had seen Captain Converse
making a Sally forth upon 'em) "captain, Wheel about your
men round the Hill, and we shall Catch 'em; there are but a
Few Rogues of 'em!" Upon which the Indians imagining,
that Captain Converse had been at their Heels, betook themselves to their Heels; and our Folks got safe into another Garrison. On the Lord's-day Morning, there was for a while a
Deep Silence among the Assailants; but at length getting into
a Body, they marched with great Formality towards the Garrison, where the Captain ordered his Handful of men to ly
Snug, and not to make a Shot, until every Shot might be likely
to do some Execution. While they thus beheld a Formidable
Crew of Dragons, coming with open mouth upon them, to
Swallow them up at a Mouthful, one of the Soldiers began to
speak of Surrendring; upon which the captain Vehemently
protested, That he would lay the man Dead, who should so
much as mutter that base word any more! and so they heard
no more on 't: but the Valiant Storer was put upon the like
protestation, to keep 'em in good Fighting trim, aboard the
Sloops also. The enemy now Approaching very near, gave
Three Shouts, that made the Earth ring again; and Crying
out, in English, Fire, and Fall on, Brave Boys! The whole
Body, drawn into Three Ranks, Fired at once. Captain Converse immediately ran into the several Flankers, and made

[1] Berwick.

their Best Guns Fire at such a rate, that several of the Enemy
fell, and the rest of 'em disappeared almost as Nimbly, as if
there had been so many Spectres: Particularly, a parcel of them
got into a small Deserted House; which having but a Board-
Wall to it, the Captain sent in after them those Bullets of
Twelve to the Pound, that made the House too hot, for them
that could get out of it. The Women in the Garrison on this
occasion took up the Amazonian Stroke, and not only brought
Ammunition to the Men, but also with a Manly Resolution
fired several Times upon the Enemy. The Enemy finding
that Things would not yet go to their minds at the Garrison,
drew off, to Try their Skill upon the Sloops, which lay still
abreast in the Creek, lash'd fast one to another. They built
a Great Fire-Work, about Eighteen or Twenty Foot Square,
and fill'd it up with Combustible matter, which they Fired;
and then they set it in the way, for the Tide now to Float it
up, unto the Sloops, which had now nothing but an horrible
Death before them. Nevertheless their Demands, of both the
Garrison and the Sloops to yield themselves, were answered
no otherwise than with Death upon many of them, Spit from
the Guns of the Beseiged. Having tow'd their Fire-Work as
far as they durst, they committed it unto the Tide; but the
Distressed Christians that had this Deadly Fire Swimming
along upon the Water towards 'em, committed it unto God:
and God looked from Heaven upon them, in this prodigious
Article of their Distress. *These poor men cried, and the Lord,
heard them, and saved them out of their Troubles:*[1] The Wind,
unto their Astonishment, immediately turn'd about, and with
a Fresh Gale drove the Machin ashore on the other side, and
Split it so, that the Water, being let in upon it, the Fire went
out. So, the godly men that saw God from Heaven thus
Fighting for them, Cried out, with an Astonishing Joy, *If it
had not been the Lord, who was on our Side, they had Swallowed
us up quick; Blessed be the Lord, who hath not given us a prey to
their Teeth; our Soul is Escaped, as a Bird out of the Snare of
the Fowlers!*[2] The Enemy were now in a pittiful pickle,
with Toiling, and Moiling in the Mud, and black'ned with it,
if Mud could add Blackness to such Miscreants; and their
Ammunition was pretty well Exhausted: so that now they

[1] Psalm xxxiv. 6.   [2] Psalm cxxiv. 2, 3, 6, 7.

began to Draw off, in all parts, and with Rafts get over the River; some whereof breaking, there did not a few Cool their late Heat by falling into it. But first, they made all the Spoil they could, upon the Cattel about the Town; and giving one Shot more at the Sloops, they kill'd the only Man, of ours, that was kill'd aboard 'em. Then, after about Half an Hours Consultation, they sent a Flag of Truce to the Garrison, advising 'em with much Flattery, to Surrender; but the Captain sent 'em word, That he wanted for nothing, but for men to come, and Fight him. The Indian replied unto Captain Converse, Being you are so Stout, why don't you come and Fight in the open Field, like a Man, and not Fight in a Garrison, like a Squaw? The Captain rejoined; what a Fool are you? do you think, Thirty men a Match for Five Hundred? No, (says the Captain, counting, as well he might, each of his Fifteen men to be as Good as Two!) Come with your Thirty men upon the Plain, and I'le meet you with my Thirty, as soon as you will. Upon this, the Indian answered; Nay, mee own, English Fashion is all one Fool; you kill mee, mee kill you! No, better ly somewhere, and Shoot a man, and hee no see! That the best Soldier! Then they fell to Coaksing the Captain, with as many Fine Words as the Fox in the Fable had for the Allurement of his Prey unto him; and urged mightily, that Ensign Hill, who stood with the Flag of Truce,[1] might stand a little nearer their Army. The Captain, for a Good Reason, to be presently discerned, would not allow That: whereupon they fell to Threatning and Raging, like so many Defeated Devils, using these Words, Damn ye, we'll cut you as small as Tobacco, before to morrow Morning. The Captain bid 'em to make Hast, for he wanted work; so, the Indian throwing his Flag on the Ground, ran away, and Ensign Hill nimbly Stripping his Flag ran into the Valley, but the Salvages presently Fired, from an Ambushment behind a Hill, near the place, where they had urged for a Parley.

And now for poor John Diamond! the Enemy Retreating (which opportunity the Sloops took, to Burn down the Dangerous Hay-Stock,) into the plain, out of Gun-shot, they fell to Torturing their Captive John Diamond, after a manner very Diabolical. They Stripped him, they Scalped him alive, and

[1] John Hill of Saco.

after a Castration, they Finished that Article in the Punishment of Traitors upon him; they Slit him with Knives, between
his Fingers and his Toes; They made cruel Gashes in the most
Fleshy parts of his Body, and stuck the Gashes with Firebrands,
which were afterwards found Sticking in the wounds.   Thus
they Butchered One poor Englishman, with all the Fury that
they would have spent upon them all; and performed an Exploit, for Five Hundred Furies to brag of, at their coming home.
Ghastly to Express! what was it then to Suffer?   They Returned then unto the Garrison, and kept Firing at it now and
then, till near Ten a Clock at Night; when they all marched
off, leaving behind 'em some of their Dead; whereof one was
Monsieur Labocree, who had about his Neck a Pouch with
about a Dozen Reliques ingeniously made up, and a Printed
Paper of Indulgencies, and several other Implements; but it
seems none of the Amulets about his Neck would save him
from a Mortal Shot in the Head.   Thus in Forty-Eight Hours,
was Finished an Action as Worthy to be Related, as perhaps
any that occurs in our Story.   And it was not long before the
Valiant Gouge, who bore his part in this Action, did another
that was not much inferiour to it, when he suddenly Recovered
from the French a valuable prey, which they had newly taken
upon our Coast.

I doubt, Reader, we have had this Article of our History
a little too long.   We will finish it, when we have Remark'd,
That albeit there were too much Feebleness discovered by my
Countrymen, in some of their Actions, during this War at Sea,
as well as on Shore, yet several of their Actions, especially at
Sea, deserve to be Remembered.   And I cannot but particularly bespeak a Remembrance, for the Exploit performed by
some of my Neighbours, in a Vessel going into Barbadoes.
They were in sight of Barbadoes assaulted by a French Vessel,
which had a good number of Guns, and between Sixty and
Seventy Hands.   Our Vessel had Four Guns, and Eight Fighting Men (Truly such!) with two Tawny Servants.   The
Names of these Men were Barret, Sunderland, Knoles, Nash,
Morgan, Fosdyke, and Two more, that I now forget.   A desperate Engagement ensued; wherein our Eight Marriners
managed the matter with such Bravery, that by the Help of
Heaven they kill'd between Thirty and Forty of the French

Assailants, without losing one of their own little Number: And they sank the French Vessel, which lay by their side, out of which they took Twenty-Seven prisoners, whereof some were wounded, and all crying for Quarter. In the Fight the French Pennant, being by the wind fastned about the Topmast of the English Vessel, it was torn off by the sinking of the French Vessel, and left pleasantly flying there. So they sail'd into Barbadoes, where the Assembly voted them one Publick Acknowledgment, of their Courage and Conduct, in this Brave Action, and our History now gives them Another.

Article XVII.

The Fort at Pemmaquid.

His Excellency Sir William Phips being arrived now the Governour of New-England,[1] applied himself with all possible Vigour, to carry on the War: And the Advice of a New Slaughter some time in July made by the Indians, on certain poor Husbandmen in their Meadows, at the North Side of Merrimack-River, put an Accent upon the Zeal of the Designs, which he was now vigorously prosecuting. He Raised about Four Hundred and Fifty Men, and in pursuance of his Instructions from Whitehall, he laid the Foundations of a Fort at Pemmaquid, which was the Finest Thing that had been seen in these parts of America.[2] Captain Wing, assisted with Captain Bancroft, went through the former part of the Work; and the latter part of it was Finished by Captain March. His Excellency, attended in this matter with these worthy Captains, did, in a few Months, dispatch a Service for the King, with a Prudence, and Industry, and Thriftiness, Greater than any Reward they ever had for it. The Fort, called The William Henry, was built of Stone, in a Quadrangular Figure; being about Seven hundred and thirty-seven Foot in Compass, without the Outer Walls, and an Hundred and Eight Foot Square, within the Inner ones; Twenty-Eight Ports it had, and Fourteen (if not Eighteen) Guns mounted, whereof Six were

---

[1] Governor Phips arrived at Boston on Saturday, May 14, 1692.
[2] Early in August, 1692. Extensive remains of the fort are still to be seen.

Eighteen-Pounders. The Wall on the South Line, fronting to
the Sea, was Twenty-Two Foot High, and more than Six Foot
Thick at the Ports, which were Eight Foot from the Ground.
The Great Flanker or Round Tower, at the Western End of
this Line, was Twenty-Nine Foot High. The Wall on the
East line, was Twelve Foot High, on the North it was Ten, on
the West it was Eighteen. It was Computed, that in the
whole, there were laid above Two Thousand Cart-Loads of
Stone. It stood about a Score of Rods from High-Water
Mark; and it had generally at least Sixty men posted in it, for
its Defence, which if they were Men, might easily have maintained it against more than Twice Six Hundred Assailants.
Yea, we were almost Ready to flatter our selves that we
might have writ on the Gates of this Fort, as the French did
over that of Namur, (yet afterwards taken by K. William)
Reddi, non Vinci potest.[1] Now, as the Architect, that built
the Strong Fortress at Narne in Poland, had, for his Recompence, his Eyes put out, lest he should build such another;
Sir William Phips was almost as hardly Recompenced, for the
Building of This at Pammaquid. Although this Fort thus
Erected in the Heart of the Enemies Country did so Break
the Heart of the Enemy, that indeed they might have call'd
it, as the French did theirs upon the River of the Illinois, the
Fort of Crevecœur;[2] and the Tranquillity After Enjoyed by
the Country, (which was very much more than Before) was,
under God, much owing thereunto: Yet the Expense of maintaining it, when we were so much impoverished otherwise,
made it continually complained of, as one of the Countryes
Grievances. The Murmurings about this Fort were so Epi-
demical, that, if we may speak in the Foolish cant of Astrology,
and Prognosticate from the Aspect of Saturn upon Mars, at
its Nativity, Fort William-Henry, Thou hast not long to Live!
Before the year Ninety-Six Expire, thou shalt be demolished.
In the mean Time, let us accompany Major Church going with
a Company to Penobscot, where he took Five Indians; and
afterwards, to Taconet, where the Indians discovering his
Approach, set their own Fort on fire themselves, and flying

---

[1] "It may be given up but it cannot be conquered."

[2] Fort Crèvecœur was the fort which La Salle built in 1680, near the site of
Peoria, Illinois.

from it, left only their Corn to be destroy'd by him.[1] And so we come to the end of 1692, Only we are stopt a little, with a very strange Parenthesis.

ARTICLE XVIII.

A Surprising Thing laid before the Reader for him to Judge, (if he can) what to make of it.

Reader, I must now address thee, with the Words of a Poet:

> *Dicam Insigne Recens, adhuc*
> *Indictum ore alio.*   Horat.[2]

But with Truths more confirmed, than what uses to come from the Pen of a Poet. The Story of the Prodigious War, made by the Spirits of the Invisible World upon the People of New-England, in the year, 1692, hath Entertain'd a great part of the English World, with a just Astonishment: and I have met with some Strange Things, not here to be mentioned, which have made me often think, that this inexplicable War might have some of its Original among the Indians, whose chief Sagamores are well known unto some of our Captives, to have been horrid Sorcerers, and hellish Conjurers and such as Conversed with Dæmons. The Sum of that Story is written in *The Life of Sir William Phips;* with such Irreproachable Truth, as to Defy the utmost Malice and Cunning of all our Sadduces, to Confute it, in so much as one Material Article: And that the Balant, and Latrant Noises of that sort of People, may be forever Silenced, the Story will be abundantly Justified, when the further Account written of it, by Mr. John Hale, shall be published: For none can suspect a Gentleman, so full of Dissatisfaction, at the proceedings then used against the Supposed Witchcrafts, as Now that Reverend Person is, to be a Superstitious Writer upon that Subject.[3]

---

[1] This was the third eastern expedition of Benjamin Church. See his *Entertaining Passages*, pp. 82–86. The site of the Teconnet fort is in Winslow, Maine, well up the Kennebec River.

[2] "I will sing a notable event, hitherto unsung by any other lips." Horace, *Odes*, III. 25, v. 7.

[3] Rev. John Hale's *Modest Inquiry into the Nature of Witchcraft* was first published at Boston in 1702. The narrative parts of it are reprinted in the next

Now in the Time of that matchless War, there fell out a Thing at Glocester, which falls in here most properly to be related: A town so Scituated, Surrounded, and Neighboured, in the County of Essex, that no man in his Wits will imagine, that a Dozen Frenchmen and Indians would come and alarm the Inhabitants for Three weeks together, and Engage 'em in several Skirmishes, while there were two Regiments Raised, and a Detachment of Threescore men sent unto their Succour, and not one man Hurt in all the Actions, and all End unaccountably. And because the Relation will be Extraordinary, I will not be my self the Author of any one clause in it: but I will Transcribe the words of a Minister of the Gospel, who did me the Favour, with much critical Caution, to Examine Witnesses, not long after the Thing happened, and then sent me the Following Account.

A Faithful Account of many Wonderful and Surprising Things which happened in the Town of Glocester, in the Year 1692.

Ebenezer Bapson, about midsummer, in the year 1692, with the rest of his Family, almost every Night heard a Noise, as if persons were going and running about his House. But one Night being abroad late, at his Return home he saw Two men come out of his Door, and run from the end of the House into the Corn. But those of the Family told him, there had been no person at all there: whereupon he got his Gun, and went out in pursuit after them, and coming a little Distance from the House, he saw the Two men start up from behind a Log, and run into a little Swamp, saying to each other, " The Man of the House is Come now, Else we might have taken the House." So, he heard nor saw no more of them.

Upon this, the whole Family got up, and went with all speed, to a Garrison near by; and being just got into the Garrison, they heard men Stamping round the Garrison: Whereupon Bapson took his Gun, and ran out, and saw Two men again Running down an Hill into a Swamp. The next Night but one, the said Bapson going toward a fresh Meadow, saw Two men, which looked like Frenchmen, one of them having a Bright Gun upon his Back, and both running a great pace towards him, which caused him to make the best of his way to the Garrison, where being come, several heard a Noise, as if men were Stamping and Running, not far from the Garrison. Within a

volume of this series, *Narratives of the Witchcraft Cases*, to which the reader is referred for fuller accounts of this painful episode of 1692–1693.

Night or two after this, the persons in the Garrison heard a Noise, as if men were throwing Stones against the Barn. Not long after this, Bapson, with John Brown, saw Three men, about a Gun-shot off the Garrison, which they endeavoured to Shoot at, but were disappointed by their Running to and fro, from the Corn into the Bushes. They were seen Two or Three Nights together: but though the abovesaid strove to shoot at them, they could never attain it. On July 14, Bapson and Brown, with the rest of the men in the Garrison, saw, within Gun-shot, half a dozen men; whereupon all the men, but one, made hast out of the Garrison, marching towards them. Bapson presently overtook two of them, which run out of the Bushes, and coming close to them, he presented his Gun at them, and his Gun missing fire, the two men Returned into the Bushes. Bapson then called unto the other persons, which were on the other side of the Swamp, and upon his call, they made Answer, " Here they are! Here they are!" Bapson then running to meet them, Saw Three men walk softly out of the Swamp by each other's Side; the middlemost having on a white Wastcoat. So being within Two or Three Rod of them, he Shot, and as soon as his Gun was off, they all fell down. Bapson then running to his supposed prey, cried out unto his Companions, whom he heard on the other side of the Swamp, and said, he had kill'd Three! he had kill'd Three! But coming almost unto them, they all rose up, and one of them Shot at him, and hearing the Bullet whiss by him, he ran behind a Tree, and Loaded his Gun, and seeing them lye behind a Log, he crept toward them again, telling his Companions, they were here! So, his Companions came up to him, and they all Ran directly to the Log, with all speed; but before they got thither, they saw them start up, and run every man his way; One of them run into the Corn, whom they pursued, and hemm'd in; and Bapson seeing him coming toward himself, Shot at him, as he was getting over the Fence, and saw him fall off the Fence on the Ground, but when he came to the Spot, he could not find him. So they all searched the Corn; and as they were searching, they heard a great Discoursing in the Swamp, but could not understand what they said; for they spoke in an unknown Tongue. Afterwards, looking out from the Garrison, they saw several men Sculking among the Corn, and Bushes, but could not get a Shot at them.

The next morning, just at Day-break, they saw one man come out of the Swamp, not far from the Garrison, and stand close up against the Fence, within Gun-shot. Whereupon Isaac Prince, with a long Gun, shot at him with Swan-shot, and in a moment he was gone out of sight, they saw him no more. Upon this, Bapson went, to carry News to the Harbour; and being about Half a mile in his

way thither, he heard a Gun go off, and heard a Bullet whiss close
by his Ear, which Cut off a Pine bush just by him, and the Bullet
lodg'd in an Hemlock-Tree. Then looking about, he saw Four men
Running towards him, one with a Gun in his Hand, and the other
with Guns on their Shoulders. So he ran into the Bushes, and turning about, shot at them, and then ran away and saw them no more.
About Six men returned from the Harbour with him, searching the
woods as they went; and they saw, where the Bullet had cut off the
Pine-bush, and where it was lodg'd in the Hemlock-Tree, and they
took the Bullet out, which is still to be seen. When they were come
to the Garrison, they went to look for the Tracks of the Strange men,
that had been seen, and saw several Tracks; and whilst they were
looking on them, they saw one, which look'd like an Indian, having
on a Blue coat, and his Hair Ty'd up behind, Standing by a Tree,
and looking on them. But as soon as they spake to each other, he
ran into a Swamp, and they after him, and one of them shot at him,
but to no purpose. One of them also saw another, which look'd
like a Frenchman, but they quickly lost the sight of him.

   July 15. Ezekiel Day, being in Company with several others,
who were ordered to Scout the woods, when they came to a certain
Fresh Meadow, two miles from any House, at some Distance from
the said Meadow he saw a man, which he apprehended to be an
Indian, cloathed in Blue; and as soon as he saw him start up and
run away, he shot at him; whereupon he saw another rise up a little
way off, who also run with speed; which, together with the former,
were quickly out of sight; and though himself, together with his
Companions, diligently sought after them, they could not find them.
The same Day John Hammond, with several other persons, Scouting
in the woods, saw another of these Strange men, having on a blue
Shirt, and white Breeches, and something about his Head; but could
not overtake him.

   July 17. Three or Four of these Unaccountable Troublers came
near the Garrison; but they could not get a shot at them. Richard
Dolliver, also, and Benjamin Ellary, creeping down an Hill, upon
Discovery, saw several men come out of an Orchard, walking backward and forward, and striking with a stick upon John Row's Deserted
House, (the Noise of which, was heard by others at a Considerable
Distance;) Ellary counting them, to be Eleven in all; Dolliver Shot
at the midst of them, where they stood Thickest, and immediately
they dispersed themselves, and were quickly gone out of sight.

   July 18. Which was the Time that Major Appleton sent about
Sixty men, from Ipswich, for the Towns Assistance, under these inexplicable Alarms, which they had suffered Night and Day, for about

a Fortnight together; John Day testifies, that he went in Company with Ipswich and Gloucester Forces, to a Garrison, about Two miles and an Half, from the Town; and News being brought in, that Guns went off, in a Swamp not far from the Garrison, some of the men, with himself, ran to discover what they could; and when he came to the Head of the Swamp, he saw a man with a Blue Shirt, and bushy black Hair, run out of the Swamp, and into the Woods; he ran after him, with all speed, and came several Times within shot of him: but the woods being Thick, he could not obtain his Design of Shooting him; at length, he was at once gone out of sight; and when afterwards, he went to look for his Track, he could find none, though it were a low miry place, that he ran over.

About *July* 25, Bapson went into the Woods, after his Cattel, and saw Three men stand upon a point of Rocks, which look'd toward the Sea. So he crept among the Bushes, till he came within Forty yards of them: and then presented his Gun at them, and Snapt, but his Gun miss'd Fire, and so it did above a Dozen Times, till they all Three came up towards him, walking a slow pace, one of them having a Gun upon his Back. Nor did they take any more Notice of him, than just to give him a Look; though he snapt his Gun at them, all the while they walked toward him, and by him; neither did they quicken their pace at all, but went into a parcel of Bushes, and he saw them no more. When he came home, he snapt his Gun several Times, sometimes with but a few Corns of Powder, and yet it did not once miss Fire.—After this, there occurred several Strange Things; but now concluding they were but Spectres, they took little further Notice of them.

[Several other Testimonies, all to the same Effect with the Foregoing, my Friend had added, which for brevity I omit: and only add, the most considerable of these passages were afterward Sworn before one of Their Majesties council.]

Reverend and truly Honoured Sir, According to your Request, I have Collected a brief Account of the Occurrences, remark'd in our Town, the last year. Some of them are very Admirable Things, and yet no less True than Strange, if we may Believe the Assertions of Credible persons. Tho' because of Great Hast, it is a rough Draught, yet there is nothing written, but what the persons mentioned would, if duely called, confirm the Truth of, by Oath.

I might have given you a larger Account; only several who Saw and Heard some of the most Remarkable things, are now beyond Sea. However, I hope, the Substance of what is written, will be enough to Satisfy all Rational Persons, that Glocester was not Alarumed last Summer, for above a Fortnight together, by real French and Indians, but that the Devil and his Agents were the cause of all the Molestation, which at this Time befel the Town; in the Name of whose Inhabitants I would take upon me, to Entreat your Earnest Prayers to the Father of mercies, that those Apparitions may not prove the sad Omens of some future and more horrible Molestations to them.

May 19. 1693. Sir,

Your very Humble Servant,

J. E.[1]

Now Reader, albeit that passage of the Sacred Story, 2 Chron. 20 : 22. *The Lord set Ambushments against the Children of Ammon, Moab, and Mount Seir, and they were Smitten*; is by the best Expositors thus understood; that there was the Ministry of the Holy Angels wondrously employ'd in this matter; the Angels in the Shape of Moabites and Ammonites fell upon them of Mount Sier, and upon this apprehended provocation they then all fell upon one another, until the whole Army was destroyed: Nevertheless I entirely refer it unto thy judgment, (without the least offer of my own) whether Satan did not now Set Ambushments against the Good People of Glocester, with Dæmons, in the Shape of Armed Indians and Frenchmen appearing to considerable Numbers of the Inhabitants and mutually Firing upon them, for the best part of a Month together. I know, the most Considerate Gentlemen in the Neighbourhood, unto this Day, Believe this whole matter to have been a Prodigious piece of the Strange Descent from the Invisible World, then made upon other parts of the Country. And the publication of this Prodigy among other Wonders of the Invisible World among us, has been Delay'd until Now, that so the Opinion of our most considerate Gentlemen about it, might have Time for a thorough Concoction: and that the Gentlemen of the Order of St. Thomas, may have no Objection to make against it. But, be it what it will, they are not a few profane Squibs from the Sons of the Extravagant Bekkar,[2] that will be a fit Explication for Things thus Attested, and so very Marvellous.

[1] Rev. John Emerson of Gloucester.

[2] Balthasar Bekker (1634–1698), Dutch theologian, who in his *De Betooverde Wereld* ("The Enchanted World," Leeuwarden, 1691, and various other editions and translations) combated valiantly the current notions respecting witchcraft.

ARTICLE XIX.

Pacem, Te Poscimus Omnes.[1]

In the year 1693 his Excellency sent away Captain Converse, to draw off the fittest of the Officers and Soldiers, quartered in the East, for a March, and causing about Three Hundred and Fifty more to be Levied, gave him, what he had merited above a year ago; even a Commission of Major, and Commander in Chief over these Forces.   While Major Converse was at Wells, hearing of some Indians, that were seen in the Woods, he Surprised them all; and finding that they had cut off a poor Family at Oyster River,[2] he gave the chief of them something of what they also had merited.   Going to Pemmaquid, after some service there, they Sailed up Sheepscote River, and then marched through the Woods to Taconet, which being Deserted by the Indians, they ranged through many other Woods; but could meet with none of their Enemies.   Repairing then to Saco, they began another Fort, which was carried on by that worthy Gentleman Major Hook,[3] and the truly commendable Captain Hill, and proved a matter of Good Consequence unto the Province.   While these Things were doing, sometime in July, the Straggling Indians did some Spoil upon Quaboag,[4] a remote Village, in the Road unto Connecticut: but Advice being dispatch'd unto the Towns upon Connecticut-River, a party immediately Sally'd out after the Spoilers, and leaving their Horses at the Entrance of a Swamp, whither by their Track they had followed them, they come upon the Secure Adversary, and kill'd the most of them, and Recovered the Captives, with their Plunder; and Returning home, had some Reward for so brisk an Action.

But now, the Indians in the East, probably Disheartened by the Forts Erecting that were like to prove a sore Annoyance to them, in their Enterprizes; and by the Fear of wanting Ammunition, with other Provisions, which the French were not so Able just now to dispence unto them; and by a presump-

[1] "We all sue thee for peace."   [2] Durham, New Hampshire.
[3] Francis Hooke, a member of the provincial council.
[4] Brookfield, Massachusetts.

tion that an Army of Maqua's, (part of those Terrible Cannibals
to the Westward, whereof 'tis affirmed by those who have
published the Stories of their Travels among them, That they
have destroy'd no less than Two Million Salvages of other
Nations about them, through their being Supplied with Fire-
Arms, before Hundreds of other Nations lying between them,
and the River Meschasippi)[1] was come into their Country,
because they found some of their Squa's killed upon a Whortle-
berry Plain: and all the charms of the French Fryar, then
Resident among them,[2] could not hinder them, from Suing
to the English for Peace.   And the English, being so involved
in Debts, that they Scarce knew how to prosecute the War
any further, took some Notice of their Suit.   Accordingly, a
Peace was made, upon the Ensuing Articles.[3]

Province of the Massachusetts Bay in New-England.

*The Submission and Agreement of the Eastern Indians at Fort William
Henry in Pemmaquid, the 11th day of August, in the Fifth year of
the Reign of our Soveraign Lord and Lady, William and Mary, by
the Grace of God, of England, Scotland, France, and Ireland, King
and Queen, Defenders of the Faith, etc. 1693.*

Whereas a Bloody War has for some years now past been made
and carried on by the Indians within the Eastern parts of the said
Province, against Their Majesties Subjects the English, through the
Instigation and Influences of the French; and being sensible of the
Miseries which we and our People are reduced unto, by adhering to
their ill Council: We whose names are hereunto Subscribed, being
Sagamores and Chief Captains of all the Indians belonging to the
several Rivers of Penobscote and Kennebeck, Amarascogin, and
Saco, parts of the said Province of the Massachusets Bay, within
Their said Majesties Soveraignty, Having made Application unto his
Excellency Sir William Phips, Captain General and Governour in
Chief in and over the said Province, that the War may be put to an
End; Do lay down our Arms, and cast our selves upon Their said

[1] Mississippi.

[2] The reference is to Father Pierre Thury, missionary at Pentagoët (Castine, Maine), but he was a seminary priest, not a friar.

[3] This peace had been forwarded by the fact that Count Frontenac, engaged in war with the Mohawks or Five Nations in New York, had summoned
to his aid many French who had been busy among the Indians of the East.   The
failure of Iberville to attack Pemaquid in 1693 when he had an advantage also
encouraged the peace party among the Abenakis headed by Madockawando.

Majesties Grace and Favour. And each of us respectively for our selves, and in the Name and with the free consent of all the Indians belonging unto the several Rivers aforesaid, and of all other Indians within the said Province of and from Merrimack River, unto the most Easterly Bounds of the said Province; hereby acknowledging our hearty Subjection and Obedience unto the Crown of England; and do solemnly Covenant, Promise and Agree, to and with the said Sir William Phips, and his Successors, in the place of Captain General and Governour in Chief of the aforesaid Province or Territory, on Their said Majesties behalf, in manner following, *viz.*

That at all time and times for ever, from and after the date of these Presents, we will cease and forbear all acts of Hostility towards the Subjects of the Crown of England, and not offer the least hurt or violence to them or any of them in their Persons or Estate: But will henceforward hold and maintain a firm and constant Amity and Friendship with all the English.

Item. We abandon and forsake the French Interest, and will not in any wise adhere to, join with, aid or assist them in their Wars, or Designs against the English, nor countenance, succour, or conceal any of the Enemy Indians of Canada or other places, that shall happen to come to any of our Plantations within the English Territory, but secure them if in our power, and deliver them up unto the English.

That all English Captives in the hands or power of any of the Indians within the Limits aforesaid, shall with all possible speed be set at liberty, and returned home without any Ransom or Payment to be made or given for them or any of them.

That Their Majesties Subjects the English, shall and may peaceably and quietly enter upon, improve, and for ever enjoy, all and singular their Rights of Lands, and former Settlements and possessions within the Eastern parts of the said Province of the Massachusets Bay, without any pretensions or claims by us, or any other Indians, and be in no wise molested, interrupted, or disturbed therein.

That all Trade and Commerce, which hereafter may be allowed between the English and Indians, shall be under such Management and Regulation as may be stated by an Act of the General Assembly, or as the Governour of the said Province for the time being, with the Advice and Consent of the Council, shall see cause to Direct and Limit.

If any controversie, or difference, at any time hereafter happen to arise between any of the English and Indians for any real or supposed wrong or injury done on one side or the other, no private Revenge shall be taken by the Indians for the same, but proper Application be made to Their Majesties Government, upon the place, for

Remedy thereof in a due course of Justice, we hereby submitting our selves to be ruled and governed by Their Majesties Laws, and desire to have the benefit of the same.

For the more full manifestation of our sincerity and integrity in all that which we have herein before Covenanted and Promised, we do deliver unto Sir William Phips, their Majesties Governour as aforesaid, Ahassombamett, Brother to Edgeremett, Wenongahewitt, Cousin to Madockawando, and Edgeremett, and Bagatawawongon, also[1] Sheepscoat John, to abide and remain in the Custody of the English, where the Governour shall direct, as Hostages or Pledges, for our Fidelity, and true performance of all and every the foregoing Articles, reserving Liberty to exchange them in some reasonable time for a like number, to the acceptance of the Governour and Council of the said Province, so they be persons of as good account, and esteem amongst the Indians, as those which are to be exchanged. In Testimony whereof, we have hereunto set our several Marks and Seals, the Day and Year first above-written.

The above-written Instrument was deliberately read over, and the several Articles and Clauses thereof interpreted unto the Indians, who said they well understood, and consented thereunto, and was then Signed, Sealed, and Delivered in the Presence of us,

JOHN WING.
NICHOLAS MANNING.
BENJAMIN JACKSON.

EDGEREMETT.
MADOCKAWANDO.
WASSAMBOMET of NAVIDGWOCK.
WENOBSON of TECONNET in behalf of MOXUS.
KETTERRAMOGIS of NARRIDGWOCK.
AHANQUIT of PENOBSCOT.
BOMASEEN.
NITAMEMET.
WEBENES.
AWANSOMECK.
ROBIN DONEY.
MADAUMBIS.
PAQUAHARET, *alias*, NATHANIEL.

JOHN HORNYBROOK,
JOHN BAGATAWAWONGO, *alias*,
SHEEPSCOAT JOHN.
PHILL. OUNSAKIS, Squaw.
} *Interpreters.*

[1] From what appears in the signatures below, it seems clear that this word should be *alias*.

ARTICLE XX.

Bloody Fishing at Oyster River; [1] *and Sad Work at Groton.*

A Years Breathing Time was a great Favour of Heaven to
a Country quite out of Breath, with Numberless Calamities:
But the Favour was not so Thankfully Enjoyed, as it should
have been. And now, The Clouds Return after the Rain.
The Spectre that with Burning Tongs drove Xerxes to his War
upon the Græcians,[2] had not lost his Influence upon our Indians. The Perfidy of the Indians appeared first, in their not
Restoring the English Captives according to their Covenant;
but the perfidious Wretches Excused this, with many Protesta-
tions. That which added unto our Jealousies about them, was,
their Insolent carriage towards a Sloop, commanded by Captain Wing; and the Information of a Fellow called Hector,
that the Indians intended most certainly to break the Peace,
and had promised the French Priests, taking the Sacrament
thereupon, to destroy the first English Town they could
Surprize. Rumours of Indians Lurking about some of the
Frontier-Plantations, now began to put the poor people into
Consternation; but upon an Imagination that they were only
certain Bever-Hunters, the Consternation of the people went off
into Security. 'Tis affirmed by English Captives, which were
then at Canada, that the Desolation of Oyster River was commonly talk'd in the Streets of Quebec, Two months before it
was Effected; for the Spies had found no Town so Secure as
That And now what was Talk'd at Quebec in the month
of May, must be Done at Oyster River in the month of July;
for on Wednesday, July 18, 1694, the Treacherous Enemy
with a great Army fell upon that Place, about break of day,
and Kill'd and Captiv'd Ninety Four, (or, an Hundred) persons; about a Score of whom were men belonging to the
Trained Band of the Town. Several persons Remarkably
Escaped this Bloody Deluge, but none with more Bravery than
one Thomas Bickford, who had an House, a Little Pallisado'd,

[1] Oyster River, the present Durham, was about twelve miles from Portsmouth, New Hampshire.
[2] Herodotus, VII. 18.

by the River Side, but no man in it besides himself. He dex-
terously put his Wife, and Mother, and Children aboard a
Canoo, and Sending them down the River, he Alone betook
himself to the Defence of his House, against many Indians, that
made an Assault upon him.   They first would have perswaded
him, with many fair Promises, and then terrified him with as
many Fierce Threatnings, to yield himself; but he flouted and
fired at them, daring 'em, to come if they durst.   His main
Stratagem was, to Change his Livery as frequently as he could;
appearing Sometimes in one Coat, Sometimes in another,
Sometimes in an Hat, and Sometimes in a Cap; which caused
his Besiegers to mistake this One for Many Defendants.   In
fine, The pitiful Wretches, despairing to Beat him out of his
House, e'en left him in it; whereas many that opened unto
them, upon their Solemn Engagements of giving them Life
and Good Quarter, were barbarously butchered by them; and
the Wife of one Adams, then with Child, was with horrible
Barbarity Ripped up.   And thus there was an End of the
Peace made at Pemmaquid!   Upon this, the Friends of Mrs.
Ursula Cutt, (widow of Mr. John Cutt, formerly President of
New-Hampshire,) desired her, to leave her Farm, which was
about a Mile above the Bank Exposed to the Enemy, on the
south side of Piscataqua River.   She thank'd them for their
Care; but added, that she believed, the Enemy had now done
their Do for this Time; and however, by the End of the Week,
her Business at the Farm would be all dispatched, and on
Saturday, she would Repair to her Friends at the Bank.   But,
alas! before the End of the week, she saw the End of her Life:
On Saturday, about one or two a Clock in the Afternoon, the
Business at the Farm was Dispatched sure enough!   The
Indians Then Kill'd this Gentlewoman and Three other Peo-
ple, a little before they had Finished a point of Husbandry
then in their Hands.   Nor did the Storm go over so: Some
Drops of it fell upon the Town of Groton, a Town that lay,
one would think, far enough off the place where was the last
Scene of the Tragedy.   On July 27, About break of Day
Groton felt some Surprizing Blows from the Indian Hatchets.
They began their Attacks at the House of one Lieutenant Lakin,
in the out-skirts of the Town; but met with a Repulse there,
and lost one of their Crew.   Nevertheless, in other parts of

that Plantation, (when the Good people had been so tired out, as to lay down their Military Watch) there were more than Twenty persons killed, and more than a Dozen carried away. Mr. Gershom Hobart, the Minister of the place, with part of his Family, was Remarkably preserved from falling into their Hands, when they made themselves the Masters of his House; though they Took Two of his Children, whereof the one was killed, and the other some Time after happily Rescued out of his Captivity.

I remember, the Jews in their Book *Taanith*[1] tell us, The Elders Proclaimed a Fast in their Cities on this Occasion, because the Wolves had Devoured two Little Children beyond Jordan. Truly, the Elders of New-England were not a little concern'd at it, when they saw the Wolves thus devouring their Children, even on this side of Merrimack!

Article XXI.

More English Blood Swallowed, but Revenged.

Reader, we must after This, ever Now and Then, Expect the happening of some unhappy Accident. The Blood thirsty Salvages, not content with quaffing the Blood of Two or Three persons, found at work, in a Field at Spruce creek, on Aug. 20, and of another person at York, the same day, (Captivating also a Lad, which they found with him;) They did on Aug. 24, Kill and Take Eight persons at Kittery. Here, a little Girl about Seven years old, the Daughter of one Mr. Downing, fell into their Barbarous Hands; they knock'd her o'th' Head, and barbarously Scalped her, leaving her on the Cold Ground, (and it was then very Cold, beyond what use to be,) where she lay all the Night Ensuing: Yet she was found Alive the Next Morning, and Recovering, she is to this Day Alive and well; only the place broke in her skull will not endure to be closed up. He had another Daughter, which at the same Time almost miraculously Escaped their Hands. But so could not at another Time Joseph Pike of Newbury, the Deputy Sheriff of Essex, who, on Sept. 4, Travelling between Amesbury and Haverhil, in the Execution of his Office, with one Long, they

[1] A treatise on fasts, forming part of the Talmud.

both had an Arrest of Death served upon them from an Indian
Ambuscado. Bommaseen, a Commander of prime Quality
among the Indians, who had set his Hand unto the late Articles
of Submission, came, Nov. 19, with Two other Indians, to
Pemmaquid, as Loving as Bears, and as Harmless as Tygres,
pretending to be just Arrived from Canada, and much Afflicted
for the late mischiefs, (whereof there was witness, that he was
a principal Actor,) but Captain March with a Sufficient Activity Seized them; as Robin Doney,[1] another famous Villain
among them, with Three more, had been Seized at Saco Fort,
a little before. Bommaseen, was Convey'd unto Boston, that
he might in a close Imprisonment there, have Time to consider
of his Treacheries, and his Cruelties, for which the Justice of
Heaven had thus Delivered him up. When he was going to
Pemmaquid, he left his Company with a Strange Reluctancy
and Formality, as if he had presaged the Event; and when at
Pemmaquid he found the Event of his coming, he discovered
a more than ordinary Disturbance of mind: his Passions
foam'd and boil'd, like the very Waters at the Fall of Niagara.

But being thus fallen upon the mention of that Vengeance,
wherewith Heaven pursued the chief of the Salvage Murderers,
it may give some Diversion unto the Reader, in the midst of a
long and a sad Story, to insert a Relation of an Accident that
fell out a little after this Time.

The Indians, (as the Captives inform us) being hungry, and
hardly bestead, passed through deserted Casco, where they
spied several Horses in Captain Bracket's Orchard. Their
famish'd Squa's begg'd them Shoot the Horses, that they might
be revived with a little Roast-meat; but the young men were
for having a little Sport before their Supper. Driving the
Horses into a Pond, they took one of them, and furnished him
with an Halter, suddenly made of the Main and the Tail of
the Animal, which they cut off. A Son of the famous Hegon
was ambitious to mount this Pegasæan Steed; but being a
pittiful horseman, he ordered them, for fear of his Falling, to
ty his Legs fast under the Horse's Belly. No sooner was this
Beggar Set on Horse-back, and the Spark in his own opinion

---

[1] Perhaps a French half-breed. The seizure of Bomazeen and others coming
under a flag of truce was regarded by the French and Indians as an act of
treachery.

thoroughly Equipt, but the Mettlesome Horse furiously and presently ran with him out of Sight. Neither Horse nor Man were ever seen any more; the astonish'd Tawnies howl'd after one of their Nobility, disappearing by such an unexpected Accident. A few Days after they found one of his Legs (and that was All,) which they buried in Captain Bracket's Cellar, with abundance of Lamentation.

Article XXII.

A Conference with an Indian-Sagamore.

But now Bommaseen is fallen into our Hands, let us have a little Discourse with him.

Behold, Reader, the Troubles, and the Troublers of New-England! That thou may'st a little more Exactly Behold the Spirit of the matter, I'll Recite certain passages, occurring in a Discourse that pass'd between this Bommaseen (who was one of the Indian Princes, or Chieftains,) and a Minister of the Gospel,[1] in the year 1696.

Bommaseen was, with some other Indians, now a Prisoner, in Boston. He desired a Conference with a Minister, of Boston, which was granted him. Bommaseen, with the other Indians assenting and asserting to it, then told the Minister, That he pray'd his Instruction in the Christian religion; inasmuch as he was afraid, that the French, in the Christian Religion, which they taught the Indians, had Abused them. The minister Enquired of him, What of the Things taught 'em by the French, appear'd most Suspicious to 'em? He said, the French taught 'em, that the Lord Jesus Christ was of the French Nation; that His Mother, the Virgin Mary, was a French Lady; That they were the English who had Murdered him; and, That whereas He Rose from the Dead, and went up to the Heavens, all that would Recommend themselves unto His Favour, must Revenge His Quarrel upon the English, as far as they can. He ask'd the Minister, whether these Things were so; and pray'd the Minister to Instruct him in the True Christian Religion. The Minister considering, that the Humour and Manner of the Indians, was to have their Discourses managed

[1] Mather himself, of course.

with much of Similitude in them; Look'd about for some
Agreeable object, from whence he might with apt Resem-
blances Convey the Idæas of Truth unto the minds of Salvages; and he thought, none would be more Agreeable to
them than a Tankard of Drink, which happened then to
be standing on the Table.   So he proceeded in this Method
with 'em.

He told them, (still with proper Actions painting and
pointing out the Signs unto them,) that our Lord Jesus Christ
had given us a Good Religion, which might be Resembled unto
the Good Drink in the Cup upon the Table.

That if we Take this Good Religion, (even that Good
Drink,) into our Hearts, it will do us Good, and preserve us
from Death.

That God's Book, the Bible, is the Cup wherein that Good
Drink of Religion is offered unto us.

That the French, having the Cup of Good Drink in their
Hands, had put Poison into it, and then made the Indians to
Drink that Poisoned Liquor, whereupon they Run mad, and
fell to killing of the English, though they could not but know
it must unavoidably issue in their own Destruction at the
Last.

That it was plain the English had put no Poison into the
Good Drink; for they set the Cup wide open, and invited all
men to Come and See before they taste, even the very Indians
themselves; for we Translated the Bible into Indian.   That
they might gather from hence, that the French had put Poison
into the Good Drink, inasmuch as the French kept the Cup
fast shut, (the Bible in an Unknown Tongue,) and kept their
Hands upon the Eyes of the Indians, when they put it unto
their mouths.

The Indians Expressing themselves to be well Satisfied, with
what the Minister had hitherto said, pray'd him to go on,
with showing 'em, what was the Good Drink, and what was
the Poison, which the French had put into it.

He then set before them distinctly the chief Articles of the
Christian Religion, with all the Simplicity and Sincerity of a
Protestant: Adding upon each, This is the Good Drink, in
the Lord's Cup of Life: and they still professed, That they
liked it all.

Whereupon, he demonstrated unto them, how the Papists had in their Idolatrous Popery, some way or other Depraved and Alter'd every one of these Articles, with Scandalous Ingredients of their own Invention; Adding upon each, This is the Poison which the French have put into the Cup.

At last, he mentioned this Article.

"To obtain the Pardon of your Sins, you must confess your Sins to God, and pray to God, That He would Pardon your Sins, for the sake of Jesus Christ, who died for the Sins of His People: God Loves Jesus Christ infinitely; and if you place your Eye on Jesus Christ only, when you beg the Pardon of your Sins, God will Pardon them. You need confess your Sins to none but God, Except in cases when men have known your Sins, or have been Hurt by your Sins; and then those men should know that you confess your Sins; but after all, none but God can Pardon them."

He then added, "the French have put Poison into this Good Drink; they tell you, that you must confess your Sins to a Priest, and carry skins to a Priest, and Submit unto a Penance enjoined by a Priest; and this Priest is to give you a Pardon. There is no need of all This: 'Tis nothing but French Poison, all of it."

The Wretches appearing astonish'd, to meet with one who would so fairly put them into a glorious way to obtain the Pardon of their Sins, and yet take no Bever-Skins for it, in a Rapture of Astonishment they fell down on their knees, and got his Hand into theirs, and fell to kissing of it with an Extream show of Affection.

He shaking them off, with dislike of their posture, Bommaseen, with the rest of them, stood up; and first lifting up his Eyes and Hands to Heaven; declaring, That God should be Judge of his Heart in what he said, he then said, "Sir, I thank you for these Things; I Resolve to Spit up all the French Poison; You shall be my Father; I will be your Son; I beseech you, to continue to Instruct me in that Religion, which may bring me to the Salvation of my Soul!"——Now God knows, what Heart this Indian had, when he so Expressed himself: to Him let us leave it.

But so much for this Digression.

Article XXIII.

More Mischiefs in spite of Treaties.

Except it were the Falling of Two soldiers belonging to
Saco Garrison into the Hands of the Enemy, who Took the
one, and Kill'd the other, some Time in March, 1695, Many
Months pass'd away, without any Action between Them and
Us, And it is Reported by Returned Captives, That the Hand
of God reach'd them, when the Hand of Man could not find
them, and a Mortal Sickness did at a Strange Rate carry off
multitudes of them.   At length, upon the Mediation of old
Sheepscoat John, once a praying Indian, of the Reverend
Eliot's Cathecumens, but afterwards a Pagan, and now a
Popish Apostate, a Great Fleet of Canoos came into an Island,
about a League from the Fort at Pemmaquid, May 20, 1695,[1]
and after they had laid still there, all the Lord's Day, on Munday morning they sent unto the English for another Treaty.
They Declared, Their Design was to Exchange Captives, and
Renew the Peace, and condemned themselves for their Violat-
ing the Peace made near Two years ago.   Eight Captives,
they Immediately Delivered up; and upon a Grant of a Truce
for Thirty Days, Colonel John Philips, Lieut. Colonel Hawthorn,[2] and Major Converse, were sent Commissioners unto
Pemmaquid, for the management of that affayr.

Our Commissioners, with Good Reason, demanding a Surrender of all the English Captives, according to former Agreement, before they would allow any New Propositions of Peace
to be offered, the Indians, disgusted that their Idol Bommaseen
was left at Boston, broke off the Conference, and went off in
Discontent.[3] Advice was immediately dispatch'd into all parts
of the Eastern Country to stand well upon their Guard; notwithstanding which, on July 6 Major Hammond of Kittery
fell into the Hands of the Lurking Indians; and the next week,

[1] Rutherford Island (Christmas Cove).   The date should certainly be 1695,
though the Lord's Day was the 19th; the *Decennium Luctuosum* gives it as 1695,
but the reprint in the *Magnalia* alters this to 1693.

[2] John Hawthorn.

[3] The Indians thought that if they gave up their captives the English should
do the same.

Two men at Exeter were kill'd by some of the same Dangerous
Lurkers. Major Hammond was now aboard a Canoo, intending to put ashore at Saco; but some of the Garrison-Soldiers
there, not knowing that they had such a good Friend aboard,
inadvertently Fired upon the Canoo; and so the Indians carried him clear away. They transported him at length to
Canada, where he met with Extraordinary Civilities; Count
Frontenac, the Governour himself, nobly purchased him of
his Tawny master, and sent him home to New-England, by a
Vessel, which also fetch'd from thence a Considerable Number
(perhaps near Thirty) of English Prisoners. In August, the
House of one Rogers at Billerica was plundered, and about
Fifteen people Kill'd and taken, by Indians, which, by appearing and Approaching, 'tis said, on Horse-back, were not Suspected for Indians, (for, Who set them on Horse-back?) till
they Surprized the House they came to. And about the same
Time, Sergeant Haley, Venturing out of his Fort at Saco, Stept
into the Snares of Death. On Sept. 9, Sergeant March, with
Three more, were Killed by the Indians, and Six more, at the
same Time, wounded at Pemmaquid, Rowing a Gondula,
round an high Rocky point, above the Barbican. On Oct. 7,
the Indians entred the House of one John Brown at Newbury,
carrying away Nine Persons with them; whereupon Captain
Greenlief, nimbly pursuing the Murderers, did unhappily so
Stumble on them in the Night, that they wounded the good
man, and made their Escape over the River. The Captain
Retook all the Captives; but the Indians, in their going off,
Strook them all so Violently on the Head with the Clubs,
which I remember a French Historian somewhere calls by the
frightful name of Head-breakers,[1] that they afterwards all of
them dyed, Except a Lad that was only hurt in the Shoulder.
Some of them Lingred out for half a year, and some of them for
more than a whole year; but if the Doctors closed up the
wounds of their Heads, they would grow Light-headed, and
Faint, and Sick, and could not bear it; so at last they Died,
with their very Brains working out at their Wounds.

But having thus run over a Journal of Deaths for the year
1695, Let us before the year be quite gone, see some Vengeance
taken upon the Heads in the House of the Wicked. Know

[1] *Casse-tête* is a frequent French word for tomahawk.

then, Reader, that Captain March petitioning to be Dismiss'd
from his Command of the Fort at Pemmaquid, one Chub[1]
Succeeded him. And this Chub found an Opportunity, in a
pretty Chubbed manner, to kill the famous Edgeremett, and
Abenquid, a couple of Principal Sagamores, with one or Two
other Indians, On a Lord's-day, the Sixteenth of February.
Some that well enough liked the Thing which was now done,
did not altogether like the manner of doing it, because there
was a pretence of Treaty, between Chub and the Sagamores,
whereof he took his Advantage to lay violent Hands on them.
If there were any unfair Dealing (which I know not) in this
Action of Chub, there will be another February not far off,
wherein the Avengers of Blood will take their Satisfaction.

Article XXIV.

Still Mischief upon Mischief.

The Next whole year, namely 1696, had it not been for the
Degree of a Famine, which the Alteration of the course of
Nature in these, as well as other parts of the world, threatned
us withal, would have been a Year of Less Trouble than some
of the rest, in our Troublesome Decad. The most uneasie
Accident of this year shall be told, when we arrive unto the
Month of August; but in the mean Time it was a matter of
some Uneasiness, that on May 7, one John Church of Quochecho,
who had been a Captive, Escaped from the Hands of the Indians, almost Seven years before, was now Slain and Stript by
their Barbarous Hands; And, on June 24, one Thomas Cole,
of Wells, and his wife, were Slain by the Indians, returning
home with two of his Neighbours, and their Wives, all three
Sisters, from a Visit, of their Friends at York: And, on Jun. 26,
at several places within the Confines of Portsmouth, Several
Persons, Twelve or Fourteen, were Massacred, (with some
Houses Burnt,) and Four Taken, which yet were soon Retaken;
among whom, there was an Ancient Woman Scalpt for Dead,
and no doubt the Salvages upon producing her Scalp, received

---

[1] Pascho Chubb of Andover is the person referred to. His military ability
was hardly equal to that of his predecessor. His action at this time was bitterly
resented by the Indians. See p. 270, *post*.

the Price of her Death, from those that hired them, and yet
she so Recovered, as to be still Alive.   Moreover, on July 26,
the Lord's-Day, the People at Quochecho returning from the
Public Worship of God, Three of them were killed, Three of
them were wounded, and Three of them were carried away
Prisoners to Penobscot; which last Three were nevertheless
in less than Three weeks returned.   But now we are got into
fatal August; on the Fifth or Sixth Day of which Month, the
French having Taken one of the English Men of War, called
the *Newport*,[1] and Landed a few men, who joyn'd with the
Indians, to pursue their Business, Chub, with an unaccountable
Baseness, did Surrender the Brave Fort at Pemmaquid into
their Hands.   There were Ninety-Five men double-Armed, in
the Fort, which might have Defended it against Nine Times
as many Assailants; That a Fort now should be so basely
given up! imitating the Stile of Homer and Virgil, I cannot
help crying out, *O meræ Novangliæ, neque enim Novangli!* [2]
and yet if you read the Story written by the Sieur Froger, how
poorly St. James's Fort in Africa was given up to the French
in the year 1695,[3] You'll say the things done in America, are
not so bad, as what have been done in other parts of the world.
The Enemy having Demolished so fair a Citadel, now grown
mighty Uppish, Triumph'd, as well they might, Exceedingly;
and Threatned, that they would carry all before them.   The
Honourable Lieutenant Governour Stoughton, who was now
Commander in Chief over the Province, immediately did all
that could be done, to put a Stop unto the Fury of the Adversary.   By Sea, he sent out Three Men of War, who, disadvan-
taged by the Winds, came not soon Enough to engage the
French.   By Land, the Indians being so Posted in all quarters,
that the People could hardly Stir out, but about half a Score
of the poor People in their Fields here and there were pick'd
off, he sent Colonel Gidney[4] with Five Hundred men; who
perceiving the Salvages to be drawn off, only Strengthened the

---

[1] The *Newport*, Captain Paxton, was cruising off the Bay of Fundy to in-
tercept French supplies, when she was taken by Iberville, on his way to the capture of Pemaquid.

[2] "O mere New England women, not New England men!"

[3] See p. 215, note 2.

[4] Colonel Bartholomew Gedney of Salem, one of the "witch" judges.

Garrisons, and Returned.   The Lieutenant-Governour, that he
might not in any other point be wanting to the Public Safety,
hereupon dispatched Colonel Hawthorn, with a Suitable
Number of Soldiers and Frigats unto St. John's, with orders
to fetch away some Great Guns that were lying there, and
join with Major Church, who was gone with Forces that way,
to attack the Fort at St. John's, which was the Nest of all the
Wasps that Stung us; but the Difficulty of the Cold Season so
discouraged our men, that after the making of some few Shot,
the Enteprize found itself under too much Congelation to
proceed any further.[1]   So we will afflict our selves no
further for this year; Except only with mentioning the
Slaughter of about Five poor Soldiers, belonging to Saco-Fort,
Oct. 13, who had a Discovery of the Enemy, Seasonable Enough
to have made their Escape; yet, not Agreeing about the way of
making it, as if led by some Fatality to their Destruction, or,
as if they had been like the Squirrels, that must run down the
Tree, Squeaking and Crying into the mouths of the Rattle-
Snakes, that fix their Eyes upon them, they went back into
the very path where the Indian Ambush was lying for them.

ARTICLE XXV.

A Notable Exploit; wherein Dux Fœmina Facti.[2]

On March 15, 1697, the Salvages made a Descent upon the
Skirts of Haverhill, Murdering and Captivating about Thirty-
Nine Persons, and Burning about Half a Dozen Houses.   In
this Broil, one Hannah Dustan, having lain in about a Week,
attended with her Nurse, Mary Neff, a Widow, a Body of
Terrible Indians drew near unto the House, where she lay,
with Designs to carry on their Bloody Devastations.   Her
Husband hastened from his Employments abroad, unto the
Relief of his Distressed Family; and first bidding Seven of his
Eight children (which were from Two to Seventeen years of
Age) to get away as fast as they could, unto some Garrison in

---

[1] Church, *Entertaining Passages*, pp. 88–99, makes the enterprise much more
of a success.

[2] "A woman the leader in the achievement."   This story of Hannah Dustan
is confirmed by John Pike in his contemporary journal.

the Town, he went in, to inform his Wife of the horrible Distress come upon them.   E'er she could get up, the fierce Indians were got so near, that utterly despairing to do her any Service, he ran out after his Children; Resolving that on the Horse, which he had with him, he would Ride away with That which he should in this Extremity find his Affections to pitch most upon, and leave the Rest unto the care of the Divine Providence. He overtook his Children about Forty Rod from his Door; but then, such was the Agony of his Parental Affections, that he found it impossible for him to Distinguish any one of them from the rest; wherefore he took up a Courageous Resolution to Live and dy with them all.   A party of Indians came up with him; and now, though they Fired at him, and he Fired at them, yet he manfully kept at the Reer of his Little Army of Unarmed Children, while they Marched off, with the pace of a Child of Five years old; until, by the Singular Providence of God, he arrived safe with them all, unto a place of Safety, about a Mile or two from his House.   But his House must in the mean Time have more dismal Tragedies acted at it.   The Nurse trying to Escape, with the New-born Infant, fell into the Hands of the Formidable Salvages; and those furious Tawnies coming into the House, bid poor Dustan to Rise Immediately.   Full of Astonishment, she did so; and sitting down in the Chimney with an Heart full of most fearful Expectation, she saw the Raging Dragons riffle all that they could carry away, and set the House on Fire.   About Nineteen or Twenty Indians now led these away, with about Half a Score other English Captives; but e'er they had gone many Steps, they dash'd out the Brains of the Infant, against a Tree; and several of the other Captives, as they began to Tire in the sad Journey, were soon sent unto their Long Home; the Salvages would presently bury their Hatchets in their Brains, and leave their Carcases on the Ground for Birds and Beasts to feed upon.   However, Dustan (with her Nurse), notwithstanding her present Condition, Travelled that Night, about a Dozen Miles, and then kept up with their New Masters in a long Travel of an Hundred and Fifty Miles, more or less, within a few Days Ensuing, without any sensible Damage, in their Health, from the Hardships of their Travel, their Lodging, their Diet, and their many other Difficulties.

These Two poor Women were now in the Hands of those, whose Tender Mercies are Cruelties; but the Good God, who hath all Hearts in His own Hands, heard the Sighs of these Prisoners, and gave them to find unexpected Favour from the Master, who laid claim unto them. That Indian Family consisted of Twelve Persons; Two Stout men, Three Women, and Seven Children; and for the Shame of many an English Family, that has the Character of Prayerless upon it, I must now Publish what these poor Women assure me: 'Tis this; In Obedience to the Instructions which the French have given them, they would have Prayers in their Family, no less than Thrice Every Day; in the Morning, at Noon, and in the Evening; nor would they ordinarily let their Children Eat or Sleep, without first saying their Prayers. Indeed these Idolaters were like the rest of their whiter Brethren, Persecutors; and would not endure, that these poor Women should Retire to their English Prayers, if they could hinder them. Nevertheless, the poor Women had nothing but fervent Prayers, to make their Lives Comfortable, or Tolerable; and by being daily sent out, upon Business, they had Opportunities together and asunder, to do like another Hannah, in Pouring out their Souls before the Lord: Nor did their praying Friends among our selves, forbear to Pour out Supplications for them. Now, they could not observe it without some wonder, that their Indian Master, sometimes, when he saw them Dejected, would say unto them, "What need you Trouble your self? If your God will have you delivered, you shall be so!" And it seems, our God would have it so to be. This Indian Family was now Travelling with these Two Captive Women, (and an English youth, taken from Worcester, a year and half before,) unto a Rendezvouz of Salvages, which they call, a Town, some where beyond Penacook; and they still told these poor Women, that when they came to this Town, they must be Stript, and Scourg'd, and run the Gantlet through the whole Army of Indians. They said, This was the Fashion, when the Captives first came to a Town; and they derided some of the Fainthearted English, which, they said, fainted and swoon'd away under the Torments of this Discipline. But on April 30, While they were yet, it may be, about an Hundred and Fifty Miles from the Indian Town, a little before Break of Day, when the whole Crew was in a Dead Sleep; (Reader, see if it prove not So!) one of these Women took up a Resolution, to imitate the Action of Jael upon Sisera;[1] and being where she had not her own Life secured by any Law unto her, she thought she was not Forbidden by any Law to take away the Life of the Murderers, by whom her Child had been butchered. She heartened the Nurse, and the Youth, to assist her in this En- terprize; and all furnishing themselves with Hatchets for the purpose, they struck such Home Blows, upon the Heads of their Sleeping Oppressors, that e'er they could any of them Struggle into any Effectual Resistance, *at the Feet* of these poor Prisoners, *they bow'd, they fell, they lay down: at their feet they bowed, they fell; where they bowed, there they fell down Dead.*[2] Only one Squaw escaped sorely wounded from them, in the Dark; and one Boy, whom they Reserved Asleep, intending to bring him away with them, suddenly wak'd, and skuttled away from this Desolation. But cutting off the Scalps of the Ten Wretches, they came off, and Received Fifty Pounds from the General Assembly of the Province, as a Recompence of their Action; besides which they Received many presents of Congratulation from their more private Friends; but none gave 'em a greater Tast of Bounty than Colonel Nicholson, the Governour of Maryland,[3] who hear- ing of their Action, sent 'em a very generous Token of his Favour.

Article XXVI.

Remarkable Salvations; and some Remarkable Disasters.

Besides a man Taken at York, in May, and another man kill'd at Hatfield, in June, and a Third kill'd at Groton; and a Fourth with Two Children carried Captives; there fell out more Mischief, with no small Mercy, on June 10, at Exeter. The Day before, some Women and Children would needs ramble without any Guard, into the Woods, to gather Strawberries; but some that were willing to Chastise them with a Fright, for

---

[1] Judges iv.   [2] Judges v. 27.
[3] Colonel Francis Nicholson, governor of Maryland 1694–1699.

their presumption, made an Alarum in the Town, whereupon many came together in their Arms. The Indians, it seems, were at this very Time, unknown to the English, lying on the other side of the Town, ready to make a Destructive Assault upon it; but Supposing this Alarm to be made on their Account, they therefore supposed themselves to be discovered. Wherefore they laid aside their purpose of attempting the Destruction of the Town, and contented themselves with Killing one man, Taking another, and Wounding a Third. But on July 4, Lord's-Day, Major Charles Frost, who had been a Person of no little Consequence to our Frontiers,[1] Returning from the Public Worship of God, in Berwick, (to repair unto which, about Five Miles from his own House, he had that Morning expressed such an Earnestness, that much Notice was taken of it,) pass'd several more Dangerous places, without any Damage; but in a place, on a little plain by the Turn of a Path, where no Danger was Expected, the Adder in the path Surprized him; the Indians having Stuck up certain Boughs upon a Log, there mortally Shot him, with Two more, while his Two Sons, that were in the Front of the Company, happily escaped; and the Two young men, that Rode Post unto Wells, with these Tidings, in their going back had their own Death added for another Article of such unhappy Tidings. About the latter End of this Month also, Three Men Mowing the Meadows at Newichawannic were themselves Cut down by the Indians; tho' one of the Mowers bravely Slew one of the Murtherers. But the most important Action of this Year was a little further off. About the beginning of July, Major March was Employed, with about Five Hundred Soldiers, not only to Defend the Frontiers, but also to seek out, and Beat up, the Enemies Quarters. In the mean time, the Lieutenant Governor, apprehending an Invasion from a Formidable French Fleet on the Coast of New-England, with his accustomed prudence and vigour applied himself to put the whole Province into a posture of Defence: And the Militia, with the several Forts, especially that of Boston, (very much through the Contrivance and Industry of Captain Fairweather,) were brought into so good a posture, that some could hardly forbear too much Dependance on our

---

[1] Commander of the militia of York County, and judge of the court of common pleas.

Preparations. But, it being more particularly Apprehended, that in the Intended Invasion the Indians, assisted by the French, would make a Desent upon our Frontiers by Land, Major March was advised therefore to Employ some of his Forces in Scouting about the Woods. Before the Major arrived at York, a party of the Enemy kill'd a man that stood Centinel for some of his Neighbours at Work in the Marsh at Wells, and catching another Alive, they carried him a mile and a half off, and Roasted him to Death: But Captain Bracket, that followed them quite as far as Kennebunk, did but almost overtake them: For truly, Reader, our Soldiers cannot, as Antiquity Reports the old Græcian and Roman Soldiers could, march at a Running pace or trot, heavily Loaded, five and twenty miles in four Hours; but rather suspect whether those Reports of Antiquity be not Romantick. Three Soldiers of Saco fort, after this, cutting some Fire wood on Cow-Island, for the use of the Fort, were by the Indians cut off; while that Lieutenant Fletcher, with his Two Sons, that should have Guarded them, went a Fowling; and by doing so, they likewise fell into the Snare. The Indians carrying these Three Captives down the River in one of their Canoos, Lieutenant Larabe, who was abroad with a Scout, way-laid them; and Firing on the Foremost of the Canoos, that had Three men in it, they all Three fell and sank in the River of Death. Several were killed aboard the other Canoos; and the rest ran their Canoos ashore, and Escaped on the other side of the River; and one of the Fletchers, when all the Indians with him were kill'd, was Delivered out of the Hands which had made a prisoner of him; tho' his poor Father afterwards Dyed among them. Hereupon Major March, with his Army, took a Voyage farther Eastward, having several Transport Vessels to accommodate them. Arriving at Casco-Bay, they did, upon the Ninth of September, come as occult as they could, further East among the Islands, near a place called Corbin's Sounds; and Landed before Day at a place called, Damascotta River;[1] where, before Half of them were well got ashore, and drawn up, the scarce-yet-expected Enemy Entertained them with a Volley, and an Huzzah! None of ours were Hurt; but Major March Repaid 'em in their own Leaden Coin: and it was no sooner

[1] Damariscotta.

Light but a Considerable Battel Ensued.   The Commanders
of the Transport-Vessels were persons of such a mettle, that
they could not with any patience forbear going ashore, to
take a part of their Neighbour's Fare; but the Enemy seeing
things operate this way, fled into their Fleet of Canoos, which
hitherto Lay out of sight, and got off as fast, and as well, as
they could, leaving some of their Dead behind them, which
they never do, but when under extream Disadvantages.   Our
Army thus beat 'em off, with the Loss of about a Dozen men,
whereof One was the worthy Captain Dymmock of Barnstable;
and about as many woundded, whereof one was Captain
Philips of Charlestown; and in this Action Captain Whiting,
a young gentlemen of much Worth, and Hope, Courageously
acting his part, as Commander of the Forces, the Helpers of
the War, which the Colony of Connecticut had Charitably
lent unto this Expedition, had his Life remarkably rescued
from a Bullet grazing the Top of his Head.   But there was a
Singular Providence of our Lord Jesus Christ, in the whole of
this matter.   For by the seasonable Arrival and Encounter of
our Army, an horrible Descent of Indians, which probably
might have laid whole Plantations Desolate, was most happily
Defeated.   And at the same Time, the Signal Hand of Heaven
gave a Defeat unto the purposes of the French Squadrons at
Sea, so that they had something else to do, than to Visit the
Coast of New-England.

Article XXVII.

The End of the Year; and we hope of the War.

O Thou Sword of the Wilderness, *When wilt thou be quiet?*[1]
On Sept. 11, a party of the Enemy came upon the Town of
Lancaster, then prepared for Mischief by a wonderful Security,
and they did no little Mischief unto it.   Near Twenty were
killed, and among the rest, Mr. John Whiting, the Pastor of
the Church there: Five were carried Captive; Two or Three
Houses were burnt, and several Old People in them.   Captain

[1] Jeremiah xlvii. 6, "O thou sword of the Lord, how long will it be ere thou
be quiet?"

Brown, with Fifty men, pursued them, till the Night Stopp'd
their pursuit; but it seems, a Strange Dog or two, unknown
to the Company, did by their Barking alarum the Enemy to
Rise in the Night, and Strip and Scalp an English Captive
Woman, and fly so far into the Woods, that after Two Days
Bootless Labour, our men Returned. November arrived,
before any farther Bloodshed; and then 'twas only of one man,
in the Woods, at Oyster River. December arrived with the
welcome Tidings, of a Peace concluded between England and
France; which made us Hope, that there would be little more
of any Bloodshed at all.

The Winter was the Severest, that ever was in the memory
of man. And yet February must not pass, without a Stroke
upon Pemmaquid Chub,[1] whom the Government had mercifully permitted, after his Examination, to Retire unto his
Habitation in Andover. As much out of the way as to Andover, there came above Thirty Indians, about the middle of
February, as if their Errand had been for a Vengeance upon
Chub, whom (with his Wife) they now Massacred there. They
Took Two or Three Houses, and Slew Three or Four Persons;
and Mr. Thomas Barnard, the worthy Minister of the place,
very narrowly escaped their Fury. But in the midst of their
Fury, there was one piece of Mercy, the like whereof had
never been seen before: For they had got Colonel Dudley
Bradstreet, with his Family, into their Hands; but perceiving
the Town Mustering to follow them, their Hearts were so
changed, that they dismissed their Captives without any further
Damage unto their Persons. Returning back by Haverhil,
they kill'd a couple and a couple they Took, with some Remarkable circumstances, worthy to be made a distinct History.
But, Reader, we are now in Haste for to have our present
History come unto an End: And though the end of this Year
did not altogether prove the end of the War, for on May 9,
1698, the Indians Murdered an old man, at Spruce-Creek, and
carried away Three Sons of that old man, and wounded a
man at York, Yet we were not without prospect of our
Troubles growing towards a period: And even in that very
Murder at Spruce-Creek, there fell out one thing that might
a little encourage our Hopes concerning it. The Murderer

<hr />

[1] See p. 261, *supra.*

was a famous kind of a Giant among the Indians; a Fellow
Reputed Seven Foot High: This Fellow kill'd the poor old
man in cold Blood, after he had Surrendred himself a Prisoner:
But behold, Before many Hours were out, this famous and
bloody Fellow accidentally Shot himself to Death, by his Gun
going off, when he was foolishly pulling a Canoo to the Shore
with it.

The last Bloody Action, that can have a Room in our Story,
is this.

The Indians, (though sometimes it hath been much doubted,
what Indians!) have in this War made several Descents upon
some of the upper Towns, that were our most Northerly Settlements upon Connecticut-River. But the Pious and Honest
People in those towns have always given them a brave Repulse,
and had a notable Experience of the Divine Favour to them,
in their preservations. Deerfield has been an Extraordinary
Instance of Courage in keeping their Station, though they have
lived all this while in a very Pihahiroth;[1] and their worthy
Pastor Mr. John Williams, deserves the Thanks of all this
Province, for his Encouraging them all the ways Imaginable
to Stand their ground. Once the Enemy was like to have Surprised them into a grievous Desolation; but He, with his Praying, and Valiant, little Flock, most happily Repelled them.
And now, about the middle of July, 1698, a little before Sun-
set, Four Indians killed a Man and a Boy, in Hatfield Meadows,
and carried away Two Boys, into Captivity. The Advice
coming to Deerfield in the Night, they presently Dispatched
away Twelve men, to way-lay the Enemy coming up the River;
having first look'd up unto the Lord Jesus Christ, that they
might find the Enemy, and harm none but the Enemy, and
Rescue the Children which the Enemy had Seized upon.
After a Travel of near Twenty Miles, they perceived the Indians, in their Canoos coming up the River, but on the other
side of it, within a Rod or Two of the opposite Shore: Whereupon they so Shot, as to Hit one of the Indians, and then they
all jumpt out of the Canoos, and one of the Boyes with them.
The wounded Salvage crawled unto the Shoar; where his back
being broken, he lay in great Anguish, often Endeavouring
with his Hatchet, for to knock out his own Brains, and tear

[1] Exodus xiv. 2, 9: Numbers xxxiii. 7, 8. A place in the wilderness.

open his own Breast, but could not: And another Indian seeing
the Two Boys getting one to another, design'd 'em a Shot, but
his Gun would not go off: Whereupon he followed 'em with his
Hatchet, for to have knock'd 'em on the Head; but just as he
come at 'em, one of our men sent a Shot into him, that Spoil'd
his Enterprize; and so the Boys getting together, into one
Canoo, brought it over to the Friends thus concerned for them.
These good men, seeing their Exploit performed thus far, Two
Indians destroy'd, and Two Children delivered, they fell to
Praising of God; and one young man particularly, kept thus
Expressing himself; Surely, 'Tis God, and not we, that have
wrought this Deliverance! But, as we have sometimes been
told, That even in the Beating of a Pulse, the Dilating of the
Heart, by a Diastole of Delight, may be turned into a contract-
ing of it, with a Systole of Sorrow, In the Beating of a few
Pulse, after this, they sent five or six men, with the Canoo, to
fetch the other, which was lodged at an island not far off, that
they might pursue the other Indians: When those two Indians
having hid themselves in the High-grass, unhappily Shot a
quick Death into the young man, whose Expressions were but
now recited. This Hopeful young man's Brother-in-Law was
intending to have gone out, upon this Action; but the young
man himself importuned his Mother to let him go: Which,
because he was an only son, she denied; but then, fearing she
did not well to withhold her son from the Service of the Publick,
she gave him leave: Saying, See that you do now, and as you
go along, Resign, and give up your self unto the Lord; and I
desire to Resign you to him! So he goes, and so he dies; and
may he be the last, that falls in a Long and Sad War with
Indian Salvages!

Article XXVIII.

The Epilogue of a Long Tragedy.

For the present then the Indians have Done Murdering;
they'll Do so no more till next Time. Let us then have done
Writing, when we have a little informed our selves what is
become of the chief Murderers among those Wretches, for

whom, if we would find a Name of a Length like one of their own Indian Long-winded words, it might be,

Bombardo-gladio-fun-hasti-flammi-loquentes.[1]

Major Converse, and Captain Alden, in pursuance of Instructions Received from the Lieut. Governour and Council, arriving at Penobscot on Octo. 14, 1698, were there informed, that Madockawando, the noted Sagamore, with several other Sachims of the East, were lately Dead. And six days after this, the chief Sachims now Living, with a great Body of Indians, Entertained them with a Friendly Discourse; wherein they said, That the Earl of Frontenac had sent them word, there was a Peace concluded between the Kings of France and England,[2] and that one of the Articles in the Peace was, for Prisoners on both sides to be Returned, and they were Resolved to obey the Earl of Frontenac as their Father; and accordingly such Prisoners of ours, as they had now at hand, might immediately Return, if we could perswade them, for They would not Compel them. When our English Messengers argued with them, upon the perfidiousness of their making a New War, after their Submission, the Indians replied, That they were Instigated by the French to do what they did, against their own Inclinations; adding, That there were two Jesuits, one toward Amonoscoggin, the other at Narridgaway, both of which, they desired the Earl of Bellomont, and the Earl of Frontenac, to procure to be Removed; otherwise it could not be expected that any Peace would continue long.[3] The Indians also, and the English Prisoners, gave them to understand, that the last Winter, many, both Indians and English Prisoners, were Starved to Death; and particularly, Nine Indians in one company went a Hunting, but met with such hard circumstances, that after they had Eat up their Dogs, and their Cats, they Dyed horribly Famished: And since the last Winter, a grievous and unknown Disease is got among them, which consumed them wonderfully. The Sagamore Saquadock further told them, That the Kennebeck Indians

---

[1] "Breathing bombs, swords, death, spears and flames."

[2] The peace of Ryswyk, September 10/20, 1697.

[3] Father Sebastian Rale at Norridgewock. "Toward Amonoscogin," on the Kennebec, were the two brothers, Father Jacques and Father Vincent Bigot.

would fain have gone to War again, this last Summer, but the other Refused, whereupon they likewise Desisted: And they Resolved now, to Fight no more: but if any Ill Accident or Action should happen on either side, he did in the Name of the Indians Desire, That we would not presently make a War upon it, but in a more amicable way compose the Differences.

That the Indian affayrs might come to be yet more exactly understood, the General Assembly of the Province Employ'd Colonel John Phillips, and Major Convers, to settle them. These Gentlemen took a Difficult and a Dangerous Voyage, in the Depth of Winter, unto the Eastern parts, in the Province-Galley, then under the Command of Captain Cyprian Southack; and the principal Sagamores of the Indians there coming to them, did again Renew and Subscribe the Submission, which they had formerly made in the year 1693, With this Addition unto it.

And whereas, notwithstanding the aforesaid Submission and Agreement, the said Indians belonging to the Rivers aforesaid, or some of them, thro' the ill counsel and instigation of the French, have perpetrated sundry Hostilities against His Majesties Subjects, the English, and have not Delivered and Returned home several English Captives in their Hands, as in the said Submission they Covenanted.

Wherefore, we whose Names are hereunto Subscribed, Sagamores, Captains, and principal men of the Indians belonging unto the Rivers of Kennebeck, Ammonoscoggin, and Saco, and parts adjacent, being sensible of our great Offence and Folly, in not complying with the aforesaid Submission and Agreement, and also of the Sufferings and Mischiefs that we have hereby exposed our selves unto, Do in all Humble and most Submissive manner cast our selves upon His Majesties Mercy, for the pardon of all our Rebellions, Hostilities, and Violations of our promises, praying to be Received into His Majesties Grace and protection; and for, and on behalf of our selves, and of all other the Indians, belonging to the several Rivers and places aforesaid, within the Soveraignty of His Majesty of Great-Britain, do again acknowledge and profess our Hearty and Sincere Obedience, unto the Crown of England, and do solemnly Renew, Ratify and Confirm all and every of the Articles and Agreements, contained in the aforesaid Recited Commission. And in Testimony thereof, we, the said Sagamores, Captains, and principal men, have hereunto set our several Marks and Seals at Casco-Bay, near Mares-

Point,[1] the Seventh Day of January, in the Tenth Year of the Reign of his Majesty, King William the Third, Annoque Domini, 1698, 9.

Subscribed by

Moxus,—and a Great Number more.

In the presence of
JAMES CONVERSE,
CYPRIAN SOUTHACK,
JOHN GILLS, Interpreter,
And SCODOOK, alias SAMPSON.

At this Time also, the Indians Restored as many of the English Captives, in their Hands, as were able to Travel above an Hundred Miles in this terrible Season of the year, from their Head-quarters, down to the Sea-side; giving all possible satisfaction, for the Restoration of the rest, as Early in the Spring, as there could be any Travelling.

The Condition of these Captives has afforded many very Remarkable Things, whereof 'tis a thousand pities that so many are lost. But because one of the Two Gentlemen Employ'd as Commissioners, for the Treaty with the Indians, took certain Minutes of Remarkable Things from some of the Captives, I am willing to give the Reader a Taste of them.

At Marespoint in Casco-Bay, Jan. 14. 1698, 9.

The captives informed me, that the Indians have Three Forts, at Narridgawog, and Narrackomagog, and Amassacanty. And at each of these Forts, they have a Chappel, and have Images in them.

They informed me, That Three Captives in one Wigwam were Starved to Death last Winter.

Mary Fairbanks, and Samuel Hutching, and some other Captives, told me, that Jonathan Hutching, belonging to Spruce-Creek, a Lad fourteen years old, They met him crying for want of Victuals, for in Two or Three Days he had nothing to Eat. Afterward, as he was going to fetch some Wood, he felt something hard in his Bosom. He put in his Hand, and unto his Astonishment, he found there Two Great Large Ears of Indian corn, which were very well Roasted. He Eat them, and knew not how they came unto him.

Some other of the Captives told me, that one Mary Catter, (which person we now brought home with us, belonging to Kittery)

[1] Now called Merepoint, in Brunswick, Maine.

her Master, and many other Indians came down to Casco-Bay. There seeing some Sloops, or shallops, they thought they were the English coming upon them, and ran away into the Woods, and left the said Mary Catter very Sick in the Wigwam, without any thing at all to Eat. They staid away many dayes; but left a Fire in the Wigwam. She Lay wishing for something to Eat, and at length in came a Turtle. She got That, and Eat it; but afterwards began to Despair of out-living the Famine, which was Returned upon her. At length, when she was very Hungry, in came a Partridge; she took a Stick and Struck it, and Drest it, and Eat it. And by that Time she was Hungry again, her Master came to look after her.

They tell of several of the Indians that have kill'd themselves with their own Guns, in taking them out of their Canoos.

Assacombuit sent Thomasin Rouse, a Child of about Ten years old, unto the Water-side to carry something. The Child cried: He took a Stick and struck her down: She lay for Dead: he took her up and Threw her into the water: Some Indians, not far off, ran in, and fetch'd her out. This Child we have now brought Home with us.

This Assacombuit hath killed and Taken this War, (they tell me) an Hundred and Fifty Men, Women, and Children. A Bloody Devil.

Thus the Paper of Minutes.

The Reader now has nothing but Peace before him. Doubtless he comforts himself with Hopes of Times better to Live in, than to Write of!

But that which yet more assures a Break of Day after a long and sad Night unto us, is, That the Best King at this Day upon Earth, and the Greatest Monarch, that ever Sway'd the Sceptre of Great Britain, hath Commission'd a Noble Person, who hath in him an Illustrious Image of His own Royal Virtues, to take the Government of these Provinces; and he is accordingly Arrived now near our Horizon. When the Schools of the Jews delivered, That there were Three Great Gifts of the Good God unto the world, The Law, the Rain, and the Light; R. Zeira[1] added, "I pray, let us take in Peace for a Fourth." All these Four Gifts of God are now Enjoy'd by New-England; but I must now ask, that our Hope of a Fifth may be added unto the Number; which is, a Governour of Signalized

[1] Apparently Rabbi Zeera, a Palestinian *amora* of the fourth century A. D.

Virtues. To the truly Noble Earl of Bellomont, the whole
English Nation must own it self Endebted while it is a
Nation, for the most Generous and Successful Zeal with which
he Laboured for those Acts of Parliament, by Assenting
whereunto, the Mighty William hath Irradiated England,
with Blessings that it never saw before His Happy Reign:
Blessings richly worth all the Expences of a Revolution.
England owes no less Immortal Statues unto the Earl of Bellomont, than Ireland unto his Illustrious Ancestors. But the
Continent of America must now Share in the Influence of that
Noble Person, whose Merits have been Signalized on the most
famous Islands of Europe; and the Greatest Person, that ever
set foot on the English Continent of America, is now Arrived
unto it. We are now satisfying our selves in the Expectations
of the Great and Good Influences, to be derived from the
Conduct of a Governour, in whom there will meet,

—*Virtus et Summa potestas.*[1]

And now, Reader, I will conclude our History of the Indian
war, in Terms like those used by the Syrian Writer at the Conclusion of his Book;

*Finis, per Auxilium Domini Nostri Jesu Christi, mense
Duodecimo, per manus peccatoris pauperis et Errantis.*[2]

Article XXIX.

Quakers Encountred.

For the present then, we have done with the Indians: But
while the Indians have been thus molesting us, we have suffered
Molestations of another sort, from another sort of Enemies,
which may with very good Reason be cast into the same History with them. If the Indians have chosen to prey upon the
Frontiers, and Out-Skirts, of the Province, the Quakers have
chosen the very same Frontiers, and Out-Skirts, for their

---

[1] "Bravery and sovereign power." Bellomont was in his province of New
York for some time before coming to Massachusetts.

[2] "Finished, by the aid of our Lord Jesus Christ, in the twelfth month, by
the hand of a poor and erring sinner."

more Spiritual Assaults; and finding little Success elsewhere,
they have been Labouring incessantly, and sometimes not un-
successfully, to Enchant and Poison the Souls of poor people,
in the very places, where the Bodies and Estates of the people
have presently after been devoured by the Salvages. But that
which makes it the more agreeable, to allow the Quakers an
Article in our History of the Indians, is, That a certain silly
Scribbler, the very First-born of Nonsensicality, (and a First-
born too, that one might Salute as the Martyr Polycarp once
did the wicked Marcion,) One Tom Maule,[1] at this Time
living in Salem, hath exposed unto the Publick a Volumn of
Nonsensical Blasphemies and Heresies, wherein he sets himself
to Defend the Indians in their Bloody Villanies, and Revile
the Countrey for Defending it self against them. And that
the Venom of this Pamphlet might be Improved unto the
Heighth of Slanderous Wickedness, there hath been since
added unto it, in another Pamphlet, a parcel of Ingredients
compounded, for mischief, as if by the Art of the Apothecary.
None but he whom the Jews in their Talmuds call Ben-tamalion
could have inspired such a Slanderer! Have the Quakers ever
yet Censured this their Author, for holding-forth in his *Alcoran*
(page 221) That the Devil, Sin, Death, and Hell, are but
Nothing, they are but a Non-Entity: And, (page 183) That all
men who have a Body of Sin remaining in them, are Witches?
I have cause to believe, they never did! Nor that they ever
advised him to pull in his Horns, from goring the sides of New-
England, with such passages as those, in (page 195) the same
horrible Pamphlet: "God hath well Rewarded the Inhabitants
of New-England, for their Unrighteous Dealings, towards the
Native Indians, whom now the Lord hath suffered to Reward
the Inhabitants, with a double measure of Blood, by Fire and
Sword, etc." And those Unrighteous Dealings he Explains to
be the Killing of the Indians, (or Murdering of them) by the
Old Planters of these Colonies in their First Settlement. Thus
are the Ashes of our Fathers vilely staled upon, by one, who
perhaps would not stick at the Villany of doing as much upon

[1] Thomas Maule had published in 1695 a work entitled, *Truth held forth
and Maintained* (New York, William Bradford), followed in 1697 by *New England
Persecutors mauled with their own Weapons* (*ibid.*), and had thereby aroused the
ire of Mather.

their Baptism it self. I must tell you, Friends, that if you don't publickly give forth a Testimony to Defie Tom Maule, and his Works, it will be thought by some, who it may be don't wish you so well as I do, that you own this Bloody Stuff: which, doubtless you'l not be so ill advised as to do. But, certainly, if the good people of New-England now make it not a proverb for a lyar of the first Magnitude, he is as very a liar as Tom Maule, they will deprive their Language of one Significant Expression, which now offers it self unto them.

Let us now leave our Friend Maule's Works as a fit Volume to be an Appendix unto the famous *Tartaretus,* and worthy of a Room in Pantagruel's Library.[1] The fittest way to answer him, would be to send him to Boston Woods!

In the mean Time I owe unto the Publick a piece of History, which it may be for the Safety of our Northern Towns, to be acquainted withal. Know, Sirs, That once the famous George Keith undertook to be the Champion of our New-English Quakers, and bid fair to be the very Dalae, or Prester John,[2] of all the English Tartars; but a Minister of Boston, upon that occasion, publishing a Book, Entituled, *Little Flocks guarded against grievous Wolves,*[3] could not but complain of it, as a very Scandalous Thing, in George Keith, to maintain the points of the Foxian Quakerism, while he really differed from them. All this while, George Keith was admired by our Quakers, as an Apostle, or an Oracle: but he, finding it impossible to mentain the gross Tenets of the common Quakers, preach'd unto them the Necessity of Believing on a Christ without, as well as a Christ within. Hereupon, there grew such alienations between him and the other Quakers, (who had been taught by George Fox, to say, the Devil is in them, who say, they are Saved by Christ without them) that he not only has written divers Learned Books, to confute those very Doctrines of the Common Quakers, which the Pastors of New-England had, upon his Provocation, Written against, but also

[1] Allusion to Rabelais.

[2] The Dalai Lama was (and is) the head of the Tibetan Buddhists; Prester John was a fabled Christian emperor of central Asia. George Keith (1639 *ca.* –1716), successively Quaker, "Keithian" or "Christian Quaker," and Anglican clergyman, had a noted part in contemporary theological controversy in England and America.

[3] A publication of Mather's own (Boston, 1691).

has therefore undergone a Storm of Persecution, from the Friends in Pensylvania: Yea, 'tis verily thought, that poor George would have been made a Sacrifice to Squire Samuel Jennings,[1] and the rest of the Pensylvanian Dragons; and that, since a crime which their Laws had made Capital, was mention'd in the Mittimus whereby Keith was committed, they would have Hang'd him, if a Revolution upon their Government had not set him at liberty. Being by the Fines, and Goals,[2] and Fierce Usages of the Quakers in Pensylvania, driven over to England, the Wonderful Hand of God hath made this very man, I think I may say, incomparably the greatest Plague, that ever came upon that Sect of Energumens. Although he do himself still retain the Name of a Quaker, yet he hath in one Treatise after another Earnestly called upon the Divines throughout the Nation more Vigorously to Employ their Talents against the Quakers, as a more Dangerous Generation of People than they are well aware; and he did in the year 1696, with the leave of the Lord Mayor, Challenge the Quakers, to make their Appearance at Turners-Hall, in the chief City of Europe; where he proved unto the Satisfaction of a vast Assembly, that the chief Writers of the Quakers assert Christ neither to be God, nor Man: and that they deny Christ to be pray'd unto; and that they had affirm'd, Christ's outward Blood shed on the Ground, to be no more than the Blood of another Saint; and that they had charged him with New Doctrine, for directing to Faith in Christ without us, as well as within us; and that at their Meetings, they had censured him, for saying, That Christ's body came out of the Grave, which they say, it never did: and many more such horrid matters.

To confirm these things, Besides the grievous Bites which Francis Bugg,[3] one of their late Friends, hath given them, one Daniel Leeds, without wholly casting off the Profession of a Quaker, hath lately Printed a Book,[4] wherein he produces above Threescore Instances of the Flat Contradictions which

---

[1] Deputy governor of West Jersey 1681–1684, and author of *Truth Rescued* (1699).

[2] Gaols, jails.

[3] Francis Bugg, at first a Friend, afterward author of no fewer than 23 writings against Quakerism, of which a dozen had already been published at this time.

[4] *News of a Trumpet sounding in the Wilderness*, by Daniel Leeds (New York, 1697).

he hath observed in the Books of the Friends, that have most pretended unto Infallibility; and he demonstrates from evident matter of Fact, that though they declared unto the World, That their Sufferings had been greater, and more unjust, than the Sufferings of Jesus and His Apostles; yet they themselves were no sooner mounted into the Seat of Government, than they fell to Persecuting as bad as any in the World. Albeit, Fox writes, They that cause People to be put in Prison, and have their Goods taken away, are Disorderly Teachers, and shall be rooted out: Nevertheless, Leeds proves by many Examples, that the Pensylvanians did it, even upon their own Friends, for meer Scruples of their Consciences. 'Tis reported, the Quakers are so confounded at this Book of Leeds, that they have been at the charge to buy up the whole Impression of it, and so to Stifle and Smother it: If it be so, I hope 'twill but produce a New Impression of so rare a Book. The Marvellous Providence of our Lord Jesus Christ having thus employ'd the Pens of the Quakers themselves, to warn you, that you beware of Quackerism, it will be a marvellous Infatuation in any of you, after this, to be led away with that Error of the Wicked. Reader, make a Pause, and here Admire the Marvellous Providence of our Lord Jesus Christ! The first and great Apostle of the Quakers, even George Fox, the Shoe-maker, in his *Great Mystery*, pag. 94, Excludes from the Church of Christ, Those who are not Infallible in Discerning the Hearts of other men. Whereas now in Spite of all their Infallibility, such Friends as Keith (and Leeds) whom they once admired, profess that they never in their Hearts Believed, as the Common Foxian Quakers do; and Quackerism Suffers from none in the world more than these. But that I may a little Suggest unto you certain Methods of Encountring those Adversaries of your Faith, which go about, seeking whom they may deceive, and whom I do here offer to prove as horrid Idolaters, as even those that worshipp'd the Rats of Egypt, if it be fairly demanded of me, I will first Recite unto you certain passages of a Discourse, which a Minister of Boston had with a very Busy and noisy Teacher among the Quakers, (and another of the Friends) in his Return from his Visitation unto some of our Northern Towns, where the Giddy People had cry'd him up for a None-Such.

Quaker. We are come to give thee a Friendly visit.

Minister. I am glad to see you at my House; you shall be welcome to the best Entertainment my house can afford you.

But will you do me the Favour to let me understand the Designs upon which you visit these parts of the Country?

Quaker. I come to preach Jesus Christ.

Minister. Excuse me—What Christ, I pray?

Quaker. The same Christ that appeared unto Abraham, and Isaac, and Jacob; and that appeared unto Moses in the Bush, and that was with Israel in the Wilderness—

Minister. I would interrupt you. I perceive, that we shall be drawn into some Discourse. Matter of Argument will occur, I foresee, in our Discourse. Argument sometimes does draw forth Words that may have too much Warmth in them. I purpose none such. But if you are sensible, that I do let fall any one such word, in our Disputation, do me the favour, to take notice of it unto me, and I'll immediately correct it. Now, if you please—

Quaker. Thou speakest very well. This is but according to the Good Report we have heard of thee.

Minister. Friend, I am sensible, that you are come among us, to preach a Religion, different from that which is commonly Preached, Professed, and Practised in the Country. If you approve the Religion of the Country, I can't see where's the Sense of it, for you to take such tedious Journeys for our Illumination. I pray, be so kind as to let me know, what point in our Holy Religion you do not Approve?

Quaker. 'Tis not my Business here to Enquire into thy Religion. I am come to preach the Religion of Jesus Christ; the same that the Holy Prophets and Apostles believed; even the inward manifestation of Christ in our Hearts—

Minister. To make short work on it; I perceive you both to be that sort of people we call Quakers. Now, there is among the Quakers that extream Uncertainty, Variety, and Contradiction, that no man can say what you hold, any further than each Individual Person will confess his own Tenets. I must therefore, pray the favour of you, to tell me; Do you own[1] George Fox's Book, Entituled, *The Great Mystery?*

[1] *I. e.*, accept, approve.

Quaker. 'Tis none of our Business to tell what Books we own, and what we do not own: and it is none of thy Business to Ask us. I say, We own Jesus Christ, and His Inward Manifestation in our Hearts. And that's Enough!

Minister. You'll Excuse me: I do again ask, whether you do own George Fox's Book of *The Great Mystery?* because doubtless you have Read it.—And if you'll ask me as much concerning any Book under Heaven, (that I have Read) whether I own it, or How much I own of it, I'll answer you with all the Freedom in the world.

Quaker. I say what hast thou to do with George Fox? or to Examine me?

Minister. Yes, Friend, I do, and must, and will Examine you. For you are come to Hold-Forth unto as many of my Flock as you can; and the Word of God bids me to Try you. And I have to do with George Fox too; because George Fox in his Writings has to do with me. And if you will sincerely tell me, whether you own George Fox, or no, I shall more probably tell, who you are. In short, if you say, you Deny and Renounce George Fox, then I must go another way to work with you. If you say, you own him, then I must endeavour to Save you from some of his Damnable Heresies.

Quaker. What heresies.

Minister. Numberless. But I do at this Time call to mind Three of them.

First, That the Soul of man is without Beginning, and Infinite. This is, if I forget not, in the 90th page of that Book.

Secondly, That it is not contrary to the Scripture, That God the Father took upon Him Humane Nature. And, That the Scripture does not tell people of a Trinity, nor Three Persons in God; but that these Three Persons were brought in by the Pope.

This is in pag. 246.

Thirdly, That they that are not compleat in Sanctification, are not compleat in Justification.

This is in pag. 284.

What say ye, Sirs?

Quaker. What hast thou to do, to Rake into the Ashes of the Dead? Let George Fox alone. Hast thou any thing to charge upon me?

Minister. I shall know if you'll tell me, whether you own George Fox, or no, And you can tell me, if you will. I would be more civil to you, Sirs.

Quaker. I never saw that Book of George Fox.

(And so said the other Quaker that was with him).

Minister. Syrs, you astonish me? What! Never see George Fox's Book of *The Great Mystery?* 'Tis impossible! this Thing is to me a Mystery! Syrs, that book is the very Bible of Quakerism. 'Tis Essential unto a Quaker, at least, unto a Teaching Quaker, as you are, to be Indoctrinated from that Book. Never see it, man!—However, if you say so, I must Believe it.

Quaker. (Fell into an Harangue, Repeating what he had Preached abroad about the Country; which, because I would mis-recite nothing, I dare not undertake exactly to Recite in this place.)

Minister. I perceive our Conversation will be to little Advantage, except we get a little closer to some certain point, which I have hitherto Endeavoured, but ineffectually

Syrs, there are several points, which I would willingly bring you to. And there happening to be several of my Honest Neighbours at hand, I have pray'd them (with your leave,) to walk in, that they may be Witnesses of what passes between us

First, I'll begin, if you please, with This.

I told you at the Beginning, I would not willingly Treat you with one Hard word. There is an Hard word, which will presently occur by the unavoidable course of Disputation. I would pray you, to ease me of the Trouble of speaking it. You shall yourself have the speaking of it.

Quaker. What's that?

Minister. I pray, Friend, what doth the Scripture say, of them that say, They know Jesus Christ, and yet keep not His Commandments?

Quaker. Nay, What dost thou say the Scripture says in that case?

Minister. You will compel me, I see—I say then; the Scripture saies, *He that says, I know Him, and keeps not His Commandments, is a Lyar, and the Truth is not in him.* 'Tis 1 Joh. 2. 4.

Quaker. And what then?

Minister. Why this then. He that says I know Jesus Christ, and yet keeps not the Commandments of Jesus Christ, is a Liar, and the Truth is not in him.

You say, You know Jesus Christ. But you must give me leave to say, That you Keep not the Commandments of Jesus Christ.

Therefore—pray Syrs, do you help out the Conclusion. I am loth to speak it. You know what it is.

Quaker. Yes, yes. We know well enough what Conclusion thou wouldst be at; thou wouldst say that we are Liars, and the Truth is not in us.

Minister. Right! Since it must be so.

Quaker. But what Commandment of Jesus Christ is there that we don't keep?

Minister. The commandment of Jesus Christ is, For His Disciples to be Baptised with Water; But you, Quakers, do not keep that Commandment of Jesus Christ.

Quaker. How dost thou prove, that Jesus Christ commanded Baptism with Water.

Minister. I know you must have the word Water, or nothing will content you; Else I would have urged, for a Sufficient proof, our Lord's Commanding His Ministers to Baptise men, (Matth. 28 : 19). This Command Expresses our Duty. 'Tis not our Duty to Baptise men with the Holy Spirit. This belongs not unto Us, but unto Him whos' that Holy Spirit is. You will not say, we Sin, if we don't Baptise the Disciples in all Nations, with the Holy Spirit. So then it must be a Baptism with Water which is there Commanded by our Lord. But, as I said, you must have the word Water, and you shall have it.

The Apostle Peter said—

Quaker. The Apostle Peter! the Apostle Peter! Thou wast to prove that Jesus Christ Commanded Baptism with Water, And now, Thou art come to the Apostle Peter!

Minister. Stay, Friend, not so fast! will you say then, that the Commandments brought by the Apostle Peter, as the Commandments of Jesus Christ, are not the Commandments of Jesus Christ? but however, I'll mend the Expression—

The Spirit of Jesus Christ in the Apostle Peter, (Now I hope it fits you!)—

Quaker. (J. S.) Thou art a Monster, all Mouth, and no Ears—

Minister.—Prethee talk Civilly; Don't make me Believe that I am at Ephesus. If I were in one of your Houses, I would not give you such Language; you had but now a greater liberty to use your Mouth than I have hitherto taken; and my Ears were patient. But, you foresee my Argument is going to pinch you. 'Tis but Civility to let me Finish it

Quaker. Thou wast to prove, that Jesus Christ Commanded Baptism with Water. And thou hast not proved it. And therefore thou Speakest Falsely.

Minister. What do you mean? These little Shuffles won't help you.

I say, the Spirit of Jesus Christ in the Apostle Peter, after our Lord's Ascension, when it was Impossible for John's Baptism (which was into the Messiah, Suddenly to come, not, already come) should[1] have place, did say, in Act. 10. 47. *Can any man Forbid Water, that these should not be Baptised, which have Received the Holy Ghost.*

Quaker. How does this prove, That Jesus Christ Commanded these to be Baptised with water?

Minister. Thus—

If Jesus Christ had not Commanded Baptism with Water, any man might have then Forbid it. But no man could Forbid it.

Therefore Jesus Christ Commanded it.

Quaker. Therefore! Therefore! Argo! Argo! Why, Dost thou think Religion is to be proved by thy Therefore's, by thy Argo's?

Minister. Friend, I perceive, the word Therefore is a very dead-doing sort of a Word to ye. I'll dismiss this Terrible Word. I'll only say, The Reason why none could forbid Believers to be Baptised with Water, was merely Because Jesus Christ Commanded it.

Quaker. *Because,* why the word Because is as bad as the word Therefore.

Minister. (*Smiling.*) It may be so. But in the mean time, you are wonderfully unreasonable! I say, why could none forbid Water for the Faithful to be Baptised?

---

[1] Corrected to " to " in the *Magnalia.*

Quaker. Who says None could Forbid Water? 'Tis only said, Can any man Forbid Water?

Minister. I pray Sirs, And is not this, None can?

But I'll bring the matter to bear upon you without those two Dangerous Words, *therefore* and *because*, at which you are so terrified.

I will put the matter into the Form of a Question. And your Answer to this Question, shall put an End to our present Velitations.

Quaker. What have we to do to Answer thy Questions?

Minister. My Question is,

Whether a man might not forbid in the Worship of Jesus Christ, what Jesus Christ Himself hath no way Commanded?

You can Answer this Question if you will; and I desire, I demand your Answer.

Quaker. What? for us to answer thy Questions! that would be, to Ensnare our selves.

Minister. I am very sensible of That. Therefore, take Notice, You are Ensnared in the Toils of your own miserable Delusions. But still I say, Answer my Question.

Quaker. Do you see, Neighbours? Friend M. was to prove that Jesus Christ commanded Baptism, and now, he's come to a Question!

Minister. So I am Truly. And I see 'tis a Question, that puts you into a Sweat. I beseech you to Answer it. I Require you to Answer it. What shall I say? I Defy you to Answer it. Pardon my Cogency; you Force me to't!

Quaker. I say, How does a Question prove, That Jesus Christ commanded Baptism with Water? And why dost thou Baptise Infants?

Minister. Nay, I'll keep you to the Question. Your Answer to the Question, will prove it; I am designing to make you your selves prove it. And, Sirs, I do here offer to you, That I will give the best Answer I can, to any Question in the world, that you shall put unto me: why are you so loth to Answer one short Question of mine?

Quaker. I be not obliged to Answer thy Question.

Minister. I must contrive some fair way to Compel some Answer unto this one Question. Give me leave therefore to tell you, That if you do not Answer this Question, you go away conquered and confounded. Yea, Sirs, I must in Faithfulness tell you That you carry away the dreadful Mark of Hereticks upon you, Even, To be Condemned in your own Conscience. You go away Self-Condemned, That you don't keep the Commandments of Jesus Christ; and Therefore That you are— what you Remember the Apostle John said concerning you.

Quaker. I don't condemn Thee for using Baptism with water.

Minister. This is no Answer to the Question still: For you don't observe it your self; neither you, nor any Quakers under Heaven. Wherefore I still urge for an Answer.

Quaker. Thou art not Civil to us. Is this thy Civility to Strangers? We have heard a Great Fame of thee, for thy Civil and obliging carriage towards others that are not of thy perswasion. But now thou art uncivil to us. That which I have to say, is, I will keep to that Book, the Bible, and I will preach what is in that Book.

Minister. (*Taking up the Bible.*) Friend, you pretend then to understand this Book. I do here make you this offer, That I will immediately Turn you to Ten several places in one Book of this Holy Bible, (the *Chronicles*) And if you can give me a Tolerable Solution of any one of them, I'll acknowledge that you are worthy to preach out of it.

Quaker. Canst thou do it thy self?

Minister. I Humbly Hope I can.

Quaker. How dost thou know that I can't?

Minister. I say you can't. Now do you Accept my offer: If you can I'll own, that I have wrong'd you.

Quaker. What's that to thee, what I can do?

Minister. Look you, Neighbours; I think, 'tis to no purpose, to proceed unto any other points, with such unreasonable Folks as these. You see, how 'Tis. If you desire it, I'll proceed.

Neighbours. No, Sir, 'tis to no purpose, they are a people of no Reason.

Quaker. Nay, Friend M—, I would not have thee to be so Hard upon us; I mean Thee no Harm. I hear, thou takest a great deal of pains for the good of thy people; And they will do well, to Hearken to Thee. I have Rebuked some of them for speaking Evil of thee. Yea, It is my Judgment, That thou, and other such Ministers as Thou art, ought Honourably to be maintained by the people.

Minister. You differ from all your Friends, methinks. What? Would you have us to be Hirelings? 'Tis very strange to hear a Quaker plead for the Maintenance of our Ministry. But for your satisfaction, I'll tell you, The people whom I Serve I never once in all my Life Ask'd for any Maintenance or Salary; and I never made any Agreement with them about any Salary in all my Life.

Quaker. I say, I would not have Thee too Hard upon us. New-England has Persecuted our Friends at a grievous Rate.

Minister. Nay, Friends, Be not you too Hard upon me, about that matter. I Approve Persecution, as Little as any of you all. I abhor it. I have Preach'd against it, I have Writ against it, I have Bewailed the mistakes that some Good men have committed in it. I would have you Treated with all the Civility, imaginable. I would not have the Civil Magistrate inflict upon you the Damage of one Farthing for your Consciences.

Quaker. But now, you may see, how the Judgments of God are come upon the East-Country, by the Indians, for your Persecution.

Minister. I can't tell That neither. For tho' I am sorry at my Heart, that ever you were Persecuted: Yet I can't say, That because Boston was guilty of Persecution, therefore Newichawannick,[1] and Casco-Bay, (places in other Provinces) that never had any such thing in it, must be cut off.

Quaker. Yes, they Persecuted at the Eastward. There were Two Women, of our Friends, cruelly Scourged there.

Minister. I suppose, you refer to a Story published by one George Bishop,[2] a Quaker: he Complains bitterly of the New-England Persecution, because there came Two Quaker women Stark Naked, into our Public Assemblies, and they were carried unto the Whipping-post for it. This was in the Northern parts of the Country, as I have been told. These Baggages, I believe, were the persecuted women you talk of!

[1] Berwick.

[2] Author of the celebrated Quaker martyrology, *New England Judged* (1661, 1667).

Quaker. Well, and what if they did appear Naked, to show the People the Nakedness of their Sins?

Minister. For Shame, Sirs, let us have no more of this Talk.

Quaker. Why didst thou treat George Keith so hardly?

Minister. He deserved it when I so Treated him. And you Quakers have since Treated him Ten Times worse than ever I did. You write whole Books of Railing against him. I never got him into Goals, and under Fines. I should have been Troubled at any that would have done so. But you have done it. Therefore, I believe 'tis best for you to leave that Subject.

And so, after a few other small Pulls, the Saw stood still: the Conference ended.

There are Five or Six witnesses, which I have to attest unto the Truth of this Relation, which I have here given, of a Conference with a Quaker, which had all the Friends far and near wondering (as well as wandering) after him. And yet these Cretians[1] boasted among their Friends, how much they had confounded the Minister in this Conference.

All that I would presume now to Commend unto those Towns, which have such Quakers annoying of them, is This: Brethren, carry it well, even with all convenient Civility and Humanity, towards this Poor Deluded People; while you Charge your Children and Servants, that they do not go unto their Meetings: and cast not your selves also into Temptation, by needlessly being There. But after all, yea, before all, make an Experiment, which the Good People at Lyn made a little while ago, with a Success truly observable and memorable.

The Quakers made a more than ordinary Descent upon the Town of Lyn, and Quakerism suddenly spread there, at such a rate as to Alarum the neighbourhood. The Pastor of the Church there Indicted a Day for Prayer with Fasting, to Implore the Help of Heaven against the unaccountable Enchantment; and the Good People presented accordingly, on July 19, 1694, their fervent Supplications unto the Lord, that the Spiritual Plague might proceed no further. The Spirit of our Lord Jesus Christ gave a Remarkable Effect unto this Holy Method of Encountring the Charms of Quakerism: It

---

[1] *I. e.,* liars; see Titus i. 12.

proved a Better method, than any Coercion of the Civil Magistrate: Quakerism in Lyn received (as I am informed) a Death-Wound, from that very day; The Number of Quakers in that place hath been so far from Increasing, that I am told, it hath since rather Decreased notably. Now let other Endangered Plantations Go and do likewise.

The Quakers are such enemies to the Holy Religion, which is the Life of New-England, That you must Excuse my concern to have you Fortify'd against their Attempts also, while I am giving you an History of your other Enemies. What all of them would be at, methinks, was a little intimated by what One of them once Declared. The Globe-Tavern was near our Publick and Spacious Meeting-House at Salem; and a Noted Quaker there caused a paper to be set up on the Door of that Meeting-House, which had such Stuff as this written in it.

> Beware, Beware, and Enter not!
> But rather to the Globe and spend a Pot.

This is but like a passage mentioned in the Life of that Excellent man Mr. P. Henry, lately published.[1] A Debauched gentleman in his Revels, Drinking and Swearing, at Malpas, was Reproved by a Quaker, then in his Company. "Why," said the Gentleman, "I'll ask thee one Question, whether it is better for me to follow Drinking and Swearing, or to go and Hear Henry?" The Quaker answered, "Nay, of the Two, rather follow thy Drinking and Swearing." Behold the Spirit of Quakerism! When I once compelled a Quaker to confess, that the Body of Jesus of Nazareth rose from the Grave, and went up into the Heavens, he begg'd me that I would not improve his confession, as if made on the behalf of all his Friends. And another of them, as I hear, publickly Held-Forth in one of his late Stercorations, That the Husks of the Swine, on which the Prodigal fed in the Parable, were the Bread and Wine, in that which People call, The Sacrament.

But what will become of those Forlorn Villages, that shall Resign themselves to the conduct of that Light within, which our Sacred Scriptures indeed never expressly mention but once

---

[1] Philip Henry (1631-1696), English non-conformist divine; biography by his son, Matthew Henry the commentator (London, 1696).

or twice, and then call it, Real Darkness; and which may lead
men to all this wickedness? There was among the Mahometans
in the Eastern parts of the World, a Sect called *Batenists*, from
the Arabic, Baten, (which signifies within:)[1] who were the
Enthusiasts that followed The Light within, like our Quakers;
and on this principle, they did such Numberless Villainies, that
the World was not able to bear them. None of all their Diabolical Raveries which I know I am now pulling on my self,
and which I value no more, than if they came from the Pouliats
of Malabar, shall frighten me from soliciting your Christian
Cares and Prayers, That you may be not over-run with English
Batenists. And I must solicitously make the Observation,
That although such a Number of Quakers in our Nation be a
dreadful Judgment of God upon men, smiting them with
Spiritual Plagues for their Unfruitfulness and Unthankfulness
under the Gospel: nevertheless, 'tis a special Favour of God,
that the Number of Quakers is no Greater; for if they should
multiply, not only would Christianity be utterly Extinguished,
but Humanity it self Exterminated. It is well known, That
when a Quaker had Stolen an Hour-glass, their Mahomet,
George Fox, (of whom Sol. Eccles, in a Sheet, call'd, *The Quakers
Challenge*, pag. 6, says, He was the Christ,) thus vindicated it,
(*Great Myst.*, pag. 77.) "As for any being moved of the Lord,
to take away your Hour-glass from you, by the Eternal Power
it is owned." Reader, Dost not thou even Tremble to think,
what a Dark land we should have, if it should ever be fill'd
with these pretended followers of the Light, who wear the
Name of Tremblers? In Truth, I know not unto what better
one might compare them, than unto the Macheveliors growing
upon St. Lucia; Trees which bear Apples of such an Odour and
Colour as invites people to Eat thereof; but it is horribly
Dangerous to do so; for there is no Antidote that can secure
a man from speedy Death, who hath once tasted of them.
The Leaf of the Trees makes an Ulcer on any place touched
with it; the Dew that falls from them fetches off the Skin;
the very Shadow swells a man, so as to kill him, if he be not
speedily helped.

---

[1] Batinites were, in a broader sense, those Muslims who found under the
letter of the Koran a hidden, esoteric meaning. Mather uses the term in a nar-
rower sense, specifically for the sect of the Assassins.

Article XXX.

Things to Come.

From Relating of Things past, it would no doubt be very Acceptable to the Reader if we could pass to Foretelling of Things to come. Our Curiosity in this point may easily come to a Degree Culpable and Criminal. We must be Humbly content, with what the God in whose Hands are our Times, hath Revealed unto us.

Two things we will venture to insert.

First, for our selves, at home, Let us Remember an awful Saying of our Goodwin,[1] quoted by my Reverend Friend Mr. Noyes, in his late Excellent Sermon at our Anniversary Election.

"As you Look for Storms in Autumn, and Frosts in Winter, so Expect Judgments where the Gospel hath been Preached; for the Quarrel of the Covenant must be Avenged."

Secondly. For the Church abroad, I am far from deserting what was asserted, in the Sermon Preached at our Anniversary Election in the year, 1696.[2] "The Tidings which I bring unto you are, That there is a revolution and a reformation, at the very Door, which will be vastly more wonderful than any of the Deliverances yet seen by the Church of God from the Beginning of the World. I do not say That the Next year will bring on this Happy Period; but this I do say, The Bigger part of this Assembly may, in the course of Nature, Live to see it. These Things will come on, with horrible Commotions, and Concussions, and Confusions: The mighty Angels of the Lord Jesus Christ will make their Descent, and set the World a Trembling at the Approaches of their Almighty Lord: They will Shake Nations, and Shake Churches, and Shake mighty Kingdoms, and Shake once more, not Earth only, but Heaven also."

Unto these two Things, my Reader will not misimprove it, I hope, if I add a Third, lately fallen into my Hands; and never yet so Exposed unto the Publick.

---

[1] Thomas Goodwin, D. D., (1600–1680), eminent English Independent divine. Nicholas Noyes, minister at Salem, preached the election sermon of 1698.

[2] By Mather himself. *Things for a Distress'd People to think upon* (Boston, 1696).

*A Wonderful Matter Incontestably Demonstrated, and much Desired
by some Good Men to be in this place Communicated.*

Mr. John Sadler, a very Learned and a very Pious man, and a
most Exemplary Christian, Lay Sick in his Bed at his Mannor, of
Warmwell, in Dorset-Shire: In the year 1663, In the Time of his Illness, he was visited by Mr. Cuthbert Bound, the Minister of Warmwell.

Mr. Sadler then desired his man, (one Thomas Gray,) to see that
there should be no body else in the Room, and Lock the Door, and
give him the Key.

He then Sat up in his Bed, and asked Mr. Bound and the Attend-
ant Gray, Whether they Saw no body? And whether they did not
hear what a person said, that stood at the corner of the Chamber?
They Replied, No. He wondered at it, and said, The man spake so
loud that the whole Parish might hear him.

Hereupon, calling for a Pen and Ink, he wrote what was told him,
and made Them set their Hands to it, for he told them the man would
not be gone, till he had seen that done.

The Articles written down were,

I.   That there would, after so many months, be a Plague in
London, whereof so many would Dye, (Naming the Number.)

II.   That the greatest part of the City would be Burnt, and
Pauls[1] he particularly show'd him, Tumbled down into Ruins, as if
Beaten down with Great Guns.

III.   That there would be Three Sea-Fights, between the English and the Dutch.

IV.   That there would appear Three Blazing Stars; the Last
of which would be terrible to behold. (He said, The man show'd
him the Star.)

V.   That afterwards, there would come Three small Ships to
Land in the West of Weymouth, which would put all England in an
uproar, but it would come to nothing.

VI.   That in the year 1688, there would come to pass such a
Thing in the Kingdom, as all the world would take notice of.

VII.   That after this, and after some further Disturbance, there
would be Happy Times; And a Wonderful Thing would come to pass,
which he was not now to Declare.

VIII.   That he and his man (Gray) should Dye, before the
Accomplishment of these things, but Mr. Bound should Live to see it.

IX.   For the confirmation of the whole, the man thus appearing, told him, That he should be well the next Day; and there would

[1] St. Paul's cathedral.

come Three men to visit him, One from Ireland, One from Guernsey, and his Brother Bingham.

Accordingly, the Day following, Mr. Sadler went abroad: And this Day there accidentally met at his House, and so Dined with him, First, the Lord Steel, who had been Lord Chancellor of Ireland, and now returning from thence, in his way to London, came to see Mr. Sadler: Secondly, Monsieur de la Marsh, a French Minister from Guernsey; and Lastly, his Brother Bingham.

Mr. Bound, and Gray, within Three Days after this, made Affidavit of it, before Colonel Giles Strangewayes, and Colonel Cocker, who is yet alive.

Mr. Daniel Sadler, and Mr. John Sadler, the Sons of this old Mr. Sadler, very serious and worthy Christians, are at this Time Living in Rotterdam; one of them is His Majesties Agent for Transportation.

Mr. Daniel Sadler, making his Applications to Mr. Bound for his Testimony about this matter, the said Old Mr. Bound, in a Letter dated, Warmwell, Aug. 30, O. S., 1697, asserts the matter at large unto him, and Subscribes, This I shall testify before the King himself, if occasion be, when he comes into England.

Yours, CUTHBERT BOUND,
yet Minister of Warmwell.

Mr. Daniel Sadler ha's this Testimony further fortifyed by a Letter from One Mr. Robert Loder; telling him, That he had met with an Old Copy of the Depositions aforesaid, which accordingly he transcribes for him; and several yet living in Dorchester affirm'd unto him the Truth of the Story.

The Copies of these Letters are now in Boston, in New-England.

Mr. John Sadler adds his Testimony, That his Father told unto his Mother, and himself, That he had been told of Remarkable Things to come to pass, particularly, the Burning of London and Pauls. But that they were not acquainted with all the matters he foretold unto Mr. Bound, and Gray. Only he Remembers well They Two were with him in his Chamber alone; and his Father went abroad within a day or two; and that, (according to the Sign he had given to them,) the Three Persons aforesaid visited him. He adds, that his Father spoke of leaving in Writing the things that had been Shown to him; and that a little after, he saw once a Thin Octavo Manuscript in his Father's Study, which he believed had those things in it; but after that, he could never find it. This Testimony is Dated in October, 1697.

A Worthy and a Godly Gentleman, at this Time Living in Roterdam, and well-acquainted with both Mr. Daniel and

Mr. John Sadler, Sends this to Mr. Increase Mather, in New-England, with a Letter, Dated, 26th March, 1698.

Reader, I am not Ignorant, that many Cheats and Shams have been Imposed upon the World, under the Notion of Communications from the Invisible World; and, I hope, I am not becoming a Visionary. But Fancies and Juggles have their Foundation laid in Realities: there would never have been Impostures of Apparitions, and of Communications from the Invisible World, if there never had been Really some such things to be Counterfeited and Imitated. Wise men therefore will count it a Folly in its Exaltation and Extremity, to Deride all Instances of Strange Things arriving to us from the Invisible World, because that Some Things have been Delusions. No, 'tis a Wisdom, that is pleasing to God, and useful to the World, for a due Notice to be taken of rare Things, wherein we have Incontestable Proofs of an Invisible World, and of the Interest it hath in Humane Affairs. The Narrative of Mr. Sadler is advantaged with such Incontestable Proofs, and contains in it such Notable passages, that I believe I do well to lay it before Serious Men; and I believe no Serious Men will play the Buffoon upon it. By no means pretend I to pass any Judgment upon this Remarkable Narrative; by no means do I presume to tell what I think of it, any more than this, that it is Remarkable. Nevertheless, for the Caution of unwary Readers, I will annex the words of an Excellent Writer upon Divine Providence.

Watch against an Unmortified Itch after Excentrical or Extraordinary Dispensations of Providence. Luther said, The Martyrs, without the Apparition of Angels, being confirmed by the word of God alone, died for the Name of Christ; and why should not we acquiesce? And he observeth how the Devil hath greatly deluded parties who have been gaping after Visions.

Nor will it be unprofitable, to recite the words of another Author, whom I must quote, as R. David Kimchi did use to quote R. Joseph Kimchi, under the Title of Adoni Avi.[1]

---

[1] Rabbi David Kimchi (1160–1235) and his father Rabbi Joseph Kimchi (1105 ca.–1170 ca.) were celebrated Hebrew grammarians, exegetes, and controversialists of Narbonne. *Adoni Avi*, "my lord father," means Increase Mather.

Evil Angels do now appear, more often than Good Ones. 'Tis an unwarrantable, and a very Dangerous Thing, for men to wish, that they might see Angels, and converse with them. Some have done so; and God hath been provoked with them for their Curiosity and Presumption, and hath permitted Devils to come unto them, whereby they have been Deceived and Undone.

More Particular Prognostications, upon the Future State of New-England.

But, Oh, my dear New-England, Give one of thy Friends Leave, to utter the Fears of thy best Friends concerning thee; and consider, what Fearful cause there may be for thee to expect sad things to come? If every Wise man be a Prophet, there are some yet in thee, that can Prophesy. Predictions may be form'd out of these

Reasonable Expectations.

I.   Where Schools are not Vigorously and Honourably Encouraged, whole Colonies will sink apace into a Degenerate and Contemptible Condition, and at last become horribly Barbarous: And the first Instance of their Barbarity will be, that they will be undone for want of Men, but not see and own what it was that undid them.

II.   Where Faithful Ministers are Cheated and Grieved, by the Sacriledge of people that Rebel against the Express Word of Christ, *Let him that is Taught in the Word, Communicate unto him that Teacheth in all Good Things*,[1] the Righteous Judgments of God will Impoverish that people; the Gospel will be made Lamentably Unsuccessful unto the Souls of such a people; the Ministers will either be fetch'd away to Heaven, or have their Ministry made wofully Insipid by their Incumbrances on Earth.

III.   Where the Pastors of Churches in a Vicinity despise or neglect Formed Associations for mutual Assistance in their Evangelical Services, *Wo to him that is alone*.[2] 'Tis a sign, either that some of the Pastors want Love to one another, or that others may be conscious to some Fault, which may dispose them to avoid Inspection; but fatal to the Churches will be the Tendency of either.

IV.   Where Churches have some Hundreds of Souls under their

[1] Galatians vi. 6.

[2] The first ministerial association in Massachusetts was formed in 1690. The movement spread rapidly, and the institution became a permanent part of New England Congregationalism. The list of "reasonable expectations" is of course one of Mather's "tracts for the times."

Discipline; but the single Pastors are not strengthened, with Consistories of Elders, or an Agreeable Number of wise, and good and grave men, chosen to join with the Pastor as their President in that part of his Work, which concerns the Well-Ruling of the Flock, there Discipline will by Degrees be utterly Lost; The Grossest Offenders will by degrees, and thro' parties, be scarce to be dealt withal.

V. Where Pastors do not Quicken Orderly Private Meetings of both Elder and Younger Christians, for Exercises of Religion, in their Neighbourhood, the Power of Religion will observably Decay, among those Christians; the Seed sown in the Publick will not so much prosper, for want of being watred in private: And when the Pastor shall fall sick, there will not be so much as one company of Christians in all his Flock that can come together to pray for his Life.

VI. Where Churches professing a Great Reformation, shall in their Constitution cease to Represent unto the World the Holiness of the Lord Jesus Christ, and of His Heavenly Kingdom, they will become Loathsome to that Holy Lord; their Glory is gone, and their Defence goes with it; the dreadful Wrath of Heaven will Astonish the World with the Things which it will do unto them.

VII. Where Churches are Loth to give unto Councils regularly, upon Complaints Enquiring into their Administrations, an Account thereof, 'tis much to be suspected, that they are Chargeable with Male-Administrations; and if the Advice of Regular Councils come once to be trod under foot by any Particular Churches, all serious men will be afraid of joining to such Unaccountable Societies.

VIII. Where a mighty Body of people in a Country are violently set upon running down the ancient Church State in that Country, and are violent for the Hedge about the Communion at the Lord's Table to be broken down, and for those who are not Admitted unto the Communion, to stand on equal Terms in all Votes with them that are; the Churches there are not far from a tremendous Convulsion, and they had need use a marvellous Temper of Resolution with Circumspection to keep it off.

IX. Where Churches are bent upon Backsliding, and carried away with a strong Spirit of Apostasie, whatever Minister shall set himself to withstand their Evil Bents, will pull upon himself an inexpressible contempt and hatred; Be his merits never so Great, a Thousand Arts will be used for to make him Little; he had need be a man of Great Faith, and Great Prayer; But God will at length Honour such a man, with wonderful Recompences.

X. Where a Fountain shall become Corrupt, there the Streams will no longer Make Glad the City of God.

XI. The Gospel of our Lord Jesus Christ, we have with much expence lately sent unto several of our Southern Plantations: if it be

Rejected, there are terrible things to come upon them; 'twere better to have Lived in Sodom, than in one of those Plantations.[1]

XII.   God prepare our dear Brethren in Connecticut, for certain Changes that are Impending over them.

Finally, there was a Town called Amyclæ, which was Ruined by Silence.[2]   The Rulers, because there had been some false Alarums, forbad all people under pain of Death to speak of any Enemies approaching them: So, when the Enemies came indeed, no man durst speak of it, and the Town was Lost.   Corruptions will grow upon the Land, and they will gain by Silence: 'Twill be so Invidious to it, No man will dare to speak of the Corruptions; and the Fate of Amyclæ will come upon the Land.

Reader, I call'd these things Prophecy; But I wish I be not all this while Writing History.

Now, if any Discerning persons apprehend any Dangers to Impend over New-England, from any of the Symptoms mentioned, it is to be hoped, they will Employ their best Thoughts, how to Anticipate those Dangers.   And whereas, 'tis the sense of all men, who discern any thing, that it is in vain to hope for any Good, until a Spirit of Grace be poured out from Heaven, to dispose men unto it; I beg them to consider, whether the only way to obtain that Spirit of Grace be not, Humbly to Ask it, by Prayer with Fasting before the God of Heaven.

It was therefore an Article in an Advice agreed by some of the principal Ministers in this Province; and with the mention of that Advice, (which doubtless, all but the Sleeping will follow) I'll conclude; "Solemn Days of Prayer with Fasting, celebrated in our Churches, to Implore the Grace of God for the Rising Generation, would probably be of blessed consequence, for the Turning of our Young people unto the God of our Fathers.   The more there is this way ascribed unto Grace, the more the Grace of God is like to be communicated; and there is in this way a natural and a plentiful Tendency to Awaken our Unconverted Youth unto a sense of their Everlasting Interests; Which, were it generally accomplished, a Remarkable Reformation were therein Effected."

[1] An allusion chiefly to the Puritan migration of 1695 to Dorchester, South Carolina.   See the Diary of Elder William Pratt, in *Narratives of Early Carolina*, in this series, pp. 189–200.

[2] See the article by Professor Ettore Païs, "Amunclae a Serpentibus Deletae," in *American Historical Review*, XIII. 1–10.

INDEX

Accomacke, location of, 25.

Adams, Mrs., of Durham, 253.

Agamagus (Agamcus, Great Tom, Moxus), a Penobscot chief, 226, 229, 233, 251, 273, 275.

Ahanquit, a Penobscot chief, 251.

Ahassombamett, an Indian chief, 251.

Albany, N. Y., Philip secures ammunition from, 64; mentioned, 68, 87, 97, 124 n., 136, 141.

Alden, Capt. John, 273.

Alderman, Mr., a guide, 104, 105.

Alexander (Moanam), an Indian chief, 7 n., 12 n., 25, 26, 31, 69, 70, 125 n.

Allen, Rev. James, 38 n.

America, English and French colonization in, compared, 3, 171; intercolonial jealousies in, 4.

American Antiquarian Society, Transactions, 122 n.

Amesbury, Mass., 224, 254.

Amonoscoggin Fort, expedition against, 225. *See also* Lewiston.

Amonoscoggin River, *see* Androscoggin.

Andrews, Lieut. Elisha, 221.

Andros, Sir Edmund, governor of New York, 9, 11, 17, 88; effect of his administration in Massachusetts, 173, 194; mentioned, 187–190, 193, 194.

Andros, Lieut. Elisha, *see* Andrews.

Androscoggin River, in Maine, 47 n., 192 n., 249, 273, 274.

Annawon, an Indian chief, 105 n.

Apannow, an Indian chief, 71.

Apequineah, an Indian, *see* Monoco.

Appleton, Major Samuel, 49, 56, 60, 245.

Aquadocta, 221.

Arrowsick Island, location of, 41 n.

Artel, *see* Hertel, François.

Ashuelot valley, N. H., 136 n., 138.

Assacombuit, an Indian chief, 276.

Assawomset pond, location of, 7 n.

Attawamhood, an Indian, 32.

Augustus Cæsar, referred to, 182.

Awansomeck, an Indian, 251.

Awashonks, an Indian queen, 25 n.; confused with Weetamoo, 25, 96.

Backus, Isaac, account of the meeting of Roger Williams and the Indians, 87 n.

Bacon's Rebellion in Virginia, referred to, 68 n.

Bagatawawongo (Sheepscoat John), 251.

Ball, Jeremiah, *see* Bull, Jeriah.

Ball, John, of Lancaster, 118 n.

Bancroft, Lieut. Thomas, 221, 222, 240.

Bapson, Ebenezer, of Gloucester, 243, 246.

Baptists, growth of, 46 n.

Baquaug River, 129, 130, 146, 147, 159.

Barbadoes, information from, 71; negroes plan an insurrection in, 72; effects of storm in, 73, 74; mentioned, 239, 240.

Barbadoes, Governor of, 73.

Barnard, Rev. Thomas, of Andover, 270.

Barret, a mariner, 239.

Bath, Me., 192 n.

Batinites, referred to, 292.

Beers, Capt. Richard, 42, 124.

Bekker, Balthasar, his *De Betooverde Wereld* cited, 247 n.

Bellomont, Richard, Lord, 181, 273; Mather's eulogy of, 277.

Belshazzar, referred to, 181.

Bennett, George, 122 n.

Bering Strait, 203.

Berwick, Me., Indian success at, 229, 236, 267; mentioned, 196, 203, 220.

Bible, Eliot's Indian, 37, 157.

Bickford, Thomas, of Oyster River, 252.

Bigot, Rev. Jacques, 273 n.

Bigot, Rev. Vincent, 273 n.

Billerica, 260.

300